South Carolina in the Civil War

South Carolina in the Civil War

THE CONFEDERATE EXPERIENCE IN LETTERS AND DIARIES

Edited by J. Edward Lee *and*
Ron Chepesiuk

McFarland & Company, Inc., Publishers
Jefferson, North Carolina, and London

Library of Congress Cataloguing-in-Publication Data

South Carolina in the Civil War : the Confederate experience in letters
  and diaries / edited by J. Edward Lee and Ron Chepesiuk.
    p.   cm.
   Includes bibliographical references and index
   ISBN 0-7864-0794-8 (illustrated case binding : 50# alkaline paper)
   1. South Carolina—History—Civil War, 1861–1865—Personal
narratives.   2. United States—History—Civil War, 1861–1865—
Personal narratives, Confederate.   3. United States—History—Civil
War, 1861–1865—Social aspects.   4. Soldiers—South Carolina—
Correspondence.   5. South Carolina—History—Civil War, 1861–
1865—Social aspects.   I. Lee, J. Edward, 1953–   II. Chepesiuk,
Ronald.
E605.S7   2000
973.7'82'0922757—dc21   00-42720

British Library cataloguing data are available

On the cover: Fort Sumter under the Confederate flag on April 14, 1861.
Sullivan's Island, South Carolina *(Corbis Images).*

Manufactured in the United States of America

McFarland & Company, Inc., Publishers
  Box 611, Jefferson, North Carolina 28640
   www.mcfarlandpub.com

For the warriors:
Obadiah, Tyre, and Tyre, Jr.

For the Civil War scholar:
Dr. Arnold Shankman

Acknowledgments

Numerous people assisted in preparing this book. Some of the Winthrop University community members who deserve special mention include our president, Dr. Anthony DiGiorgio, and his executive assistant, Dr. Katherine Holten. Assistant archivist Gina Price White always serves as a valuable ally with projects such as this one. Taylor Glass, our institution's computer wizard, calmly came to our rescue on more than one frustrating occasion. The history department's administrative assistant, Carol Hanlon, an Illinoian by birth, became an honorary Southerner as she resurrected Obadiah Hardin and the others on the manuscript's pages. And we thank the donors who have loaned their treasures to our archives.

In everything we do, our spouses, Ann-Franklin and Magdalena, patiently allow us to embark on adventures such as the compiling of this book. We thank them for their unwavering love. And Elizabeth, a daughter of the Confederacy even though she does not understand any of this, is acknowledged for her bottomless pool of energy, which inspired the editors to complete this book.

Contents

Acknowledgments   vi

Preface   1

1. Eyewitness to Fort Sumter   5
2. Bathed in Blood   13
3. For the Widow Hardin   19
4. I Am Nearly Crazy   29
5. Lieutenant Watson's Camp Reminiscences   76
6. For My Only Living Daughter   80
7. Trapped on Union Soil   93
8. Augustus Franks, German Confederate   99
9. My Dear Elodie   106
10. A Grand C.S.A. Victory   110
11. Our Banner Is Waving   120
12. Thirteen Hundred Miles from Any Place   126
13. Not Just a Man's War   129
14. In the Midst of Life, We Are in the Midst of War   133
15. The Ground Where I Lay   138
16. There Is a Place We May Meet   145
17. The Lost Cause's Last Rites   149
     Conclusion   154
     A Note on Sources   157

Notes   159

Index   183

"It is sweet and honorable to
fight for one's country."
Horace, *Odes*, Book III
65–8 B.C.

Preface

In the last winter of the Lost Cause, the frigid wind came whirling into Columbia, South Carolina, from the northwest. From the south came a force much more menacing: Union general William Tecumseh Sherman, "Tecumseh the Great," and his 62,000 troops. Thus, on February 17, 1865, Columbia, the proud capital of the proud state where cotton had once been king, was squeezed between the elements: the brisk wind and the brutal general who had remarked, quite succinctly, that "South Carolina has bet on the wrong card."[1]

Four years earlier, the scene had been quite different. There had been celebrating in the streets and laughter in the air. South Carolina had left the Union in December 1860. By February 1861, the Confederate States of America had been born in Montgomery, Alabama. Some South Carolinians, in typical South Carolina modesty, whispered that Columbia, with its magnificent capitol building under construction, would be a more fitting location for the citadel of States' Rights.[2]

But in the four years since, the ringing of church bells and the swaggering boasts and the joyous laughter had long passed, replaced by battlefield defeats—some small, some large (Dranesville and Gettysburg); by deaths of beloved leaders who left their children fatherless and their wives grieving widows (Captain Obadiah Hardin and General Stonewall Jackson); by pain and deprivation on the homefront; and by a sinking realization that the cause was, indeed, nearly lost.

As the sun rose on February 17, the gray defenders, under the command of General Wade Hampton, evaporated like mist. At the Columbia railroad depot, an angry crowd assembled. Some wished to escape Columbia; others were disillusioned by the collapse of their ill-conceived nation. Some people vented their rage on the stockpiles of supplies that had reached the end of the line. An eyewitness described the scene this

1

way: "Whilst at the depot of the South Carolina railroad, a reckless mob, composed of both sexes and colors were plundering its contents in search of treasures of every description which had been accumulated there." Barrels of gunpowder were ignited and about forty individuals perished in the inferno.[3]

By 11:00 A.M., Sherman entered Columbia and met with mayor Miles Goodwyn, pledging to shield the city from abuse by the conquerors. After all, the commander had fond memories of the four years, 1842–1846, during which he had been stationed in South Carolina. When the general had crossed the Savannah River, however, he had vowed, "As for that hotbed of secession, Columbia, I shall lay it in ashes." Earlier, he had promised to make South Carolina "feel the hard hand of war." And his soldiers, as they flowed across the rain-swollen Congaree River, chanted, "Hail Columbia, happy land! If I don't burn you, I'll be damned."[4]

Therefore, the stage was set for an explosion far larger than the one at the railroad depot. While no evidence exists that Sherman personally ordered the torching of Columbia, his army was athirst for swift and harsh punishment to the rebels. A forty to fifty mile pathway had been burned and slashed across Georgia, to the outskirts of Columbia. Sherman had faked an eastward turn toward Charleston, but the capital city was his real target. His troops lived off the land, butchering livestock, trampling fields, and terrorizing civilians. Sherman's pledge to the mayor to protect the city from destruction seems to have been impossible to honor. After the war, he testified, "The feeling [of vengeance against South Carolina] was universal, and pervaded all ranks….We looked upon South Carolina as the cause of our woe [and thought] that she thoroughly deserved extirpation."[5]

"Extirpation" is defined as pulling up by the roots. Sherman's march was "extirpation," a form of total war which mocked the desperate condition of the ill-fed and ill-supplied remaining southern troops. The Confederate soldiers seemed impotent as women, children, and the elderly felt the harsh slap of Sherman's presence deep in the South's heartland.

Impotence, hopelessness, helplessness, crushing defeat, extirpation — words which lack power — typified the rebels and their bewildered families. Whether the city was burned by General Hampton's men who perhaps carelessly ignited cotton bales (the precious cotton) as the wind swirled about, or by undisciplined Union soldiers, drunk on whiskey and victory which warmed their souls, the destruction could not have been stopped. Even if Sherman had tried to hold back the flames, he would have failed. The burning of Columbia ripped the heart out of South Car-

Main Street, Columbia, S.C., February 18, 1865, the day after Union General William T. Sherman entered the city. (Courtesy Caroliniana Library, University of South Carolina.)

olina and shattered the will of the rebels to continue their drive for independence. The populace had been crushed by the invasion of their homeland and, in a real sense, the flames consumed their spirits, singed their psyches, scorched their proud hearts, and scarred them forever.

We argue that the war that climaxed with the torching of Columbia is not ancient history in South Carolina. Generations of the state's schoolchildren read Mary C. Simms Oliphant's *The History of South Carolina*, which calls the Civil War "a disaster from which South Carolina is still recovering." The war is only yesterday to many southerners. Some Confederate widows lived long into the twentieth century. Emotions flow forth concerning the battle flag which flies amid controversy over South Carolina's statehouse; African Americans consider it a tribute to slavery, while some whites believe it deserves honor as part of the state's heritage. Every town in South Carolina, it seems, has a monument to the southern soldiers. The one in York stands like a gray sentinel; "To our Confederate Dead," the inscription reads. The Sons of Confederate Veterans and the United Daughters of the Confederacy meet in the memorial's shadow each May to commemorate the Lost Cause.[6]

The scars of the Civil War are fresh ones and they get reopened on a regular basis. Refighting the war (or reenacting it) has become popular and serious for thousands of men and women. Movies like *Glory* and *Gettysburg* are immensely popular—as are the 50,000 books on the ordeal which line library shelves. But would any sane person wish that the war had turned out differently? Did not human bondage deserve extirpation? Was the South's cause not immoral? Did the "hotbed of secession" not receive its just desserts? What, exactly, went through the minds of southerners as they ruptured the Union and fought—and sacrificed—for the Confederacy? Why did they not yield and furl their banner? Why does the banner still summon forth the ghosts of 1861–1865? How did it come to this?

In this book we use some of the magnificent holdings of the Winthrop University Department of Archives and Special Collections to take a fresh look, at the beginning of a new century, at South Carolinians and their Confederate compatriots and the scars inflicted by the Civil War. These letters, diaries, and journals are windows through which we can glimpse the effects of this war upon its contemporaries.

We have attempted to reproduce the text of the documents as accurately as possible. Spelling and punctuation errors are sometimes retained; corrections discussed in the endnotes. Editorial insertions are enclosed in brackets.

We commence our study with an eyewitness account by a federal private of the April 1861 bombardment of Charleston harbor's Fort Sumter.

Chapter 1

Eyewitness to Fort Sumter

With the passage of the Ordinance of Secession on December 20, 1860, South Carolina presented demands to President James Buchanan calling for the removal of all Union troops from Charleston Harbor and forfeiture of all federal property to the state. Six days later, Major Robert Anderson, the commander of the Union forces at Charleston, secretly removed his troops from Fort Moultrie on Sullivan's Island to what he believed would be a more defensible position at Fort Sumter. When Buchanan refused to agree to the demands of the South Carolina commissioners, Confederate troops seized the United States arsenal at Charleston.

Buchanan then attempted to relieve Anderson's garrison by sending the *Star of the West*, an unarmed warship loaded with provisions and reinforcements. Heavy fire from shore batteries repulsed the ship, and it was forced to return to New York.

On April 6, the new president, Abraham Lincoln, notified South Carolina authorities that a ship was on its way to Charleston, carrying no troops but only provisions for Fort Sumter. But on April 11, suspicious of the movement and fearful of a prolonged federal occupation, Gen. Pierre G. T. Beauregard, the local Confederate commander, demanded that Anderson surrender immediately. Anderson's offer to surrender in a few days when his supplies would have been exhausted was refused by Confederate authorities. At 4:30 in the morning of April 12, the Confederate shore batteries opened fire on

Institute Hall, Charleston, S.C. Delegates signed the Ordinance of Secession here on December 20, 1860, setting the stage for the confrontation of Fort Sumter four months later. (Courtesy Winthrop Archives.)

Fort Sumter. The next day, after a bombardment of thirty-four hours, Anderson surrendered. The Civil War had begun.

Two of the most unique and significant reports concerning these momentous events are to be found, not in an American archival institution but in Belfast at the Public Records Office of Northern Ireland. They are the letters of John Thompson, a private who was part of the federal force at Fort Sumter, serving in Company E, 1st United States Artillery.

Not much is known about the life of Private Thompson. According to his military records preserved in the National Archives in Washington, he was born in Anticlave, County Londonderry, Ireland. On September 25, 1856, at the age of twenty-two, he enlisted at Philadelphia. With blue eyes, fair complexion, and dark hair, he stood five feet five inches tall. Given the style and content of the letters, it is curious that

Thompson gave his occupation as a laborer. His wife Mary Charlotte was with him at Sullivan's Island at least in September 1860 for she is listed as a sponsor at the baptism of a child of another Irish garrison member. Thompson's term of service expired on September 28, 1861, and he was discharged.

The first of two letters, both written to his father, Robert Thompson of Anticlave, gives a graphic account of the tensions and events in the "cold war" period preceding the bombardment. The second letter, written a few days after the evacuation of the federal troops from Fort Sumter, describes the atmosphere in the garrison while it was under heavy fire.[1]

Fort Sumter So. Carolina
February 14th 1861

My Dear Father

Your letter dated January 11th has been duly received, and I am exceedingly glad to hear of your welfare. You are anxious you say in your letter to know all the war, or properly speaking the rebellion of South Carolina. I shall endeavor to describe what has come under my notice. Ever since the election of President in November last great dissatisfaction has prevailed in the Slave States, and during December this State formally sexcede from the Union, and openly threatened to take forcible possession of the Forts, Arsenals and other public property in this harbor. This they were certain could be easily accomplished, as two of the three Forts in this harbor were without any Garrison, and the third, Fort Moultrie, being garrisoned by only seventy five United States Artillerymen.[2] Certain of success they vigorously set about warlike preparations, all the time keeping a very strict watch on the helpless little Garrison of which I formed a member. Steamboats were nightly set to watch us to prevent our moving to Sumter, a far more formidable, may I say almost impregnable work, situated directly opposite us, and distant about a mile. Our Commander set about fortifying himself in Moultrie, with such unparalleled vigor that our opponents soon became thoroughly convinced that he intended to make a desperate stand in the position he then held, and the duty of watching us was performed with a laxity corresponding to the strength of their conviction. So completely did our Commander keep his own counsel, that none in the garrison officer or soldier ever dreamed that he contemplated a move, until the movement had actually been made. On the night of the 26th Dec. shortly after sun down, we were formed in heavy marching order, and quietly marched out of the Moultrie leaving only a few men behind on Guard, and embarking on board a number of small boats that in readiness were safely landed in Sumter. The consternation of the Carolinians may be imagined next morning when they observed Fort Moultrie enveloped in flames and smoke and at noon saw the Stars and Stripes proudly waving from the battlements of Fort Sumter. What they feared, and endeavored to prevent, had taken place, and they had the pleasure of witnessing Uncle Sam's troops in a position scarcely assailable in any other way than by the slow process of starvation. During the night of the 26th the men left behind spiked all the guns, and then set fire to the gun-carriages etc. at the abandoned Fort and then left it to quietly be taken possession of by the troops of South Carolina. This they were not long in doing, they can scale the walls of an *unoccupied*[3] Fort with a gallantry highly commendable. In fact their martial ardor seemed to have taken a turn in this direction for the same day they assaulted the remaining empty Fort in the harbor and amid shouts, exultantly raised their Palmetto flag to announce their bloodless victory. Of course they were boiling over to attack Sumter, and tear down the cursed Stars and Stripes, but of course they haven't done it yet, and if they do and live it will only be to repent their rash folly and mourn their loss. Fort Sumter which we now occupy is a five sided brick work, walls from 12 to 5½ feet thick mounting three tier of guns of the heaviest caliber, and completely surrounded by water. It is situated on the very edge of the ship channel, so that every vessel passing in or out of the harbor passes directly under our guns. In fact, it is the key of the harbor and completely commands all the other fortifications. Sumter was far from being in a defensible condition, very few guns were mounted and everything was in admirable confusion. However, we went to work assisted by 50 to 60 laborers, and now we can say *We are ready*. The Carolinians have been by no means idle all this time however. At the nearest point of land on Morris Island about 1400 yds. distant they have constructed very formidable batteries, and are now I may say just as ready as we are. We are in daily expectation of a commencement, which must come from them as our orders are to act strictly on the defensive. That they intend to bombard us is evident, and that they will attempt to breach this work at its weakest point is equally sure, but we are sure their attempt will prove a failure. They may starve us out and harass us meantime by shelling our position, but we all feel confident that assault if attempted will prove a signal failure.

Inside here we are all, thank God, in excellent health and spirits, in fact a more contented lot of men would be hard to scare up. We are only seventy-five in number and have now only about twenty laborers,[4] the rest having taken their leave of us, no doubt thinking discretion was the better part of valor, and we are opposed to at least ten or twelve thousand Carolinians,[5] our Commissariat scarcely in a condition to stand a long siege, cut off by the batteries of the enemy from reinforcement and supplies, depending on them for mail facilities etc.; and yet we are confident and contented because we all see the strength of our position and know that the chivalry of South Carolina are effectually scared to attack the frowning fortress the possession of which they so much desire. So matters stand at present, but how long they may continue so is a mystery.

You need not be in any unnecessary anxiety on my account, for to tell the truth in spite of all their bluster I am almost sure they never will fire a shot at us, indeed I think they are only too glad to be left alone. I am in excellent health, and hope you all are enjoying that same blessing. At the expiration of my time I shall doubtless return to see you all and give you an account of America verbatim. Keep up this correspondence. A letter from home is very refreshing in a place like this. I will endeavor to keep you posted when opportunity offers regarding events on this side Jordan. Give my respects to all my friends and acquaintance, and believe me

> Your affectionate son
>
> John Thompson

> Fort Hamlton[6] New York
> April 28th 1861

My Dear Father,

I have just received your welcome letter and am exceedingly glad to hear of your welfare. Since I last wrote I have passed through not a few exciting scenes. In my last letter I brought the history of our present difficulties down to our safe arrival in Fort Sumter. Well as time wore on the clouds of disunion thickened around us and we were being gradually hemmed in by formidable batteries erected under our very noses. Our Government suffered matters to go so far that the reinforcement or relief of Sumter was declared an impossibility to any force under twenty thousand men. Thus we were left at the mercy of the rebels, dependent on them for supplies and completely surrounded by their hostile batteries. They no doubt expected that we would surrender without a blow, but they were never more mistaken in their lives. Our supply of breadstuffs was fast giving out and the Carolinians knew it. They had cut off all communication with the shore, and starvation was staring us in the face. We had been on _____ rations for a long time and on the 8th of April a reduction to half rations was made and cheerfully submitted to, the hope of being re-enforced or withdrawn having not yet entirely left us. On the eleventh one biscuit was our allowance, and matters seemed rapidly coming to a crisis. The rebels had doubled their watchfulness and we were certain that something was in the wind. On the afternoon of the 11th about 4 o'clock, three officers from the rebel army made their appearance under a flag of truce, and formally summoned our gallant Major to surrender. This of course he refused to do. About one o'clock on the morning of the 12th another messenger notified us that Genl. Beauregard, the rebel commander would open fire on us immediately. This message found our little garrison, only 71, enjoying their usual repose, but they had taken the precaution of moving their blankets under the bombproofs in anticipation of a bloody melee before morning. The word was quietly circulated through the men that it was time to be up and get ready. At 3 o'clock we hoisted our colors the glorious "Star Spangled Banner" and quietly awaited the enemies fire. Long before daylight, at 4 ½ A.M., the first shell came hissing through the air and burst right over our heads. The thrill that ran through our veins at this time was indescribable, none were afraid, the stern defiant look on each man's countenance plainly told that fear was no part of his constitution, but something like an expression of awe crept over the features of everyone, as battery after battery opened fire and the hissing shot came plowing along leaving wreck and ruin in their path. The rebels for some time had all the play to themselves as our batteries were not opened until six and a half in the morning.[7] It would be useless for me to attempt to describe the scene for the next four hours. If viewed from a distance it must have been grand. The men were eager for the work, and soon had become perfectly familiarized to the bursting of bombshell, not that they had forgotten the destructiveness of these customers. The nimbleness with which they dodged into the safest corner on the approach of one of these messengers put that question beyond doubt.

   The battle raged on both sides for about two hours, when the fire from Fort Moultrie began to slacken. This, added to the fact that we had nobody hurt on our sides raised a cheer from our begrimed cannoneers, and the bombardment continued. We had been playing on the magazine of Moultrie with considerable effect. For the Carolinians admitted that they left the Fort entirely for some time thinking we were using red hot shot. The batteries doing us most damage were on Morris Island, distant about 1400 yards mounting heavy 8-inch Columbiad guns, and what was worse for us a 24 pounder Rifled Cannon throwing shaft and shell similar to those used with the Armstrong gun. This shot with astonishing precision. Almost every second shot would come in through the embrasure, and those who failed to come in had struck all round the embrasure knocking it completely out of shape and endangering the men's lives inside from the shower of broken brick knocked loose at every shot. Here we had three men slightly wounded in the fact not so severely as to require the services of a surgeon. Towards mid-day we could distinctly see a fleet of three war vessels off the bay, and we were certain they were an expedition fitted out to relieve us, and the hopes of speedily getting assistance compensated for the lack of anything in the shape of dinner. The action continued without any unusual occurrence until dark when the word was given cease firing for the night. After loading our guns with grape and canister and posting a sufficient guard we went to sleep by our guns in the safest places we could get. So ended the first days bombardment with none injured on our side, it was something miraculous, and as our Commander said, certainly, "Providence was on our side." The damage done to our Fort however was considerable. Our quarters, especially the officers, were knocked into a cocked hat, and had been three times on fire from the bursting of shell. The enemy kept up a slow but steady fire on us during the entire night, to prevent our getting any rest, but they failed in their object, for I for one slept all night as sound as ever I did in my life. We confidently expected the fleet to make some attempt to land supplies and reinforcements during the night, it being as dark as pitch and raining, but we were disappointed. Morning dawned and with appetites unappeased and haggard look although determined and confident, all took their positions for the days work. The second day opened on us with a fair prospect for us, we could distinctly see the destruction our first days fire had worked, and our guns were all just as we wanted them, so we anticipated a good days work. But alas, shortly after we had got everything in full blast, the quarters were again observed to be on fire. The enemy seeing this cheered and doubled their fire with red hot shot, and it very soon became apparent that the quarters must be allowed to burn. Our magazine was becoming enveloped in flames and our own shell were constantly bursting around us and the increased fire of the enemy made our position at this moment not to be envied. Forty barrels of powder taken from the magazine for convenience had to be thrown into the sea to prevent an explosion,[8] and the fire from our guns for the time being ceased, we only returning a shot every two or three minutes to let them know we were not giving up yet. The heat and smoke inside was awful. The only way to breathe was to lay flat on the ground and keep your face covered with a wet handkerchief. About this time we had our first man seriously but not fatally wounded. A large piece of shell tearing some frightful flesh wounds in his legs. He is now doing well. As the smoke began to clear away a little and our batteries about to be opened more generally, some excitement caused our cannoneers to congregate on the left where I was stationed. All were armed with their muskets. It turned out to be Col. Wigfall[9] with a white flag. Myself and another countryman were at the embrasure when the individual above mentioned made his appearance, and we stubbornly refused him admittance for a while, but he begged so hard, exhibited the flag he carried and even surrendered his sword, that at last we helped him in. He begged us to stop firing. An officer answered "We obey no orders here but those of Major Anderson." He then desired to be shown to the Major who at this moment made his appearance. He begged the Major "For God's sake to stop firing and they would grant any terms." This the Major after a little deliberation deemed satisfactory and the word was passed "cease firing." Previous to this however Wigfall had been waving his handkerchief from an embrasure, but the smoke was so thick that it could not be seen, and the batteries who were not aware of Wigfall's presence still kept firing. At the rebel gentleman's request the white flag was shown from our ramparts, and the firing ceased. As soon as all was quiet the flag of truce was hauled down, and our Commander submitted or rather dictated his terms; which were that we should leave with the honors of War, salute our flag, and be furnished with transportation anywhere north we desire. Thus ended the fight and here I am without a scratch, no one being wounded in the fight but the man above alluded to.[10] I forgot to mention that during the fire on the second day our flag was shot down, but it only remained down a few moments when it again floated from our ramparts nailed with ten-penny nails to a stick.

Your affectionate son

John Thompson

Chapter 2

Bathed in Blood

Reflecting on the ill-fated warriors who had served the Lost Cause, General Fitzhugh Lee observed "the bulk of the fighting material of the South were men who could not well afford to leave their little farms or moderate business for any purpose, as the daily bread of so many others depended on their daily labor." These soldiers, Lee wrote, "were intelligent and thinking men, and in instruction and training were far above the average soldiers of the world." Among these gallant Confederates was thirty-three year old Captain Obadiah Hardin, a farmer from western Chester County, South Carolina. The father of five young children, Hardin left his family and fields in early 1861 and headed, as an officer in the Sixth South Carolina, toward a bloody Virginia rendezvous with destiny.[1]

As the Civil War erupted, cotton was the undisputed king in Chester County. And a member of the royal court was Hardin, one of thirteen children. Hardin had matured in a rural region isolated from the remainder of the state. The capital city, Columbia, was sixty miles away. Chester County was frozen in time, clinging to a social and economic code that propelled young farmers—or "planters" as they sometimes considered themselves—to the heights of power. Land and slaves were symbols of wealth and Hardin, a member of a prominent family, owned both.[2]

In Hardin's judgment, the North threatened his way of life economically, politically, socially, and militarily. His spouse, Paulina Worthy Hardin, saw a different danger. After Hardin was elected commanding officer of the Chester Guards, he faced a dilemma: Would he be required to leave his native state in order to preserve South Carolina's bid for independence? A review of his correspondence with Paulina reveals that she wished him to stay close to home and not join any military force which would take him far from his children and crops. Who would discipline the children? Who would keep an eye on the eight slaves? Who would plow the fields and harvest the cotton?

In Charleston, Obadiah, still a member of the home guards, wrote Paulina this letter during the summer of 1861.

Dear Paulina, if I do join the Confederate army don't think that I have forsaken you and the children. And I don't want you to forsake me. You can say you have not but when you say that you never will write to me again if I leave the state. If I join the army, I don't expect to leave the state. Every captain has joined but me. Paulina, I had a very bad dream last night. I dreampt that all the abolitionists were marching down through our country and that I had not joined the army to keep them back and I was in a heap of trouble about it. No person has tried to get me to join since I came here. They have been very cool on the subject. I don't know what to do. No body persuades me any way at all.

Paulina be as easy as you can under the circumstances for I know you don't have any idea the trouble that I am in. I don't care about everybody knowing what I write. Perhaps it would be better for me not to write so much. I must close by telling you to kiss the children for me. Your ever affectionate and true husband

Obadiah.[3]

The confused and lonely soldier scribbled on the back of the letter "write soon if you can. It will give me great pleasure to hear from you."[4]

Within a month, Captain Hardin had joined the Confederate army and was stationed in Virginia. The following is a September 1861 letter to his wife:

Dear Paulina, you wanted me to send you word when I was coming home. I would do it with pleasure if it was possible but that is what nobody can tell. And I assure you it would be a great pleasure to me to walk home some evening and I will come home as soon as I can. I wish that peace could be made and let us all come home. But, alas, we will not all ever get home. We have already lost over fifty of our regiment and it is very probable if we ever get in battles that some others will not live to get home. As for myself, I feel thankful that I have been blessed with good health so far and trust to a kind Providence for

Captain Obadiah Hardin. (Courtesy Tyre Lee Family.)

health and I also feel thankful that you and our dear little children have been blessed with tolerable good health so far and I still hope and trust that I will soon see my Dear Wife and children in good health. I know that you have trouble and difficulties to contend with but it is the best to be patient and take things as easy as you can.... Paulina I will send you as much money as you will spend when I get it and I don't think there is any doubt but that I will get it this week. Tom Wright said he had borrowed some money from you. I have no objections of you lending him some money if you have it to spare. I would not sell any cotton yet if I was there. It may get higher between now and spring and if it don't you can keep it one year longer. After a while I will want some more things if I can get them. I sleep cold every night. There is me and Billy Cook and Bill Sanders sleeps together. We have eight blankets between us but they are too light. We have to lie on four and cover with four. If I get a chance I will get me two more, I could have got them the other day and thought I had some for myself but had to let some other men have them that had but one. Write soon to your affectionate husband

Obadiah.[5]

A later letter asked Paulina for a pair of pants. He signed that brief correspondence "Your true Husband until death."[6]

As autumn's shadows descended on Richmond, Obadiah
became depressed. A November 1861 letter focuses on a disgraced
kinsman who had resigned from the army and was returning
to Chester County.

Paulina, you said you was all anxious to hear about Eli's coming home.
Well I think you all know by this time if you and Tom Wright have got
my letters but I will tell you again and as I have written to you before I
would rather you could hear it from somebody else before you told it. He
has resigned but I told him he had better resign for he had been of no
use to the company him nor John either and I am in hopes that John will
resign. I will tell you what all of the liars have done and how they have
treated me. Bill Sanders too. They all went home and left their commis-
ary bills for me to pay the best way I could and I have paid it for us all
for two months and theirs is one month behind. Yet you need not say anything about it until you hear everything about it. They said they would
pay it when they got the money and I will let you know all about it sometime. But the truth is them very three men out to have been the last men
in my company to grumble about pay....

Paulina you need not say anything about them everybody in this regiment shall know how they have done. There is a good many already
knows them as well as I do. I look for Eli to come back but not to this
Regiment. I think he will go to the fourth where his brother-in-law is.
He never can get in this regiment any more or I don't think he can. He
may get in the Fourth South Carolina Regiment and he may not try to
get in anywhere.

Paulina as I have told you so often I will try to do my duty and when
I get off I want to come out honourable and with nothing against me....

Paulina how glad I would be to see you and our dear little children
now. I was looking at your likeness just now and I wish it was you that I
could see and talk to. Oh when will my wish come true?

Obadiah.[7]

Captain Hardin's wish remained unfilled. On December 20,
1861, the Sixth South Carolina, under the command of Colonel
Secrest and under the overall direction of General J.E.B. Stuart,

ROLL OF THE DEAD.
South Carolina Troops, Confederate States Service.

NAME.	District.	Age	Rank.	Co.	Regiment.	Date of Death.	Cause and Place of Death and Remarks.
Hanly A				C	3rd S.C.V.	Aug 18.'64	Died pris. at Pt. Lookt. Md.
Hanna D Pinckney	Marion	25	Priv	J	10th	Sep 14	Pneumonia Tompkinsville Va
" Jas D	"	30	"	J			Measles in S.C.
" Y H I			"	Y		Sep 9.'62	Bt at Richd
Hanvey Jas	Abbeville	44		16	19th	Oct 10.'63	Dis in Ky.
Harb Alfred	Edgefd	18	"				At Shelbyville Tenn
Hardin N. H			Capt	B	P. S. S	Sep 4.'62	Kd. b. Sharbsbg Md
" C. N			Priv	K	2d S.C.Res	'65	Mdrd at Dingles Mills S.C. Ap. 10.'65
" Elias Nathanl	Pickens	17	"	K		Lee Ap 18.'65	At Summerville wd d thru stomach Ap. 9
Hard John Stuart	Edgefd	20	Major	4th		Sep 20.'63	Kd. l. Chickamauga
Harden Cornelius	Horry	17	Priv	A	26th	Ap '62	Dis. Waccamaw Se
Harden A			"	B	5th	Ap 29.'62	Bt at Richd
" Thos	Chester	20	"	C	5th	Dec 20.'61	At bat Dranesville Va
" Obadiah	"	35	Capt	"		Dec 26.'61	Of wds . " "
Hardick A M	Horry		Priv	C	10th	Dec 31.'62	Kd. b. Murfreesboro Tenn
Hardwick A H			"		Smiths Batt	June 24.'62	Charleston S.C.
" Valentine	Horry	18	"	C	26th S.C.V.	Ap '62	Measles at Camp Jackson
Hardy J			"	Y	Hamp Leg	Dec 4.'64	At Richd
" Jul			"	F	1st S.C.V	Ap 21.'63	Chronic diarrhoea in pris
" Jas Hayward	Newberry	25	"	D	5th	May 25.'64	Dis. at home
Hare J H			"		Ingles S.C.Vol		Dis. in No. Ca.
Harget Eli			"	J	1st S.C.V	Sept 4.'64	Of wds rec in battle
Hargrove J H	Marion		"	R	1st S.C.Ar	Nov 4.'61	At bombardment Pt. Royal S.C.
Harken H C	Charleston		"	B	4th	Nov Dec 18.'62	b. Fredericksbg
Harkness Hm St.		17			Stuarts Cav	Dec 4.'61	Typhd near Manassas Va
Harley Rchd Sr	Barnwell	20		D	5th Cav	Mar 18.'65	Drowned in Dupt R. N.C. whilst dischg of duty
" Jos M	Colleton	24	"				
" Virgil	Barnwell	20	Serg		1st S.C.V	July 5.'62	Kd. near Richd
Harllee Robt Armstrng	Marion	19	"	J	8th	Feb 29.'62	Pneumonia in camp near Romney
Harman J LO	Orangebg		Priv	J	25th	Sept 1.'63	Dis. near Wilmington N.C.
" Hm N.D	Newberry	25	"	D	13th	May 12.'64	Kd. b. Spottsylvania C.H.

This page from South Carolina's official "Roll of the Dead" includes an entry for Obadiah Hardin (14th line from top). The death date (Dec. 26, 1861) is incorrect. Hardin died on Jan. 1, 1862, of wounds suffered at the Battle of Dranesville on Dec. 20, 1861.

became part of a disastrous encounter with Union troops along the Leesburg Turnpike. The Battle of Dranesville provided Obadiah Hardin an opportunity to do his "duty." Paulina would, through an act of courage on her husband's part, become a widow and their children would become fatherless. Captain Hardin stepped forward himself to carry the flag. As Union cannons fired down upon the outnumbered Confederates, who had come in search of food and supplies, Hardin was mortally wounded. He would die in a Richmond hospital on January 1, 1862, on the first anniversary of South Carolina's secession. In his official report, General Stuart reported "the Sixth South Carolina, under the fearless Secrest, did its whole duty, let the list of killed and wounded and her battle flag, bathed in blood, with its staff shivered in the hand of the bearer, be silent but eloquent witnesses."[8]

Chapter 3

For the Widow Hardin

While Captain Obadiah Hardin fell tragically at the Battle of Dranesville in December 1861, the Sixth South Carolina Regiment fought on until, after four grueling years of combat which thinned its ranks considerably, the men in ragged gray stood as witnesses at Appomattox Courthouse. Then, in the spring of 1865, the survivors staggered home to their farms. One of these warriors, Captain J. M. White, prepared a detailed review of the unit's service record. As he passed through Chester County, White delivered a copy of this document to Paulina Worthy Hardin. Scribbled atop the copy are the words, "For the Widow Hardin."[1]

The 6th South Carolina Regiment Volunteers

The 6th Regiment, S.C. infantry entered the state service April 11th 1861 for twelve months and was mustered into the Confederate service during June and July, 1861. Subsequently it was broken up and a number of the men re-enlisted in the Palmetto Regiment South Carolina Sharp Shooters, the 5th Regiment South Carolina Infantry, the 13th Battalion, South Carolina Infantry and the 17th Regiment South Carolina Infantry. In February, 1862, the remainder re-enlisted for two years or the war and were re-organized into six companies which were joined on March 27, 1862 by a company of re-enlistees[,] men from the 9th Regiment South Carolina Infantry. These seven companies formed the 1st South Carolina Battalion of re-enlisted volunteers. They were increased to a regiment April 22, 1862 by the addition of three more companies of re-enlisted men from the 9th Regiment South Carolina Infantry and designated to the 6th

South Carolina 6th Regiment re-enactors' flag. (Courtesy Scott and Glinda Coleman.)

Regiment South Carolina Infantry. A number of men from the old 5th Regiment South Carolina Infantry and a few recruits were also assigned to the various companies.

Date: April 11, 1861
Company A, 6th South Carolina Regiment, Volunteers
Company Muster Roll
    Muster Roll of Captain A. J. Walker's Company, in the 6th Regt. S.C.V commanded by Col. Secrest, called into the service of the Confederate States in the Provisional Army, under the Provisions of the Act of Congress passed Feb. 11, 1861 and by an act of Louisiana Congress the 11th day April, 1861 (date of muster) for the term of 12 months unless discharged sooner.
    Certificate of Mustering Officer:
    "I certify on honor, that I have carefully examined the men whose names are born on this roll, their horse, and equipment, and have accepted them into the service of the Confederate States for the term of 12 months from this day of April 11, 1861."

Major John Dunovant, June 19, 1861
Station: Summerville, South Carolina
Also included Company B commanded by Capt. L. Strait

Station: Germantown, Virginia
Date: June 19 through August 31, 1861
Left Camp Woodward near Summerville, S.C. July 16, 1861. Proceeded via Charleston, S.C., Wilmington, N.C., Weldon, N.C. and Petersburg, Virginia where it arrived on the 18th of July, 1861.
Left Richmond on July 20th arrived at Manassas Junction on the 21st to participate in the battle. On the 28th July marched to Lee's Farm four miles to Camp Pettus, joining the 3rd Brigade, 1st Confederate Army of the Potomac. Struck camp August 12th and marched 5 miles to Camp Pettus, Fairfax County, Virginia.

Station: Germantown, Virginia
Dates: September-October 1861
Camped near McLean's Ford, Virginia
The regiment left camp on September 10, 1861 and marched to Falls Church for picket duty, 14 miles distance. On the 13th one Yankee was killed when he advanced to close to our lines. We skirmished with the enemy pickets driving them from there position. Several enemy were killed and several were taken prisioner.
Returned to Germantown on the night of the 14th Sept., 1861. Marched to Lewisville and returned to Peach Grove Road. Marched 10 miles to picket and marched to Germantown on the night of the 27th.
On Oct 1st left camp for picket duty to Mill's Road marching 5 miles. Returned on the night of the 16th to camp at Germantown, Vir. On the 17th we pitched tents near McLean's Ford on Bulls Run. On the 25th marched to Mackley's Farm 5 miles distance and returned to camp at McLean's Ford on the 26th Oct. 1861.

November-December 1861
Station: Centreville, Virginia
On Nov. 7th we started picket duty to Post #5 a distance of 5 miles

and returned to camp near McLean's Ford on Nov. 11th. On Nov. 12th we struck tents and returned to Centreville, a distance of 3 miles. On Nov. 29th started picket duty to Post #5 a[nd] returned 12th December, 1861. Started with right wing of the regt. on picket duty to Post #5 and returned Dec 16th, 1861.

On Dec. 20th at 4:30 AM under Lt. Col. Secrest reported to Brig. General J.E.B. Stuart as a part of the escort for a wagon train in search for forage. A superior force of the enemy was encountered near Dranesville with 2 of our men severly wounded along with many others wounded and killed. Killed and wounded are as follows. Lt. Moon, Capt. Hardin, Capt. Jerome, J. J. Barber, A. J. Barnes, Pvt. English, Hardess, Johnston, McKeown, Sebitts, Caldwell, McGill, Cook, Robinson, Hoffman, Price, Bowman, Means, McFadden, Wylie, Kirby, Pots, Sibley, Barnes, Byers, Mobley, Hollis, Blair, Elliott, Sanders, Licas, Abell, Boyd, Lipsey, Shular, Douglas, Sgt. Farris, Campbell, Hamilton, Merritt, Sadler, Crosby, Patterson, Whitesides, Scales, Petty. The battle lasted 1-1/2 hours afterward the regiment returned to camp arriving about 10 PM that night after a march of 32 miles.[2]

Dates: December 31st-1861 to April 20, 1862
Station: Centreville, Virginia

Left camp at Centreville March 20th 1862 and marched to Orange Court House a distance of ten miles. Pitched camp at Orange Courthouse on the 21st and camped there untill April 6th 1862. Struck camp on the 6th April and marched to Louisa Courthouse, a distance of 20 miles. Struck camp at Louisa Court House on the 12th and marched to within 2 miles of Richmond, Vir. on the 17th, struck camp and took the boat to York Town, Vir. arrived there the same day.

Station: Centreville, Virginia
Dates: January, February, March, April 1862

Left camp at Centerville, Vir. and marched to Orange Courthouse a distance of ten miles on March 10th, 1862. Nothing of interest happened on the march. Pitched camp at Orange Courthouse on the 21st and camped there untill April 6th, 1862.

Struck camp on the 6th of April and marched to Louisa Courthouse a distance of 20 miles.

Struck camp at Louisa Courthouse on the 12th and marched to within 2 miles of Richmond.

On the 17th struck camp and took the boat to Yorktown, via the boat and arrived there the same day.

May-June 1862

Station: Near Richmond, Virginia

Left Yorktown on the 3rd of May, 1862. Arrived at Williamsburg on the evening of the 4th. The company with the regiment went on picket duty. Participated in the Battle of Williamsburg. Left camp at Williamsburg on the 6th and arrived at the Chickahominy River. Left there on the 11th and proceeded towards Richmond on the River Road and camped at the Laurel Hill Church on the 27th and marched 2 miles N.E. of Richmond. Left camp on the morning of the 27th with 2 day's rations in our haversack. Marched to Seven Pines (also known as Fair Oaks) and encountered the enemy at 3:15 PM. We succeeded in driving him from four different camps. We camped in the 4th Enemy Encampment that night. We were commanded by General Wilcox. We loss eight men killed and 20 wounded in the battle out of Company A. Returned to camp on the 2nd day, June 1862. On the 21st June we left camp and proceeded to New Bridge and camped there that night. On Friday the 28th engaged the enemy and had three men severly wounded but none killed.

On the 30th we marched in the direction of Charles City Courthouse. The regiment engaged the enemy but Company A had been thrown out as skirmishers to protect our flank and did not get into the battle but was exposed to the enemy fire all the while. None killed or wounded.

May 1st 1862 encamped at Yorktown. Evacuated and commenced a retreat. Fought actively at the Battle of Williamsburg May 8th 1862. Lt. Campbell and Private Hugh Smith was killed. We continued the retreat and encamped in the vicinity of Richmond May 20th 1862. Engaged the enemy May 31st at Seven Pines with a loss of 13 wounded and one killed. Engaged the enemy June 27th at Gaine's Mill and had 4 wounded. On June 30th 1862 on Monday we engaged the enemy all day driving there pickets while reconnoitering his front lines. Actively engaged the enemy in the evening and opened the fight by a charge on the enemy's battery. 1 killed and ten wounded.

Station: Culpeper Courthouse, Virginia
Dates: September–October 1862

On Sept. 1st we marched from Manassas toward Fairfax Courthouse marching five miles and camping there. Left Fairfax on the 4th and camped near Dranesville. Marched from Frederick City on the 10th arriving at Hagerstown, Maryland on the 18th. Left Hagerstown on the 14th. Marched to Boonesboro and engaged the enemy at that same day. We were in support of General Daniel Harvey Hill (This was the great grandson of Col. William Hill of the Revolutionary War. Gen. D. H. Hill was born on Allison Creek, Bethel Community, York County, South Carolina at the old site of Hill's Iron Works.) On the 15th left Boonesboro and arrived that evening. The 16th was spent with the two armies shelling each other at Sharpsburg. On the 17th engaged the enemy in the Battle of Sharpsburg and defeated them. Remained on that battlefield resting and on the 19th crossed the Potomac River at Shepardstown. On the 28th arrived near Winchester and marched to our present camp near Culpeper, Vir on the 31st Oct.

November–December 1862
Station: Fredericksburg, Vir.

The regiment remained in camp in the vicinity of Culpeper C.H. untill the 21st when it struck camp and arrived at this place on the 23rd Nov. 1862. On the 13th December the enemy crossed the river and endeavvard to break our lines of battle on the right. They were repulsed with a great slaughter. The enemy recrossed the stream in the middle of the night. This regiment was held in reserve and was not engaged.

January–February 1863
Station: Chester Station, Virginia

The 6th South Carolina Regiment, Volunteers received orders on the Sunday, Feb 15th, 1863 to rejoin Pickett's Division at Richmond. We struck camp at Hamilton's Crossing near Fredricksburg, Vir. On the 18th we joined the division and marched four miles from town and on the 19th marched through Richmond and camped that night three miles outside the city in the direction of Petersburg on the Telegraph Road. On the 21st we again took up the line of march toward the present camp. The road was very muddy, the weather was extremely cold and disagreeable.

Dates: March–April 1863
Station: Near Suffolk, Virginia

The regiment removed from camp near Chester Station, Vir. via the R & P Railroad on the 1st March 1863 and arrived at camp near Petersburg on the evening of the same day. Remained there untill the 9th March. Struck camp on the 10th and arrived in the vicinity of Franklin March 13th. Stayed there untill Arpil 10th and left camp near Franklin for Suffolk marching some four miles and camped there. Broke camp and arrived near Blackwater May 5th, 1863.

Dates: May–June 1863
Station: Near Richmond, Virginia

On the 3rd of May 1863 the 6th S.C. Regiment Volunteers returned from the front lines of Suffolk. On the 15th we skirmished with the enemy near Carsville. Left on the 16th taking the rail cars to Weldon, N.C. On the 19th returned to Blackwater. Marched from Blackwater to Iron Station on the 21st and arrived at about 9:30 PM. This being a distance of 24 miles. Left there and took the cars to Petersburg, Vir. We were reveiwed by General D. H. Hill on the 28th. Left Petersburg on the cars for Richmond reaching our present camp on the Charles City Road that day on the 28th.

Dates: July–August 1863
Station: Petersburg, Vir.

On July 1st the regiment skirmished with the enemy near Turnstall Station. Left camp on the Charles City Road and proceeded to the Chickahominy River on the 2nd July, 1863. There we participated with the enemy in a skirmish. No one was killed or wounded. Returned to the camp on the morning of July 4th, 1863 (Independence Day) left the Charles City Road Camp and moved to Brook's Turnpike. Left there on the 28th July and moved to Petersburg. On Friday July 31st the company was sent to strengthen a detachment under Capt. Foster at Stony Creek. Returned August 2nd to Jackson Hall.

Dates: August–To December 1863
Station: Morristown, Tennessee

On Sept. 14th 1863 the 6th S.C. Regiment took the rail cars to join the army of Tennessee. We reached the railroad terminal on the 20th of Sept. and united with General Hood's division on the 21st. On the night of October 28th with the rest of Jenkins Brigade we made a night attack upon the enemy in Lookout Valley. We lost 16 men. On November 5th we left Lookout Mountain for East Tennessee.

From November 6th we marched through Tiners Station, Cleveland, and Sweetwater, Tennessee. Part of our journey being taken on the Georgia and E. T. Railroad. From Sweetwater we crossed the Tennessee River and were threatened by the enemy on the 14th. On the 15th we took the line of march driving the enemy before us all day. On the morning of the 16th Company A skirmished with the enemy. At Campbell's Station we had 2 killed and 8 wounded. Arrived at Knoxville, Tenn. on the 17th and stayed there untill December 5th 1863. Marched through Rogerstown and Brans Station and engaged the enemy on the 21st December. We then camped near Morristown.

Dates: January-February 1864
Station: Bulls Gap, Tennessee

Left camp to forage on the 14th of January, 1864. On January 15th the regiment marched from Morristown, Tenn. five miles on the road to Dandridge. On the 16th we marched 6 miles father. On the 17th we skirmished with the enemy at Dandridge. One man was killed and three wounded. The regiment returned on Jan. 19th to winter quarters at Morristown, Tenn.

On the 23rd we marched to New Market, Virginia a distance of 17 miles. Left New Market and marched to Strawberry Plains, Tenn. a distance of 6 miles on Feb. 13th, 1864. On the 22nd we marched back to New Market and on the 23rd to Panther Springs. Marched to Russellville on the 24th and then to Bulls Gap on the 26th.

Dates: March-April 1864
Station: Mechanicsville, Virginia near Cotham Station

On the 28th of March 1864 the 6th S. C. Regiment left camp near Bulls Gap, Tenn. and arrived at camp near Zollicoffer, East Tenn. on the 1st day of April, 1864 having marched a distance of seventy-five miles. On the 17th April we were transported by rail to Charlottesville, Virginia. On the 28th April 1864 we left Charlottesville. We arrived at this present camp after marching a distance of seventeen miles.

Dates: May–June 1864
Station: Petersburg, Virginia

Left Gordonsville on May 4th 1864 and marched in the direction of Fredricksburg Virginia. We arrived at the Wilderness Battlefield on the morning of the 6th of May, 1864 and participated in that battle sustaining a loss of three men killed and 15 wounded. We left the Wilderness Battlefield on the night of the 7th and marched toward Spotsylvania Courthouse arriving there on the 8th. We remained there untill the 22nd when we marched toward Hanover Court House Junction. We had a skirmish with the enemy on the 28th and had one man killed. We left Hanover Junction on the 28th and marched to Cold Harbor. Left that place on the 11th June to Petersburg, Virginia.

Dates: July–August 1864
Petersburg, Virginia

The regiment remained in the trenches at Petersburg untill the 29th of July when it marched to the north side of the James River near Chaffin's Bluff. We laid quietly in camp untill August 14th when the enemy drove in our pickets. Our left line had a severe fight. This regiment was not directly in the fight and lost only a few men. We returned to Petersburg, Vir. on the 24th August 1864.

Dates: September–October 1864
Station: Trenches between the Charles City Road and the Williamsburg Road, Virginia

On the 2nd of Sept. the regiment moved from Petersburg, Virginia to Swift Creek and returned on the 4th Sept. 1864. On the 16th we moved down the Boydton Plank Road and after two or three days moved back toward Petersburg. On the 29th September we struck tents and camped at Fort Gilmen for the night. We moved down opposite Fort Harrison and participated in the assault on September 30th, 1864. We loss 142 men killed and wounded. We slept on our guns on the night of October 6th 1864.

We engaged the enemy on Oct 7th 1864 on the Darby Town Road and lost 30 men killed. Was engeged again on the Darby Town Road and loss one man killed on October 13th. On the 27th we loss one man on the Williamsburg Road.

Dates: November–December 1864
Camp near Richmond, Virginia
    Engaged the enemy lines on the north side of the James River on the 10th of December. Lost two men. We left the trenches on the 14th December and marched to New Market attacking the enemy trenches. We loss one sgt. and one private. On the 22nd December the regiment was ordered to move to the right and accupy the lines vacated by Hokes Division. Having remained one day was ordered back to it's original position. On December 23rd 1864 the regiment took the cars to Gordonsville and spent the night in the cars. The weather was extremly uncomfortable due to the extreme cold. The crowded conditions and body lice made the night most miserable and intolerable. We had about 65 men on the box car. The car was filled with horse manure. Left Gordonsville on the 24th and returned to camp on the 25th December, 1864, Christmas Day. Christmas dinner consisted of green apples, uncooked corn from the mules' trough and corn stalk roots.

Dates: January–February 1865
Station: Trenches near Richmond, Virginia
    Camped in the trenches near Richmond, Virginia on the Williamsburg Road.

Dates: March–April 1865
Station: With General Lee at Appomattox Courthouse vicinity. Present for surrender. Headed home to South Carolina.

Chapter 4

I Am Nearly Crazy

The year is 1861. David Harris leaves his 500-acre farm, eight miles southeast of Spartanburg, and marches off to war to defend the Confederacy.

His 34-year old wife, Emily Harris, must manage the best she can, no easy task when you consider she has seven children and has to supervise ten slaves.

Before leaving, David has kept an accurate record of his farm work, hoping that it will make him a better farmer. He asked Emily to carry on with the journal. Fortunately for history's sake, she does, leaving a remarkable record of what it was like to be the wife of a soldier and farmer during one of American history's most turbulent periods.

And fortunate, indeed, is the Winthrop Archives, for the Emily Lyles Harris journals are now a part of its holdings. For sheer historical value, the Harris journals are one of the Winthrop Archives' most valuable and fascinating collections.

They offer an unusual, penetrating insight into what womanhood and motherhood were like in rural America in the mid-nineteenth century.

Since marrying in 1846, Emily's life was hard. She gave birth, raised children, made and mended clothes, tended the garden, cooked, cleaned, and performed the many other duties that society expected of the 19th century woman.

When learning that he would soon be conscripted for service with the South Carolina state volunteers, David began to worry about Emily. He knew Emily would be a good mother and would work hard, but he wondered if she might not be "much at a loss with the management of the farm and negroes."

Emily, too, had her doubts. The day after David left, she wrote for the first time in the diary: "The trial had come at last ... how I shudder to think that I may never see him again. A load of responsibilities are resting upon me in his absence but I shall be found trying to bear them as well as I can."

Almost as soon as David departed, Emily began to face a myriad of problems—the presence of the farm, dealing with her children, managing slaves. At times Emily seemed overpowered by life's many details and the diary poignantly conveys this:

> If I am always to live as I have the last few months I shall soon tire of life and be willing to die. It seems that I have to think for everyone on the place ... every little things has to pass through my hands.

Grasping for a reason to explain her predicament, Emily began to slowly blame the Confederate government for taking away her husband and making life miserable. Emily became so disillusioned with the war effort that, by 1865, she began hoping for a quick defeat.

If the Harris journals were nothing more than an exercise in self-obsession, they would still be a valuable record of the Civil War's impact on one Southern family. But Emily commented on the lives and fortunes of those around her.

In one entry she catches the mood of the Confederacy on the road to defeat:

> How We pity the brave men who are engaged in these battles.... Everybody is anxious and gloomy. Constantly We are hearing of some brave man who had fallen and whether an acquaintance or not he is somebody's son, somebody's friend, some face will grow pale at news of his death, perchance some heart break, some soul pray, in its anguish, for death.

As the situation became more desperate, Emily began to worry about her slaves over whom she felt to be losing control. In early 1865 she wrote that "the negroes are becoming so impudent and disrespectful that I cannot bear it." A few months later, Emily wrote, "The negroes are all expecting to be set free very soon and it causes them to be very troublesome."

Spartanburg district was in a frenzy during the last few months of the war with word about General William T. Sherman's burning of Columbia. Like other South Carolinians, Emily and her neighbors knew that Sherman considered the state to be "the hellhole of secession" and so expected the worst. "I am nearly crazy," Emily wrote, to describe her fear that the Yankee army was marching on Spartanburg. But Sherman never came near Spartanburg; instead, he marched on Camden.

Emily managed to prevail. Shortly after, David returned safely and once again took up the journal.

Once again, like most women from that period, Emily's life is obscure. We must rely on family tradition. After her husband died in 1875 at age 54, Emily lived with her children until her death in 1899. Emily's death was as dramatic as many of her journal entries. She died from a stroke suffered in a dentist's chair.

1862

November 23. Sunday. But little work has been done since Mr. Harris left except some little jobs that he directed. It rained all night one night. Was he sheltered? This morning little D.G. was fretted about something and he run crying out to the gates where the hogs were being fed, I know, expecting to be taken up by his father. The tears would come a little in spite of me but I choked them down because the children seem sad enough without encouragement. It has always been my lot to be obliged to shut up my griefs in my own breast. I wish he was here to tell me whether to have some hogs killed tomorrow or not. Mary Harris is with me to night. She is crying for her absent husband and I must laugh and be gay on her account. Truly I have no time to grieve.

November 24. KILLING HOGS. This morning being cold and frosty I had eight of our hogs killed selecting for that purpose, according to my husbands directions, the smallest and least promising. They weighed as follows: 196, 170, 166, 161, 114, 120, 121, 110, amounting to 1148 [1158] lbs. The day's work was troublesome and I missed my best friend very much indeed. Just after dark, to my unspeakable surprise he stepped in. It made us all very glad but his visit is only for a few days. He was sent home by the authorities to warn some laggard numbers to join their company. I received a letter from him a little while before he came which was the first he ever wrote to me in his life except a little note the morning after he left home.

November 25. To day Elifus and York are ditching in the Buffalo Bottom. Edom and Will clearing a new ground on the same branch a little higher up and the negro women are helping me do up the lard and sausages. The new ground was commenced a few days ago and I hope the negroes will be able to get on well with it without their master. To day I finished weaving up my wool. I have made into cloth this fall, about 65 lbs. of wool. Some jeans I have sold for $3.50 cents per yd.

November 28. KILLING HOGS. To day Mr. Harris took the cars for the camp again. I do not feel quite as bad as when he first started. We had six more hogs killed. They weighed as follows: 146, 190, 220, 206, 205, 261, averaging 204⅔ lbs. We have one more to kill and then our year's allowance of meat will be hard in. I am afraid it will be short but our carn would not justify any more meat. In the evening cousin H. Allen called and I paid her from flour I borrowed last summer.

November 29. Ditching in Buffalo bottom and clearing. All doing as well as could be expected in the absence of our Head.

December 1. Carried a piece of cloth to Miss Polly Smith to weave. I find it utterly impossible to get my weaving and sewing done this winter without help. Went to Gleen's Spring and bought some buttons for Mr. Harris's clothes and a five gallon pot. I saw some more pot ware which I wanted badly but let it alone lest I might want the money worse for something else.

December 2. All going well as far as I can judge but tonight it is raining and cold and a soldier's wife cannot be happy in bad weather or during a battle. All the afternoon as it clouded up I felt gloomy and sad and could not help watching the gate for a gray horse and its rider but he came not, though all his family are sheltered and comfortable the one who prepared the comforts is lying far away with scanty covering and poor shelter. "The soldier in his tent."

December 4. Had a stack of hay hauled from forest bottom and commenced regularly feeding our cattle. For a year or two our cattle have seemed to decline. I think because we have too many for our plantation and now that the forest bottom from which we have usually obtained large quantities of hay has passed into other hands I feel sure we shall have to reduce the numbers of our stock. The present crop of hay is the last we shall have from that place. This evening I went around to all our barley pastures. They look fine and I think will make a change in the condition of our cattle. The calves and donkeys are rejoicing in it every day. Threatening rain. Is my Husband sheltered?

December 5. Night has at last put an end to a very troublesome day. I have had company last night and to day. It has rained all day, the children have been cross and ungovernable. Old Judah and Edom are both sick. Ann is trying to weave, and a poor weave it is, the sewing must be done, every thing must be attended to; Laura is coughing a rough ominous cough, has scarcely any shoes on her feet, and no hope of getting any this week, West has the croup. I am trying to wean the baby and the cows laid out last night, and last and worst of all I know my husband is somewhere miserably cold, wet, and comfortless. "The soldier in his tent."

December 14. At home. Husband gone to the army again, every thing resting on me, children troublesome, company forever, weather very cold, negroes in the newground, cows, calves, and sheep on the wheat. To day I have heard that the Yankees were shelling Charleston. Oh! God preserve my husband!

December 17. Weather excessively cold. Anxiously expecting news from Charleston. Mother almost insane. Negroes in the new ground and killing beef. I almost wretched.

December 19. All well, weather moderately cold, newground getting on well, housework slowly, no letter from Mr. Harris since he left, false report about the shelling on Charleston.

December 22. Weather moderate. All tolerable well. Sent some raw hides to the village to Charles Thompson to be tanned. No letter from Mr. Harris yet. I am almost crazy.

December 24. Christmas Eve! How different from any I have spent. War raging in the land. Husband away in camp. [I am] afraid to look into the "dark and shadowy future." Had a stack of hay hauled from forest bottom. Sent York with the four eldest children in the rockaway to the village to spend the night and Christmas day. Let them have pleasure while they can. A kind and merciful God is over us all.

December 25. Christmas day has past off pleasantly. The negroes seem disposed to be quiet and obedient. The weather is scarcely cold enough for us to need a fire. Sis and Mary Harris have spent the day with me. We had a nice turkey for dinner. The children have got home from the village without accident, and better than all, I have had two letters from my absent husband. I wished last night for a letter from him, as best thing I could have for a Christmas gift, and Fortune graciously sent me two.

1863

January 1. KILLING HOGS. I have sickness in the family, yet this new year's day I have felt in good spirits and hopeful. I cannot tell why unless it is because Mr. Harris writes me so many kind letters. I had one today and two yesterday. A little thing sometimes makes our cheerfulness or sadness for the whole day. I had the last one of our hogs for this year killed today. It weighed 180 lbs. Our number of hogs this year was 15. Their average weight was 170⁶⁄₁₅ lbs., the whole amount 2,556. Our usual allowance is 3,000 but these are war times. I pray God that next New Year may find our country at peace and my husband at home.

January 2. Weather fine but cold. Sick [are] all convalescent. Had a letter from Husband. If I had the time to spare I don't know to what extremes I might go in writing to him. I can scarcely refrain from writing a letter to him every night. I could not have believed I should have enjoyed his letter so much. To day I agreed to let Mr. Zimmerman have three common sized cows and two small yearlings for the sum $127. I hope I have done well to sell them.

January 6. To day and yesterday I have had the hands hauling leaves and raking up manure but things don't go on like they did when Dick was at home. I have had a letter from him every day for some time. He is a kind and faithful husband.

January 10. We are all pursuing the even tenor of our ways without much trouble or disturbance any way. Old rose, a good old cow, died this week and I sold one for $35.00. Three rainy days this week. FIRST LAMB, FIRST LAMB.

January 17. Saturday night all well and weather cold, extremely cold. One lamb has made its appearance this week and young brindle has had a calf. I have sold a little beef for $13.00. I have been sick, and very sick to see Mr. Harris.

January 19. Cold rain. Yesterday the weather was so extremely cold that I thought I should be saving ice to day but rain has put an end to the ice. The family are all suffering from colds and sore throats. YOUNG PIGS.

January 20. Rain all night and all day. Forest up to the bridge. To day we discovered in her bed the white sow with six nice pigs.

January 22. Sold Landford [a] cow for $28.00. Weather warm. Little Dixie sick, not well myself. Negroes cleaning out hill side ditches.

January 25. YOUNG PIGS. During the week. Elifus has discovered that we have some more pigs [born to] the spotted sow. We do not know how many. We have not yet found the bed. The weather now is quite pleasant but news from Mt. Pleasant[1] is unpleasant and that makes me feel unpleasant. My soldier is tired of his tent.

January 28. I have just ascertained that the black spotted sow has only two pigs and they bad looking. Snow on the ground this morning. All gone by night. Family not well, negroes doing nothing but eating, making fires and wearing out clothes.

January 29. To day we are plus a lamb and minus a calf. Nothing lost by the swap. I'd rather have a nice young lamb than a poor lousy calf. The weather is cold and very little work is being done in or out doors. Husband will soon be home and I fear he will be much disappointed in the quantity of business that has been done in his absence.

February 3. SNOW. SNOW. This morning when I waked I found a heavy snow on the ground. Thought it would soon be melted, but it has since turned very cold and there is a probability of our having snow for some days. I have heard of some fighting near Charleston and I am now looking with painful anxiety for a letter from Mr. Harris to tell me whether he is preparing to meet the foe or start home.

This morning when I went out to see about our sheep I found that something had eaten three lambs. One had been eaten a day or two ago. I am extremely sorry for the loss for the sake of the loss and for Mr. Harris' sake who has taken so much pains with and is so proud of his fine sheep. The day has been extremely cold. The snow is still on the ground and the North wind is howling frigidly around the house. Sis Camp left her old home to day for good and all, and I reckon it will be a long time before we will see her again.

February 5. SNOW. SNOW. All night it snowed and hailed and blowed and snowed and hailed. All day has been freezing cold. I have never seen but once before so much snow on the ground. This is the day that Husband was to have started home from the war but his letter last night says he will have to stay until the 20th. Old white sow got in the yard last night and eat up a little lamb which I had been nursing during the day. If crying would have brought it back I could have easily done it. It seems like I must let them freeze or be eaten up, one or the other. Five have been destroyed.

February 6. Willie has just got home from Charleston where he has been nearly two weeks visiting his father in camp. He has many wonders to tell. HAULING ICE. I have had the ice house cleaned out this evening and prepared for the reception of ice but I expect it will turn warm by morning. How badly I do want Mr. Harris at home.

February 7. HAULING ICE. Had two loads of ice put in the house, one from Enoch Smith's pond and one from our fish pond. It is a little over an inch thick. Just read a letter from Mr. Harris telling me that he will probably be pressed into service for thirty more days. "Hope deferred makes the heart sick."

February 8. Good skating this morning, but now, at night the weather is warmer and I reckon the skating and the ice saving are over for this winter.

February 12. Nothing new. Weather very warm and cloudy. Elifus working for Billy Ray at $1.00 per day. Edom, Ann, Nerve in the new ground. Will and York hauling hay from forest bottom. To day I have warped forty yards of fine cloth. I am going to sell ten yards of it when it is wove which will bring me ten dollars and pat for the weaving of it and get me a bunch of thread. The thread in the whole piece is worth $12.00, the weaving $6.00, the dyeing $2.00, the spooling and the warping $4.00. The cloth when it is done will be worth $1.00 per yd. What a time for speculation.

February 14. FIRST GARDENING. To day I have had the garden ploughed and such seeds planted as should have been a month ago. I have made the garden extremely rich to try to make up lost time. We shall need a good garden worse than usual this year. We have scarcely enough corn and meat, and no wheat. Never since we kept house has our table presented so little variety as at present. My heart grows anxious as I sit down to the table and look at the hungry mouths that are gathered around it. A letter from Mr. Harris last night tells me that he will be home Wednesday night then all things will be bright again. The house is needing its band.

February 18. It rained all day yesterday, all night last night and is still raining. This afternoon I am to send to the station at Cedar Spring to bring Mr. Harris home from the war. His time of service for the present is at an end and he is still alive and well. I did intend to go myself and meet him but the weather is so wretched bad and it is so dark and cloudy that I am afraid to undertake it lest he might fail to come and I be obliged to drive home in the dark which I could not do with safety.

February 21. MR. HARRIS HOME FROM THE WAR. Saturday night. The weather is still raining. There has been but little sunshine this week though we did contrive to get our Irish potato seed ploughed up to day. They should have been planted three weeks ago. We expected to have had some for sale, but like every thing else which I build hopes upon, they have come out at the little end of the horn. Self sucking cow had a calf last night. If she attempts to suck herself again we must put a muzzle on her, we want milk to bad at this table to afford to feed cows on it. Agreeable to orders, last Wednesday evening I sent the carry all and buggy to the station at Cedar Spring to bring Mr. Harris home. A miserable and anxious night I spent watching for his arrival and wondering what horrible accident could delay their coming. At last about 12 o'clock York came home leaving the buggy broken down on the road. The cars had not come, and the people had given them out for the night. I went to bed, but only to dream of the crushed and mangled body which I thought, like as not, was lying somewhere on the road between here and Columbia. I arose quite early, ate a few mouthfuls of breakfast, and started to the station to hear news [from] the returning soldiers. I could scarcely hope it would be good, for we all knew that some accident on the road must have detained the cars. Just as I started I heard the whistle and hurrying on, met my soldier husband trudging along home on foot, looking extremely well and soldier like. An accident had occurred on the road but no one was hurt, so all the anxious hearts were relieved. Thursday and Friday passed off pleasantly with us all, but several things have combined to put Mr. Harris out of humor today. Our stock are not looking as well as he thinks they should. Perhaps if he had been at home he would have given them more corn than they had, but with all my pinching and saving I think our corn will not hold out till new corn comes. I was afraid that he would not be pleased with us all, but I've done the best that I knew how to do. Another thing that has cost me a severe scolding is the manner in which I have kept this journal. I think that I had better not undertake it for him any more, then he will be spared the pain of scolding me, and me the pain of being scolded. My husband is a man of fine and sensitive feelings, easily irritated, but a choice, superfine husband withall.

September 13. Last Friday morning Mr. Harris left home for the hard and perilous life of a soldier. This is the first time since he started that I have felt sufficiently composed to write a sentence. Why should I tremble so? His life is in the hands of God in all cases and surely he is safer at the post of duty than elsewhere. Last night we had thunder, lightening, and a little rain. To day is extremely hot.

September 18. To day I have had some cane and some wood hauled and tomorrow I shall commence making molasses. I have not had a letter from Mr. Harris, and I am not well and as blue as indigo.

September 19. MAKING MOLASSES. PLANTING ONIONS. PUTTING UP FATTENING HOGS.

September 21. FROST, not severe.

September 24. Finished saving fodder. Gathered a little corn. Received from Bomar's mill 907 lbs. of very nice flour made from 25 bushels of wheat. I am very busy making molasses. Today I have made 10 gallons. Just received a letter from Mr. Harris. He is well and satisfied for which I am thankful.

September 28. Threshing barley today. Things go on slowly when Mr. Harris is gone. I am afraid he will not be convinced when he comes home that I have done the best I could. PRICES. We find it takes a great deal of money to get on with. In a letter Mr. Harris wrote me from Charleston he gave me some of the market prices—beef $1.00, pork $1.50, onions $25.00 a bushel, potatoes $15.00, geese $9.00 per poun[d], chickens $3.00 each, mutton from 75 cents to $1.00, butter $8.50, common pumpkins $1.00. Three years ago who would have believed this?

September 30. FIRST NEW CORN MEAL.

October 3. All this week has been spent threshing oats and barley. We have all done the best we could. Our crop of small grain this year is fine. Sixty-nine bushels barley, twelve rye, two hundred and eighteen wheat and one hundred and twenty eight oats.

October 5. Making molasses. The cane in the bottom pull green but I dare not wait any longer. The weather is very fine. Finished spinning wool. Wool rools are selling at $7.00 per lb., linsey $5.00 per yd. and jeans $10.00. Our sheep are fat and fine.

October 6. Making molasses, and breaking up last year's barley patch to sow again in barley.

October 11. Finished breaking up barley patch. Molasses mill broken down. Business gets on slowly, slowly. Oh! if Mr. Harris could be with us just one week to set us straight. How many unhappy restless women this war has made. When will it end?

October 13. Commenced sowing barley.

October 15. We have had an awful storm of wind, rain, and hail blowing down fodder stacks, hay stacks, fences, and trees at an alarming rate. All well for which I hope I am thankful.

October 18. Cloudy and warm. All quiet about Charleston but daily expecting the Yankees to break loose. Yesterday we broke to pieces the molasses mill for good and all. I have made eighty gallons of good molasses. I have three or four loads of can left which I may have made [away] from home and give the third for making it.

October 21. Finishing sowing the Barley field. Weather very fine. No very severe frost yet. No news from the war.

October 24. Raining a little. I am having the crib cleaned out and a little wood hauled preparatory to doing a good weeks work next week gathering corn. Finished picking over the cotton yesterday evening. I get letters daily from Mr. Harris which are a guide and comfort to me during his absence.

October 26. GATHERING CORN. Weather still very unpleasant. No news from the war. People are in great trouble about getting as much, and such food as they want. WE can scarcely buy leather or hire work done except for something to eat. Butter is selling in the village at $4.00 per lb., leather the same, jeans $10.00. Cotton cloth from $2.00 to $3.50 per yd. Factory yarn $20.00 per bunch.

October 28. Finished gathering the corn at the home plantation. Had only fifteen loads. Mr. Harris is at home on furlough. I am suffering severely with my sore foot which I scalded several days ago. Mr. Cunningham is here fixing our plows for sowing wheat. The weather is pretty cold, but quite favorable for out door work.

October 29. CORN. Commenced hauling corn from Buffalo bottom.

November 7. SOWING WHEAT. Today Mr. Harris left me again for the camp. During his stay at home his regiment has been removed from Greenville S. Car. I always feel extremely bad when he leaves me. I shall never get used to being left as head of affairs at home. The burden is very heavy, and there is no one to smile on me as I trudge wearily along in the dark with it. I am constituted as to crave a guide and protector. I am not an independent woman nor ever shall be.

November 9. SEVERE FROST & ICE. DIGGING POTATOES. Find our potatoes small and few. To night it is cold and cloudy and seems likely to snow. A letter from Mr. Harris tells one that he has arrived safe at camp near Greenville. I wish I could have the privilege of tucking the blankets around about him and making him comfortable this bleak night. They have an excuse for tents and I will try to be thankful. Oh! pity the "Soldier without a tent."

November 10. Still digging potatoes.

November 11. Finished digging potatoes. Put them into the potato house at once. We have tried various ways to keep them and have never been successful. This time we tumbled them into the potato house as soon as we got them out of the ground. I took no pains to wrap them or to air them. I except them to rot, but if they don't we will eat them.

November 17. Finished Sowing wheat at home and commenced in Buffalo bottom. I went to the village to day. Sold some ordinary homespun for $3.25 cents per yd. I made a few purchases. The prices of everything is distressing. I came home feeling very restless and confused about many things. The weather is cold.

November 18. Still sowing wheat. Mr. Finch has helped us three days with three plows. The weather again is mild. The ground has not been to wet to plow since we commenced sowing wheat.

November 24. Rainy and disagreeable. I have had a trying day. If I am always to live as I have lived the last few months I shall soon tire of life and be willing to die. It seems that I have to think for every one on the place. My brain is feverish with the effort to think of all that needs attention. Every little thing has to pass through my hands in some way. Will I ever have my husbands help again?

PRICES. Yesterday I went to the village to try to make a full return to the tax collector, but he was not there. It is said that it must be done before the 25th or we [will] be double taxed. I shall risk it. If I take many more trips up there through the cold, neglecting business at home (I have been there three times) it will be double taxing any way. I saw jeans retailing at $15.00 per yd., cotton cloth at $2.00, $3.00 and $4.00. Turkeys are $10.00 a pair, butter $3.00 per lb., homemade molasses $5.00, leather $9.00 per b., good cotton cords $50.00. I gave for large buttons enough to put to a coat $2.95.

November 25. Today we have heard that Lieut. R. P. Miller was killed in battle in Tennessee last Friday. Many a tear will fall for that young man. Though he had neither wife nor mother and few relatives he had made himself many friends.

The weather is fair and pleasant. I have also pleasant news from my husband. A lady told me yesterday that she had just bought two pair of good cotton cards and paid $50.00 a pair. When and how will it all end?

November 26. BUTCHERING. To day we have killed ten hogs weighing as follows 145, 203, 180, 205, 125, 108, 161, 86, 140, 204. The day has been cold and clear. Fine weather for saving our meat.

November 30. This morning the weather is extremely cold and there is frost and ice plenty. The hands are trying to plow but it is bad work. I have some barley and wheat to sow yet. I am busy cutting out winter clothing, every thing is behind time and I'm tired to death with urging the children and negroes to work.

December 1. YOUNG PIGS. YOUNG PIGS. Within the last two days two spotted sows have had pigs, one seven and one eight.

December 3. FINISHED SOWING BARLEY in the big field by the gin. COMMENCED sowing wheat in the mill pond meadow. To day I went to the tanyard at Walnut Grove and bought 73 lbs. of leather at $5.00 per lb. I should not have been able to get it at that if it had not been promised to me months ago.

There is no good news from the war. God only knows what is the future of the Southern Confederacy. If any one should raise the veil of futurity and ask me to look I should not have courage to do it. There is not a ray of light to be seen. All is black darkness around and before us. Heaven help us!

1864

March 1. About 3 o'clock this morning Mr. Harris again left his home for the "soldier's tent." He has gone into Confederate service and there is no telling when I shall see him again. After he had started and I had cried until I could cry no longer I slept a little nap, waked with the heaviest heart I ever had and spent a sad and lonely day with no company but little D.G. Pour little fellow, he was happy as a bird little knowing the dangers to which his best friend is exposed.

March 2. A little rain last night. Sold a gobler for $10.00.

March 3. NEW FLOUR. To day I sent 26 bushels of wheat to mill which made 885 lbs of flour.

April 20. Finished planting the upper field to day and commenced the lower one. The weather is still very cold and it has commenced raining again. I saw two or three stalks of corn up to day but they were badly frost bitten.

April 21. Who can read the signs of the times? Watchman, tell us of the night!

April 22. Friday. Today I went to the village and drove old Press. I paid to the government the tenth of our bacon which amounted to 138 lbs. Dr. Dean has bought some corn at $12.00 per bushel, he is going to try to buy me some but is not certain he can get it. I received warning to send a fourth of our slave labor to the coast immediately. I shall try to pay for a substitute and if I cannot get one I suppose I will be compelled to send one of our negroes, but they shall not budge till they are literally compelled to go. I've sent my husband and that is enough for me to do. A negro was hung today and two more are waiting to be hung in June. I feel bad, there is nothing to feel glad about. All is darkness.

After supper. I have just received a letter from Mr. Harris. The first since he left. He is in low spirits. I am very sorry for him, I can only help him by trying to do my duty at home. The weather has turned warm at last, we are all rejoiced and I am having corn planted in a hurry. I humbly hope and pray that we may make our bread this year. Heretofore, my husband has been a corn seller instead of buyer.

April 24. Sunday, raining again, weather warm. Our garden is beginning to improve. This warm shower is acceptable. FIRST LETTUCE.

April 25. This morning, the ground being too wet to plow, I mounted old Press and went in search of corn. After riding till noon without hearing of a grain for sale I landed at home almost tired down. Every body else is done for planting but us. I feel impatient and worried. There is not much pleasure in life when ones husband is in the army and no corn in the crib.

April 26. PLANTED SUGAR CANE.

April 27. Planted cotton at the old Golightly house. The weather is very fine and all natur seems engaged to make amends for the tardiness of Spring.

April 29. FINISHED PLANTING CORN. To day I have employed one horse and hand in a fruitless search for corn. I can hear of none for sale. I do not expect our family will actually starve but if I cannot buy a little corn to feed our horses we will perish next year. In this fearful crisis is the Almighty for us or against us?

May 1. Sunday, warm and cloudy. Passed a quiet day at home which has rested and refreshed me very much. Plowing the corn at Camp place. Youngest large faced cow has a young calf at which event we are all rejoiced. SHEARING SHEEP. Weather cold and windy, almost cold enough for frost but it is the third of May and I'm ready for the shearing and we will risk it. Finished shearing the sheep. We sheared only twenty eight, thirteen of them ewes. The wools of the twenty-eight without washing weighed ninety six pounds. The wool of two that died during the winter was six pounds, which makes us one hundred and two pounds.

May 5. Plowing corn in upper field the first time. Replanting at Camp place. I get letters almost daily from Mr. Harris. He is on the way to Green Pond S. Car[olina]. where he will probably be camped for a time. I ought to be thankful that he is well and cheerful. Garden is looking well, salad plenty at last. May 11. We have had a little rain this evening and I have had thousands of cabbage plants set. One of the sows has one small Pig and some one has stolen another which would have had pigs. We have had six fat shoats stolen since Christmas. Oh! If I could discover the rogue. A bloody battle is being fought in Virginia, so far our troops are victorious.[2] Every Christian ought to be engaged in prayer for surely the crisis must be at hand. Every heart should bow in prayer for our success, and for the souls of those who give their lives for their country.

May 12. MADGE HAS A MALE COLT.

May 13. We have had a good season, not before we needed it. The ground is now to wet to plow and the hands are replanting corn. Our rye is heading out of our wheat and oats are still low. We are anxiously awaiting the heading of our wheat to feed our horses. Our corn is nearly gone and I've tried in vain to buy. I don't know what to do next. In all the darkness which surrounds us we at last see a few gleams of light. Our army has been successful at every point. The shout of victory comes to us from all parts of the Confederacy, but alas! with it the wail of the widow and orphan.

May 15. Sunday evening. The day has been cool, cloudy and rainy. We are all well, and, as yet have not suffered for food or raiment. I have had no company today and it has been to me a day of rest. I feel refreshed and strengthened for the duties of another week.

The battle still goes on in Virginia and the news of victories is coming on every breeze. How we pity the brave men who are engaged in these battles. How we sympathize with the anxious hearts which almost stand still with suspense as the turn and listen in every direction for the last scrap of news from the battle. These hearts are more to be pitied than those that lie cold and still on the bloody field. They are "Where the wicked cease from troubling and the weary are at rest."

May 18. Plowing and replanting corn in the barley field. Weather pleasant but not as warm as we desire. The sounds of bloody strife still comes with every train from Virginia. Every body is anxious and gloomy. Constantly we are hearing of some brave man who has fallen, and whether an acquaintance or not, he is somebody's son, somebody's friend. Some face will grow pale at news of his death, perchance some heart break, some soul pray, in its anguish, for death.

May 19. This evening we had a nice warm shower. A fine swarm of bees came out today. The first good swarm we have had. I have just had a very pleasant letter from Mr. Harris. He is on the Carolina coast doing picket duty. I miss him very much in all my undertakings but the privation may be of service to me in after life and if he is of service to his country, I ought to be reconciled, for truly our country needs help in her fearful struggle for life.

May 20. Commenced plowing over the corn the second time. The cotton is just up and looks weakly. I had it plowed over, praying it will improve it. Our old horse Press has given out. I am a good deal troubled about it. I shall have to send wheat to mill this week and after that I shall have to send of go to hunt some corn and if I am so lucky as to find it, then it will take both mules two days to bring it home. All this time the plows should be running. I am not very well and am almost worried to death. The soldiers wives who have nothing but what they draw from the government are better off and happier than I.

May 23. Monday. Laid by Irish potatoes. Examined our ice, found it keeping tolerably well. Dr. Lund, Mrs. Dean and Mrs. Gwin Harris and her children spent the day. All well.

May 24. Today I spent with Mrs. Billy Ray and enjoyed it very much. The hands are plowing over the lower field. We have there a good stand of corn and it looks well. We planted this corn some weeks after the land had been broken up and then plowed out the middles before we drove out the plows. I do not know whether to call this the second plowing or not. I am a young farmer though not a very young woman. The weather is warm and it is thundering and raining a little.

May 25. Planting First Potato slips this morning.

May 26. To day I have attended the funeral of aunt Jane Wells. We had thunder lightning and rain during the service. I have had a letter from Mr. Harris telling me that he is quiet well and going to Adam's run. Our troops in Virginia are still bravely and successfully fighting our foes. Truly the country is pouring out its blood freely to win our freedom.

May 27. Early this morning I took York, the mules and rockaway and started to Mrs. Alexander's in quest of corn. I had the good luck to get the promise of ten bushels at $7.50 per bushel. When I reached home I was tired and low spirited. I have heard that one bushel of corn at home was worth two abroad, but I never realized it before.

May 29. I have just returned from a visit to the village. I went up yesterday morning. While there I made a return of our property and to the assessor tells me our tax (Confederate tax) will be $581.45. I have the means to pay it, but if we continue to be taxed during the next year as we have last I am afraid our means will utterly fail. I must comfort myself with "Sufficient unto to day is the evil thereof." I gave $5.00 for a pound of soda, $1.00 for a paper of needles, $4.00 for a spool of white cotton thread, $4.00 for a quire of paper.

May 30. To day our girl Minerva GAVE BIRTH TO A FINE BOY.

May 31. I have been quite busy today, scouring and scalding. Our hands are plowing over corn second time, and hoeing and thinning it out. Our corn looks as well as other peoples, but not very well. I have just received a letter from Mr. Harris telling me that he had been in a small fight with some Yankee boats. I have been trying to get a petition signed to have him detailed as a farmer, but he tells me that his officers are determined to disapprove it. Now of course there is no hope but for him to remain there and fight our foes. I feel just as much like fighting our men who, standing at the head of affairs, are the cause of keeping such men as him in the field, as I do the Yankees.

June 5. Sunday morning. The weather is warm and rainy. I have not seen the sun since last Thursday. Since it commenced raining we have set a great many cabbage and potato-slips. As usual, I shall employ myself today in writing to Mr. Harris. I shall be troubled some to find wherewith to fill a letter but letters, he says he must have, and I must try to give him what comfort I can. It is little that he can have at last. Oh! "When this cruel war is over."

June 6. My Birthday, I am thirty seven years old. I can scarcely see to live as many more.

June 8. It has rained a great deal the last few days. We have not been able to plow and I am distressed about our crop. I am an inexperienced farmer and I do not know how much the danger is of getting behind. I am like one walking in the dark. We have just finished hoeing the cotton. Our corn has been plowed and hoed twice but the upper field. We go into that tomorrow or next day. To day I have been again in search of corn and found none. Thank the Lord we have wheat plenty.

June 12. Sunday morning. The weather is bad. It is raining and has been raining or cloudy for more than a week. During this time but little work has been done in the crop and what plowing and hoeing has been done will do but little good. Our wheat looks fine. Farmers tell me that it will not till well. I must not fret about that, over which I have no control. The family are all unwell. Vomiting and diarrhea is the order of the day. Elifus has gone to see his wife, Lucy buried. Last Sunday we planted the last corn we shall plant this year for Roasting ears.

HOG STEALING. Today after many preliminaries and several postponements we undertook an examination of some negroes to try to discover who it is that has been stealing our hogs. We have evidence sufficient to bring heavy suspicion on Gwin Harris's Pink. He has sold pork, beyond a doubt, and he grows separately. They all told different tales, but all agreed that Pink had sold pork. He says he got it from our boy, Elifus but has no proof. I believe that Pink sold our hogs and I do not believe more about it. Dr. Dean, Gwin Harris and Harvey Underwood assisted me, but if Mr. Harris had been at home I think the thief would not have escaped. Thinning sugar cane and hoeing and thinning corn in upper field.

June 15. Fair weather at last. For more than a week we have had cold, cloudy weather with considerable rain. I have been trembling for the wheat, but I believe it has escaped unhurt. Yesterday I finished robbing bees. I found the hives moderately well filled. Mr. Moorman came down and staid all night. He brought me some nice fan handles and I've been busy all day making fans.

June 16. This morning we had to assist our old horse, Press, to rise. We will soon have his skin. The weather is warm and pleasant.

June 18. This morning it is raining. I am having the garden hoed out. I staid all night at Gwin's and helped Mary nurse her sick children. OLD PRESS is dead. The boys are skinning him. I expect his hide will be more valuable to us than he was.

June 21. Finished planting potato slips. Finished thinning corn for this year. Finished plowing upper field. Commenced it on the 10th with three plows. Stopped two or three days for wet weather.

June 22. Last Sunday I received a letter from Mr. Harris telling me that he had applied for a furlough and would probably be at home in a few days. No one can guess how glad I was. Last evening I sent to the station to bring him home but, Alas! I only got a letter telling me to look for him no more present. I tried to look the disappointment directly in the face but it cost me a few tears nevertheless. I did so much hope that he should get home to help me with a heavy harvest and various other perplexing matters. It is bad for the house to be deprived of its band. We hear that the yankees are making a desperate attempt to take Petersburg. We have been very successful all this Spring. If we have a reverse now, The Lord save or we perish.

June 23. COMMENCED WHEAT CUTTING. Col. Harris and Gwin Harris and family spent the day with me. The old man thinks our corn crop looks fine and that our wheat will be found rather light. He has promised me a hand during harvest. We had cucumbers for dinner to day. We are having a plenty of vegetables now, and are all able to do them justice. Miss Jinnie has dismissed school this evening for a few weeks.

June 26. Sunday and one of the hottest Sundays I have ever seen. Our ice is keeping up pretty well. We are enjoying it [in] this weather. It is a source of great grief to me that the one who provided it cannot now enjoy it. He is in a hot climate with no one to give him a glass of ice water. To day some-one sent from the village to beg some ice for a dieing soldier. I gave it to him with a prayer that my husband might receive a similar kindness should he ever need it.

June 29. We have four cradles. We had a nice shower this afternoon. It came too late to spoil any wheat. We are done all but the white wheat and nearly done that. I do not much like the white wheat. It is too easily injured by wet weather. The oats are waiting for the sickle so that we go on with our small grain until we are done with it. The oats are very fine. I shall know more about the wheat when it is threshed. It has been considerably injured by wet weather.

July 1. Finished cutting the wheat and rye. Commenced the winter oats and found them too green. Tried barley and found it so low that it all fell through the cradle. I want to pasture it awhile and plow it about the last of August. I think it will make me another pasture. This morning I had a letter from Mr. Harris. He tells me that there is no chance of him to get a furlough. I did not know how much I had hoped for it until I found that hope destroyed. I must flounder along without him. I may have to do without him forever. He tells me that his mess includes himself and one other, and they two draw 1½ gal meal, 1 qt. flour, 3 qt. rice, 1½ lbs. of meat and a tea cup full of salt for five days. TO DAY I HAD SOME CORN PLANTED.

July 2. Early this morning I had the two mules put to the rockaway, and drove to town myself, carrying Laura and Luella to attend the commencement at the Female college, and to fly around a little. Willie went to come back with me and assist me in case of an accident. When I reached Col. Harris I found the family considerably agitated in consequence of a robbery which had taken place night before last. Some one took a trunk out of the old man's bed chamber, opened it, took out all the money that was in it ($100.00 in specie) and some other valuable things, then kindly left the trunk in the portico. While in town I bought a paper of pins for $2.00, A steel pen 25 cents, Pack of envelopes $2.50, Quire of paper $2.50. Black pepper is selling at $16.00 per lb., Sorghum syrup (molasses) $25.00 per gal., Lucifer matches 25 cents per block. The weather is extremely hot. The thermometer stands at 100 degrees. We are needing rain.

July 4. The children have been fishing in our pond and have caught three suckers each over a foot long. Great rejoicing with them. To day we have commenced plowing again. I find some corn over at Camp place, which I had intended to plow again, too large. We shall have to "let it rip." All is well, for which I pay to be truly thankful.

July 8. They have had a battle on James Island[3]—are still fighting there. Mr. Harris is there. I feel very anxious, but why should I? The decrees of fate are unalterable. The weather is hot and we are needing rain. Cutting Spring oats and fretting because I cannot hire help. Our oats are very fine and I do hate to lose them.

July 9. What times! What times! We do have with our harvest. We have the finest oats in the country. When I tell my friends, to they all cry out "save them, save them." But how can we do everything? I have nearly run myself and all the rest down and still there is oats, oats, oats. If I hire much more we will have nothing to feed hirelings with. I can find no one willing to cut oats for anything but wheat. What is best to do I can't tell. Oh! me Oh! my. No rain yet. We need it badly.

July 11. Last night we had a small shower. I have five hands and a wagon and team hired. We are trying to save our grain. Some are cutting oats and some are hauling up wheat. I have rented a wheat pasture at the rate of $1.00 per day for 12 hogs. I find that our ice is melting very fast.

July 13. To day we finished hauling wheat and rye. We are still cutting oats. It is now raining beautifully and we are glad to see it, but I hope it will clear off tomorrow so that we can go to hauling up the oats. To day I paid $3.00 for a pound of coperas[4] and sold a half gallon of molasses for $12.00. Leather is selling at $17.00 per lb.

July 14. Last night we had a good rain. This morning I had some cabbage set out. I do not much expect them to live. As it is too wet to haul the oats or to cut, the hands have been laying by the sugar cane.

July 18. Sunday morning. All well and quiet at home. A letter from Mr. Harris tells me that he is not very well. I feel a little anxious about him. The weather is fair and pleasant. The children are reading and everything seems to enjoy the calm of this beautiful Sabbath day. The Sabbath is a great mercy to mankind.

The weather is cool, cloudy and rainy. We are very busy laying bye corn. Hauling up oats, etc. We have at last finished cutting our large crop of grain. Part of our extensive pasture is open and our hogs, cows and horses are living high. I have just read a letter from Mr. Harris. He is quite well which makes me feel a good deal better that I did this morning. We are rose across. The school commenced again this morning, and the children had all their books and papers, pens and pencils to parade. By the time they were fairly off my patience was worn out. Several unpleasant things assailed me during the day, until I could only find relief in tears. "There are moments in life when teeming with sadness, There seems in our pathway no gleaming of gladness." Mr. Harris tells me that he bought a pound of sugar for $7.00 in Charleston. It sells for $10.00 in Spartanburg.

July 19. Laura is sick. Judy is sick. Ned is sick, and Edom has gone to see his daughter—Leah—buried. Rain this morning.

July 23. Finished hauling up the oats. Laid bye the barley field corn and sorghum. Today I sent ten bushels of wheat to Thompson's mill. For the first time in six months I went to church. I heard no sermon nor no news except that two women, both members of the church, had had a fist and skull fight and beat each other black and blue. I had a letter from Mr. Harris that tells me that he has been in great danger of being killed by the fire. He has at least discovered how it feels to be shot at and missed. The weather is really cold. I could have enjoyed a fire all day.

July 24. Sunday. The weather is still cold. I've had fire all day. The girls went to church at Cedar Spring. Caught old Will stealing eggs. He steals and lies and disobeys all laws with the utmost impurity. Oh! that some kind providence would rid me of him.

July 27. Today and yesterday Mr. Allen has been threshing our small grain. We have made 149½ bushels of wheat, 229 oats, and 13 rye. The weather is quite cool and cloudy with little rain. Busy laying bye corn. Finished cutting oats. Our wheat has turned out very badly. We have not made a half crop. When expenses of saving and threshing are all paid, there will be none to spare. I feel almost sick to think of all the trouble we had sowing and cutting and hauling and threshing and at last we've only made as much as we can eat. It is no small matter to feed the hands and mules of the thresher, and it is no small matter to feed the reapers that I have had to feed. I have worked hard with brain and muscle this summer. I cannot whether with it all we shall make expenses. I feel low spirited. We have suffered for rain. This forenoon we had a good season. I hope it will improve the appearance of our upland corn. Our ice is all melted. We have news of a victory at Atlanta.[5] This victory has been hoped for a long time. I suppose the battle still goes on. No letter for me tonight.

July 29. Rain plenty at last. A very hard shower is now falling. Roasting ears. We planted a little corn on the 19th of March and another lot on the 14th of April. The latter yielded the first roasting ears. Both lots were equally fertile. It is no use planting corn in cold weather. It will not grow till warm weather comes.

July 30. To day I went to the village and carried a box filled with good things for Mr. Harris to be sent to him tomorrow. When I came home I found a letter from him telling me that he was now getting plenty to eat, which was not the case all the time. His mess includes himself and one other man. For a while drew for five days 1½ gallons meal, 3 qts. rice, 1¾ lbs. bacon, a half pint of salt. Their horses are poorly fed generally. The day he wrote, six ears of corn were given to 24 horses. I think the government should take care of their Calvary horses, for they seem to be very scarce and difficult to obtain. During the past week we have been eating a very nice fat mutton, the first I have allowed myself since the war commenced. Weather warm and cloudy.

August 1. Things are out of order as usual on Monday morning. The air is so still and hot that one feels a sense of suffocation. It is quite cloudy and will rain directly.

We still have a good deal of hoeing to do. It worries me. If Mr. Harris had been at home the last row would have been hoed in the month of July and we could have had the month of August for improvements but Alas! Alas!

August 2. Hoeing and laying bye cotton. This afternoon we had a small shower. The weather is now very warm with plenty of rain.

Billy Ray is home on a furlough. He belongs to the same Regt. with Mr. Harris but he is so busy telling all about the war that he tells but few particulars about the camp on James Island. I do not like his politics, but about the bad management of the men at the head of the nation, he is about half right. We have some very bad laws and some that oppress the people very much and still don't answer the purpose. The tax in kind is a perfect torment to the people and is so managed as not to feed the army. Thousands of bushels of corn rotted at the depots where it was delivered to the Government and now our calvary horses are starving and soldiers sometimes near it.

August 2. Wool. Wool. I have had my wool washed and weighed. It lost in washing just thirty pounds. Wool is now worth $20.00 per lb. in a rough state and $25.00 in rools. Our legislators intended prices to fall this autumn but as yet I see no indication of it.

August 4. Today I have had my late corn and cane plowed. It looks promising. I have spent the day at Billy Ray's very pleasantly. I have received the rent wheat from Mr. White—ten bushels and three gallons. That will add a little to our Wheat crop. CUTTING INDIGO.

August 5. A little rain today. This morning the hogs have been put into the Buffalo pasture. The cotton is laid bye.

August 6. Churning indigo. I do not much expect to succeed with my indigo. It is a new business, entirely, to me.

August 7. Sunday. Someone has stolen a few fine watermelons from me today and I am now indulging in the feelings which are uncongenial to the Sabbath day. I feel very unforgiving.

August 10. Breaking up and manuring a turnip patch today. I never will fail again to have my turnip patch made in the Spring and ready before this time. Many people have sown their turnips but perhaps I'll have good turnips late. Mr. Moorman is staying all night with us. We want a little rain. We are having a few very good watermelons. Mr. Harris tells me that they are selling in Charleston from $5.00 to $10.00.

August 14. Sunday night. Today the girls went to church at Philadelphia. I passed the day pleasantly, reading for my own and the children's benefit, writing to Mr. Harris, and fixing a box of good things to send to him by Billy Ray. After the box left home I heard that Billy would not start until Tuesday. I am very sorry. Some of the things will spoil before they reach him. The weather is excessively hot and dry. We want rain.

Thoughts of the business of this week are beginning now to exclude the mental calm which is our duty to encourage on the Sabbath day. As far as I can now judge no time in April or May ever presented as many things to be attended to in one week. I must go on patiently.

August 15. A nice shower to day. Billy Ray will leave for the Camp on James Island in the morning. I have sent Mr. Harris a few nice things which will keep his wife, children and home fresh in his memory.

I have agreed to give $2.00 per yd. for the making of jeans. I furnish the warp, coloring and wool rools. Wool at the lowest is $15.00 per lb. (Some say rools are $25.00) Factory yarn such as we use for jeans is worth $30.00 a bunch. What will jeans be worth?

August 16. To day Mr. Jesse Barnett commenced making us a molasses mill. I had some indigo cut, the turnip patch plowed and plowed again and harrowed and put in nice order for sowing. It has been a very busy day. My feet are sore. I am sore, heart, soul, and body.

August 20. This morning I had my own turnips sown. We had a good rain yesterday and again this afternoon. This is Saturday night. It has been a week of weariness and trouble. Many trifles have occurred to make me feel unpleasant. Many things which I thought to have done have been left undone. I have at last made a little indigo which has the appearance of indigo.

This morning we heard of another battle, another victory and the fall of several young men—true and brave. Lemuel Moorman, the only brother of our esteemed young friend, and teacher Virginia, is among the slain. His father, mother and sister all looked to this young man for support and guidance. The piteous shrieks of his sister are now ringing through the house. "Oh! how can I live without my brother?" How few have escaped the bitterness of this cruel war.

August 21. Sunday. Afternoon. Mr. and Mrs. Moorman came down last night and have just left with Miss Virginia who wishes to rest from her school a few days and remain with them until she may hear the particulars of her brothers death. I had no letter from Mr. Harris last night nor the night before. I feel restless and anxious.

August 24. Putting away our wheat and oats in boxes and fixing up various little matters which have been waiting for the finishing of the crop. Our molasses mill is finished. I think it is a very good one. It cost me $30.00 in money besides the work of three hands nearly a week. I got no letter from Mr. Harris tonight. I feel disappointed.

August 25. Today we have commenced plowing barley and cutting wood to boil molasses with. I have seldom seen an August as uniformly hot as this has been. I am almost afraid to plow the mules. I have been offered two stacks of hay for the cutting. Should I sow the barley and cut the hay? The family are all unwell.

August 27. Today I have ridden many miles among the neighbors in search of soap. I found two pounds at $1.50 per lb. I am tired and thoroughly sick of trying to live and make and keep something for the children. Every thing I lay my hands on seems to fail. I thought I would have a splendid barley pasture. The barley was not cut, only pastured a little while. When I look at it last there was a seed plenty on the land. Now I believe it is all gone, where I cannot tell. The negroes say they have kept the hogs out. I have missed the chance to save some hay thinking that the barley, plowed in now, would perhaps be worth the most.

There is no pleasure in life and yet we are not willing to die. I do not know how it might be but I feel like I should welcome the Messenger if it were not for those who need my services here a while longer.

August 30. Today we have commenced Pulling fodder at Camp Place. The mornings are quite cool and the days quite hot. Miss Virginia has got back and again taken her post as teacher. She looks sad and heart broken.

Peace conventions are being held in the North, an armistice is talked of, and peace flags have been raised in New York. I tremble for fear it is too good to be true, or may amount to nothing.

September 3. I have been a good deal grieved lately about old Mr. Landford selling an old still kettle which he had borrowed from us. He loaned us one to use for a molasses boiler while he used ours for distilling. He, in some strange manner concluded that the exchange was final and finding he could get a good price (as he thought) for ours he sold it and appropriates the money. I thought I had a good copper boiler to last me for years but it is straw. I am sick of losses crosses and disappointments.

We had a nice little shower and I am having parts of our turnip patch resown. I am sick of life.

September 6. Yesterday I went to the village. The trip was extremely unpleasant in many respects. I intended to come home last night but was prevented by a storm. If I had been alone I would have started before the storm. I was dreadfully put out by being compelled to stay. When I reached home I found the negroes skinning two of my finest milk cows. A tree fell across the fence of Dr. Dean's cane patch. They walked in and killed themselves eating cane. No one can tell how I feel at the loss of these cows. I have had some feelings about it which I have never had about the loss of property before. It will cause us, White and black, to sit down to many dry suppers. Time has been that if we needed a milk cow we could go and buy one. Now we cannot. We have not the means and besides, we could scarcely find the cow if we had. Milk cows are selling at $500.00.

The prospect for Peace is not so bright as it has been, or as we thought it was. Atlanta has fallen into the hands of the enemy[6] and McClellan a man favoring a continuation of the war has been nominated for next Yankee President. The weather is cool, and cloudy. We had plenty of rain yesterday.

September 7. I am boiling my dead cows and skinning off the grease to make soap. The meat is excellent food for the hogs. The hands are busy gathering fodder. I am busy doing everything.

Mr. Harris has sent the boys some hats made of rushes tied together with strong thread. One of them he made himself. Quite an achievement. He also sent me some rice which I valued highly. Anything which will keep life in the human body is now fully appreciated by me.

September 9. Gwin Harris has made some molasses today in iron vessels which he likes very much but I now taste iron in it. Mr. Landford came according to promise and mended the old copper boiler. If it will do we will use it henceforth. Gwin and I are in copartnership. Gwin helped about the mill and puts up the furnace for the use of them one year. Gwin dont like the mill. He thinks nothing but iron mill or iron cogs will save all the juice. He thinks he can haul his cane to a better mill, and pay toll for making, and get more molasses besides getting rid of the boiling. If he tries is and finds it so I shall profit by the experiment and haul mine to a better mill too.

September 10. Today I killed three stands of bees to get some honey for winter use. I find my bees doing tolerable well. In the afternoon I went to the tan yard to get some goat skins which had been tanned for me. I found them not quite ready. I carried my two cow skins to be tanned. I came home last and found my three year old baby being rocked to sleep.

The weather has been unfavorable for saving fodder but is now better. We get on slowly at that, as with everything else.

September 17. Saturday Night. Nothing of importance has taken place in our family during the week. I have made a little molasses for old Mrs. [Alice] Hawkins, more for her accommodation than mine. I took the third for grinding and boiling. Those who make molasses for the "third," which is customary, do not make expenses. So I think. Our hands are still saving fodder.

The news from the army is anything but cheering. The Confederacy seems ready to cry out "Lord save or we perish." Letters from Mr. Harris are not cheerful. A sadness seems to have enveloped him. They are half fed and half paid. Their horses are not fed at all. Flour is selling at $1.00 per lb. Sweet Potatoes $2.00 per qt. Irish $1.50 and other things in proportion. The infantry privates are paid $12.00 per month, the calvary $24.00. How many months of wages will it take to buy a bushel of sweet potatoes? May a merciful God send wisdom to the men who stand at the helm of the nation.

The yellow fever is in Charleston.

September 20. NEW CORN. To day we gathered a load of corn from Camp Place. I have put up nine hogs to fatten. It is all we have that are large enough. I may put up some shoats after a while.

September 21. Raining. Raining

September 23. Still Raining. Bill Camp and Sis staid all night at Gwin's on their way home from Dr. Bennett's. Time has been when they would have stopped here. But Alas! the friendship which once bound us together has been shattered, and can never be repaired.

September 27. Saturday night. Nothing has been done this week to make us either richer, wiser or happier. It has rained nearly all the week. We have finished, or rather quit PULLING FODDER. I am now ready to make up our molasses, and the trouble and distress that it has cost me and my friends to get me fixed for it is all most without parallel. The sum total of it is Dr. Dean had mercy on me and loaned me two boilers, and Gwin Harris had mercy on me and came and made the furnaces. The old copper kettle which I expected to boil in has "gone up the spout."

September 30. MOLASSES. I am so busy that I can hardly spare a moment from my journal. I had a great deal of trouble to get fixed for making molasses but at last I am fairly into it. I have an excellent mill and two large boilers. I thought the mill was not good but I find it very good. I have some of the very finest cane. Every farmer should not try to make his molasses. It should be managed after the fashion milling. Until it is so managed I think it will not prove a blessing to us. The improvements which we would make on our farms between the laying by and gathering of crops, now give place to making molasses.

October 1. To day I have made twenty gallons of molasses. It was a very hard days work. A hard shower fell on me while I was dipping up the last. I do not feel in the mood to journalize. I labor under many difficulties and get on slowly with all I undertake. I surely am a bad manager. The great trouble is, there is no one on the place that has the welfare and prosperity of the family at heart but me. No one helps me to care and to think. Our man Edom is very sick with typhoid fever. We do not expect him to recover. Losses, crosses and disappointments assail me on every hand. Is it because I am so wicked?

My husband and children are well. Let me be thankful.

October 8. FINISHED MAKING MOLASSES. Saturday night. Such a weeks work I have never done before. My molasses has turned out very well. I have made something over a hundred gallons. We have had rain twice during the week which interfered with my work considerably. Through much tribulation I have finished. I have not injured the boilers (They were borrowed) which relieves my mind of a great load of anxiety. I could have paid the owner what they cost him, but I could not have replaced them. The weather has suddenly turned very cold, almost cold enough for frost. Our sick negro is no better, or if he is we cannot discover it. I expected him to have seen a change before now. Typhoid fever is slow fever. I must wait patiently. I very much fear that we all have more of it in the family.

The yellow fever is still in Charleston, too close to James' Island. We have had another battle, another victory and have as usual paid dearly for it. Numerous brave, prominent, promising young men of Spartanburg are reported dangerously wounded. Where are the ones to fill the places of the gifted so have yielded up their breath in this awful struggle?

October 9. Sunday morning. The weather is fair and bright and cold. I have seen no frost yet. It seems quite cold enough for it.

The girls and their teacher have gone to church. I am alone in the house, though not lonely. I'm never lonely. Time never hangs heavily on my hands. I've always more for hands and brain than they can possibly do. As the years roll on, cares and anxieties, and theirs are mine, consequently more are multiplied day by day. Will it continue so to the end? Life is not desirable for life's sake, but for the sake of those who need my services. I wonder how they feel who profess to think this life is all.

October 11. We have another case of fever. I fear two more. The first case is no better. I have spent the afternoon in search of some one to spin and weave wool. I could have finished working up my wool at home, but for the sickness of the family.

Trouble assail me on every hand. I find my molasses barrels leaking. Surely I have more ill luck than any one else who ever tried to make a support from their family. Gathering corn at Camp and Golightly Places. First Frost.

October 13. We made six loads of corn on the other side of Buffalo. Today I am having some small lots sowed in rye. Some are picking cotton and some are planting onions. The rye and onions should have been planted in September but thus it is that a large crop of molasses interferes with other important business. I should have been able to sow a very good pasture the first of this month if the family had been well. As it is I must give it up. Our fever patients are all better but one. The weather is extremely cold for the time of the year. The Peace question is agitating the public mind.

October 16. Sunday. I have had company today contrary to my wish. The family are all unwell. Is it the sorghum syrup which has disordered us all? I have craved a few quiet days and for several weeks they have been denied me. I may as well give it up and resign myself to live in hub-bub all my life. I have been so troubled with sickness and company and business that I have neglected to note in this journal several important occurances. Mr. Harris will be disappointed in the journal when he sees it. I have been compelled to leave some things undone which he would have done. In that case I have tried to attend to the most important first.

Fattening hogs have been up nearly a month. We have one very large white sow which I expect to make very heavy, seven ordinary hogs, seven small ones, and that is the dependence for bacon another year. It is not enough but it will have to do. We have a very fat hog in the yard which I may perhaps conclude to add to the file. The weather is still cold and clear. Our sick negro gets neither better nor worse. The house is quiet at last.

October 17. Finished first picking over cotton. The weather is cold. The family are sick. I am very well myself. If I was sick what would become of the rest? I think I am of use to the family.

October 18. PICKING PEAS. It seems that I cannot spare time to pick them but surely I ought to save enough for seed. The weather is cool, pleasant and a little cloudy.

The sick of the family are all improving except Luella, who is quite sick with sore throat. Miss Virginia was too unwell to attend her school today. The children have all been at home. I have been much troubled by their noise and confusion which has caused me to ask myself what I should do with them when the school was out, and then what should I do with myself if I had no children.

Mr. Harris tells me that the troops on Jame's Island are not starving but next to it. Sprouted peas boiled without meat and cold rice was their bill of fare when he wrote last. He had given a woman $2.00 for a quart of sweet potatoes.

October 19. More sickness. Picking peas. Hauling wood. Weather fine. Government agent called on me but did not impress anything I had because I had nothing to spare and am a soldier's wife.

October 21. The weather is fine. I had my dried beans picked today and commenced gathering corn in the upper field. The squirrels are playing havoc with it.

It is seldom I stop to think of how I feel, much less write about it, but tonight I feel so unusually depressed that I cannot [help] half casting about in my mind to see what is the matter. I left home about eleven o'clock to drive with Mary and Gwin by special and urgent request, to celebrate the anniversary of their marriage. I forgot to tell all I wanted to carry with me. I lost some money. I felt unwell. I came home and found my sick ones not so well, I heard that our troops on Jame's Island were ordered to sleep with their shoes and cartridge boxes on. After supper the topic of conversation was, Death. Our faithful dog—Bony has howled ever since dark. What ails me I do wonder?

October 22. Saturday night. Today I have spent at Dr. Dean's. It is the first time I have gone from home except on business since Mr. Harris left home in April. The sick of the family are all convalescent, still I felt as if I ought not to leave them. When I came home I found that all had gone on well in my absence. Each member of the family had done their duty. The weather is cold and windy. I think we will have heavy frost in the morning. The hands have been pulling down corn in the fresh field by the gin.

October 23. Last night some one stole one of our fattening hogs, skinned it and left the skin for our share. I have had the good luck to get a very large fat hog, which has been gone from home nearly a year. I shall fatten and kill him if some one this lawless land does not kill him for me. Col. Harris is spending the night with me. I am glad to be under the same roof with him. He is my husband's father and is my disinterested friend.

October 24. I am in a peck of trouble. I have a whole field of corn pulled down and nothing to put it home. Our oxen cannot be paraded. Elifus and York have spent the whole day in search of them. I am awfully afraid they have broken into someones corn field and killed themselves eating peas. They are very mischievous. One of them has to be chained head to foot all the time.

Several members of our family are still quite unwell. I have no joyful feelings this night, nothing to make me glad and many would say nothing to make me sorry. Calico is selling at fifteen dollars per yard.

October 25. Found the runaway oxen and finished hauling the barley field corn (four loads). I took a long ride today to see about some spinning and weaving. My wool is all spun.

Last night some one stole some molasses from Dr. Dean out of a barrel which sat right under his bedroom window. The lawless are getting bold and bolder. Shooting them is the only remedy.[7]

October 27. This has been a very rainy day. We found one of our fattening hogs dead today. I had it skinned and the meat boiled to save the grease for soap. Another of our largest hogs will soon have pigs so we cannot kill her. That will take three from the number we intended to kill. If all had done well we would not have had half enough. Dr. Dean kindly came over and mended up my old carry all. Once in a while the soldiers wife receives a favor. I have been looking for Mr. Harris home. I have been dreadfully disappointed in not getting a letter today from him to tell me when to send to the station for him. I should grieve for him to have to walk home this rainy night.

Last night at one o'clock I was roused to hear Edom was much worse. I hastily dressed and went to him finding the negroes all assembled to see him die. He was suffering with colic. I gave him a dose of whiskey and red pepper which soon relieved him.

Gwin and Laura have had a shooting match this afternoon. Laura shoots well. With a little practice she would make as good a marksman as her father. There is no telling but the times may demand the use of her skill.

October 29. HUSBAND AT HOME. Last night at the hour of midnight I heard a familiar step on the threshold of our home. The joyful news quickly brought the children out of their beds. After we all had hugged and kissed our best friend, we raised a light to gaze upon and scrutinize the beloved features which had begun to be something belonging to the past. Six months in camp has changed him but little in my eyes. Some of his friends say he looks haggard and worn. I don't think so but I wonder that he is not. A man who loves his home as Mr. Harris does, suffers heavily when separated from it. His arrival has dispelled all gloom for the present.

October 30. Sunday night. Today we had friends to dine with us. Dr. Dean and his family, Gwin Harris and his, and Billy Ray and his. We all enjoyed the day, but Sabbaths should be spent in a different manner. Mr. Harris and Billy Ray have been in camp together and have been almost starved for a few months. I have never seen men eat like they do. I cannot blame them. I know they cannot help it. I can only hope they will not do the job which the Yankee's shell has as yet failed to do.

November 5. Saturday night, This week has passed away. I can scarcely tell how I have been very busy making winter clothing. The out door work gathering corn and hauling wood has gone on during the year.

We had a few rainy days and some freezing mornings. Mr. Harris has been quite busy making arrangements for the welfare of his family. He has a furlough of only two weeks.

This afternoon we butchered the fattest kid I ever thought of. It is the second I have had killed since Mr. Harris came. I never can enjoy eating when he is starving in camp, therefore I will use them while he is here.

November 6. Sallie Owens spent the day with us. In the afternoon I carried her home in the buggy driving Madge and making a short visit to Mattie Ray and Annie Dean. Not the way to spend the Sabbath.

Since dark it has commenced raining.

November 8. The weather is warm as May and very cloudy and damp. Yesterday was quite rainy. The hands have been hauling in the fodder from the upper field, it being too wet to haul corn. Mr. Harris is about to swap Madge for (he thinks) a better horse. He has brought the horse home to try him a few days.

This is the day of Northern Presidential election. The last one brought about a horrible war. Let us hope this will bring us peace.

November 15. There are days of glad meetings and sadder partings. Yesterday morning at five o'clock I started my husband once more to do battle for his country.

The weather is quite cold. We finished digging potatoes and sheltering from the cold our cabbage. This afternoon I took a short ride on our new horse. I do not like him much for the saddle. His paces are too rough. He will suit Mr. Harris for a war horse very well. I want to call him Billy Button in honor of this horse which Mr. Harris rode when he came a courting but the children are begging to call him Roland. I don't know which it will be.

November 18. DONE PICKING COTTON. I went to town today and drove our new horse, Roland. I am pleased with him. I paid $6.00 for a pound of soda and $5.00 for a paper of pins. Everybody seems to be distressed about the war. The dark days have surely come. The Confederacy! I almost hate the word. May the Lord have mercy and incline our hearts to do his will.

November 20. A dark cold cloudy day. Miss Virginia and Laura and Ella have been from home since yesterday morning. I and the small children have had a quiet Sabbath day.

November 21. Monday night. It has rained all day and rains on. When will we get to sow wheat? I have been having some corn shucked and shelled to send to mill while the ground is too wet to plow. I am trying hard to make a support.

I have not been well today. The children have been confined to the house. Their noise and confusion and the trials that I see in the future have made me a miserable day. I have felt crazy. I could almost feel the wrinkles coming on my face and the hair turn gray on my head. A few more years of this kind of life will wear me out. I feel old and miserable and ugly. I see no pleasure. I try to see none. I have ceased to expect it. I expect no more rest this side [of] the grave. The wants of the family are never satisfied and their wants weigh heavily on me. I have often heard my old mother in law say that they who raised the most children had the most trouble. My eyes are failing. I can hardly write by candlelight. I shall soon be blind. I suppose that when I am no longer of use here I shall be called hence.

November 22. Gave $25.00 for a coffee pot.

November 23. Cold, freezing cold, extremely cold. Ice everywhere. Every body shivering. Since dark Walter Mitchell and Anna have come to spend the night with us. I have sent Elifus to the village with the wheat which I owe the Government. It is one of the bad terms of the Confederacy, that, no matter how little we make we must give the tenth to the Government. Give it whether we have enough for ourselves or not.

Some of our hands have been cutting corn stalks. I am trying to get all things in readiness to sow wheat if ever the weather permits it again. I have had news from Mr. Harris since he reached camp. He is all safe and sound at his post ready to "strike for our native land."

November 24. Commenced sowing wheat. The weather is still severely cold. The ground thawed a little after noon. George Camp is staying all night. All is well.

November 25. Today our school closed for this year. Miss Virginia was to have taught a year but the weather being so extremely cold and her health not very good, I thought it best for the school to close. I would be glad to employ her another year.

Mr. Harrison Bagwell is to crop with us next year. He done his first days work with our hands today. We have had a terrible time trying to mind up the old gears so as to get through another year. I go forth into the "shadowy future" but not without a fear. I can see no more beyond the next crop. After that there will have to be a general remodeling of every thing, Everything.

Today we found another hog skin. The hog was killed in the lower field. It appeared to have been done some days past. The skin appeared to have been taken off hastily or carelessly. I may never find the thief but if ever I do they will have to leave for parts unknown. I think our hogs are killed for revenge as well as gain. We have insulted a negro who is smart to be detected in his villanery.

November 26. Saturday. Dr. Dean and his family dined with us today also George Camp and Harriet and Mary Harris and her children. During the day Dr. Dean and George captured Sam, a runaway negro that once belonged to him. The event saddened us all for the remainder of the day. The weather is pleasant and we are getting our wheat in very fast with five plows.

November 28. Today we finished sowing wheat in the Barley field and commenced in upper field. The fine large hog which we secured about a month ago thinking it was ours which had been gone a year was claimed, proven and carried away today by Sam Means's overseer. Alas! for our hopes. I wonder how many more losses and disappointments I am to have in the hog business.

The weather is pleasant. The family have colds. I have been trying to get some shoes made but have not succeeded. Every ones attention is now strained Yankeeward. Surely the end is near. God humble us and help us.

November 29. The weather is delightful. We sit all day without a fire. The wheat sowing has been going on bravely. I have been out again today to try to get my shoemaking done. One man says he will do my work if I will pay him in wool or wheat. I have neither to spare.

November 30. After supper. The family are all sitting in the piazza. Today I have heard of robbery of various kinds. A party of deserters have robbed Dr. Mills who lives about thirty miles from us. Several negroes belonging to our neighbors have been stealing on [a] small scale to the great annoyance of their owners and others. Times are getting more desperate everyday. Some say the war will continue four years more. If it does we will be nowhere and nobody. Prices. Turkeys are selling in Charleston at $50.00 a pair. Chickens $25.00. Butter $10.00 per lb. Soldiers are paid $12.00 a month and half fed, half clad.

December 6. The deserters and tories are still advancing. They are now threatening Fingerville. The old men and boys are gone from Spartanburg village to check their progress. Fourteen year old boys have shouldered their guns and gone.

The weather is still beautiful and we are getting on finely sowing wheat. The family are all well and have, yet, the necessities of life. I have sold a lot of jeans, thirty or forty yards for $25.00 per yard. Who will reap the wheat we are now sowing? I feel enveloped in uncertainty. It is time for the Confederacy to invoke the aid of the Almighty God, for the arm of man seems powerless to some. Our esteemed friend and teacher left us last Sunday morning. I hope she will find friends wherever she goes.

December 7. Another hog skin has been found today. It was found in the upper field and appears to have been taken off four or five days. Last night it rained. It is now fair and very warm. We finished sowing wheat in the upper fields today. It took five plows eight days and two or three hours to do the upper field.

December 8. I went to town today to inquire about various matters of business. I had a cold disagreeable day. I paid my tax in money which amounted to $428.00. I paid $7.00 for a fine tooth comb. I paid $4.00 for a paper of needles. The band of tories and deserters who threatened to make a raid on Spartanburg have vanished. I brought home with me two bushels of thin straw wheat. It is said to yield more than the May wheat.

Decmeber 9. When I waked this morning it was sleeting. It has sleeted all day and is still hailing. The weather is extremely cold. I had a housefull of company today. Dr. Dean's family and Sis Camp and four of her children. Notwithstanding the weather is cold and the ground covered with hail, we all enjoyed the day. I had a little beef butchered this morning.

December 11. Sunday night. Cold and clear and bright. The full moon is shining on the snow and every thing is freezing. How are the poor Soldiers faring tonight. I have heard that Col. Harris has slipped and fallen on the sleet and hurt himself. I am anxous to hear how much.

December 12. I think it is the coldest weather I have ever seen. Mr. Bagwell is moving into the Camp house. Elifus is sick, the other negroes have been cutting and hauling wood.

December 16. The weather is warm and cloudy. I am anxious to kill hogs but must wait for a change. A little rye has been sown today. I feel distressed but am trying to be composed and hopeful. I have just heard that Mr. Harris' regiment has been sent to meet the great terror of the Confederacy, [Gen William T.] Sherman. I have learned through negroes that three Yankee prisoners have been living for several days in our gin house and been fed by our negroes. The neighbors are now watching for them with their guns.

December 18. Sunday night. This day has been spent in great restlessness and anxiety. We had heard that Mr. Harris had left James Island on some dangerous and uncertain expedition, we know not when. Last this afternoon we received a letter from him. He is still safe. Sherman is advancing on Savannah[8] and people are beginning to think we must give up the struggle. The weather is very warm. We have needed no fire since morning. Cornelia Camp spent the day with me.

The search for Yankee prisoners on our premises ended without success or information except the unmistakeable evidence that some one or more had been lodged and fed in and about our gin for some days. We tried to get the negroes to tell something about it, but in vain. We could hear their telling each other all about it but they would tell us nothing. I feel quite unwell tonight. I don't know what is the matter with me.

December 19. Finished sowing wheat. The weather is warm and cloudy.

December 20. Finished sowing winter oats at Camp Place. It is raining again. I am not in the humor to journalize and have nothing of importance to record.

December 21. Clear, cold and windy. Letters from Mr. Harris tell that he is in great danger at Coosawhatchie.[9] The war is growing more desperate everyday. Troubles are thickening around us. York and Old Will had a fight this morning.

December 22. Today we have butchered ten hogs weighing 181, 200, 182, 115, 150, 100, 105, 152, 130, 91 amounting to 1407, averaging $140\frac{7}{10}$. We have one more to kill which we hope will outweigh all the others.

The weather is bitter cold and windy. I had the meat salted as soon as we could cut it up. It is the first time I have ever salted meat the same day it was killed. It would have been hard frozen by morning.

December 23. Weather extremely cold. Finished doing up lard and sausage. Worked very hard indeed. Wonder if I will do up lard and sausage another year.

December 25. Sunday evening. Christmas day. It is not a merry Christmas to me. True I am in a comfortable house with the comforts of life plentiful around me, the family area, all well and happy, but the "Head of the family, the King of the household" is now in the Confederate camp exposed to the Yankee shells. Any moment a shell may send him into the presence of God. But why should I suffer more anxiety than when he is under his own roof by his own fireside? When his mission on Earth is accomplished he will be called hence.

The day is dark(,) still and cloudy. The children are all visiting and bent on fun and frolic. Let them be merry while they may.

December 26. Another still dark very quiet day. I was sick last night. I am still too weak to sit long. What time I can I must write to the "Soldier in his tent" who is sadly in need of kind and hopeful words. Rain last night.

December 29. This is a fair and bright cold day. The family have all left home but little D.G. and I and one servant. I have never passed so quiet a time in my life. I have indulged in many strange sad thoughts today upon the past and future. Much such dreaming is not wholesome for the mind but it is seldom I am allowed to indulge. Soon the children will come in noisy swarms and then my busy life will commence again. The past and future will give way to the stern necessities of the present. It is best so.

December 30. Today I have been mending and darning some old clothes and knitting socks for Mr. Harris. Will he ever wear them? I have had no letter from him in two days. I feel uneasy. I have been very much provoked by the negroes leaving home without leave and staying over their time. I think if We all live to see another Christmas that I give them but two or three days to idle or worse than idle away. My children are as bad as the negroes. I wish Christmas could come "like a thief in the night."

December 31. The pulse of the year grows faint. A few more throbs and We will place it among the things that were. How many of our fellow beings have been hurled into the presence of God during this year. How many tears have fallen from loved ones bereaved? How many graves and prayers have gone up from our blood stained land.

What an eventful year it has been. How its hoary head is crowned with thrilling and painful memories for years to come. Few have been made to rejoice and many to mourn. The Nation mourns and bleeds. Wounded from crown to sole it is now intervention of the God of battles our once proud Confederacy must sink to rise no more. This is not alone the opinion of an ill judging woman but of the greater part of the Solomons of the land. To our private family there has been but little change. Our children are reaching toward maturity and receiving impressions which will blossom and bear fruit in coming years.

We have made enough of the necessaries of life this year. Corn wheat oats and meat, not enough meat of not as much as We are used to, but enough to make us very thankful that it is no less.

During this year I have had trials only known to myself and in which no one did sympathize. My Husband has been at home but two weeks since the middle of April and I have struggled faithfully, if not successfully to some, from diminishing our little property. I have had some losses and many crosses and disappointments to contend with. Many times I should utterly fail to continue the struggle if I had no children. I sometimes feel very lonely and sad. I'm without father[,] mother[,] brother or sister. No one seems to think that I ever sigh for love and kind words.

There has been no death and but one birth in the family during the year. All seem well and contented. We have felt but little of the horrors of the war in our circle. We ask and well We are unanswered. What is there for us among hidden gifts of the next year?

1865

January 1. New Year. Sunday morning. It is a cold bright day. The children are all engaged with some book and We are all as happy as the gloomy aspect of the times and the dangerous and critical state of our country will admit. Our best friend, the King of the household, the Head of the family[,] is exposed to the inclemency of the winter and the shells of the enemy, lying in trenches at Coosawhatchie, cold shivering and hungry, struggling almost without hope for the independence of the Confederacy. The war goes on with unabated fury. Many are crying out for peace. Many are willing to unite again with the hated Yankees rather than continue the hard and seemingly hopeless struggle. Our state, which has until recently stood like the land of Goshen amid the plagues of Egypt[,] is now threatened with the dreadful ravages of the foe. I do say fervently— Let God's will be done, and let the right cause triumph as it most certainly will.

January 2. Monday night. Mary Gwin Harris and her children spent the day with us. The weather is very cold. We are having a hard winter. The negroes have been getting firewood. The girls have been preparing stocking thread and all are falling into ranks for another year's struggle with the giant, Want.

January 3. This morning We commenced cutting wood for a coal kiln. In the afternoon it rained a little and I put some of the hands to shucking the governments corn. I must pay it soon.

I have had Laura and Luella washing some today. I think if I learn them to wash, it will make them more careful with their clothes and can do them no harm whatever. I have been knitting and planning work for the others.

Old Will came to me and asked me to give him "a paper" and let him go and hunt him a home. York has given him a whipping and he wishes to leave the place. I'm in trouble. York must be corrected for fighting the old negro and there is no one willing to do it for me. It seems that people are getting afraid of negroes.

I had three letters from Mr. Harris dated at Coosawhatchie. He is suffering with cold and hunger and trying to do a soldier's duty. The army is in low spirits.

January 4. I have spent this day at Mrs. Moss's and returned quite unwell. I hear that Charleston is evacuated by the Confederate troops.[10]

Devoted city! How We do hate to give it up, and proud old fort Sumter that has stood so bravely the most skillful and energetic bombardments of the foe. It is only rumor but We fear it is too true. The weather is cold and clear.

January 5. To day I went to town. I never saw the roads so extremely bad before. I tried to attend to some business but failed to get it properly done. I found the Harris family in a state of confusion and trouble on account of Uncle Jimmy Harris arresting a negro boy, Jack, belonging to Julia Harris, for stealing Sallie Owens' dog. I believe they will go to law about it. I discovered that Bill Camp had served us another mean trick. I expect it will end in a lawsuit. The difficulty is one which has grown out of the thread trade which should have been settled by law instead of arbitrators. The grievance is just as bad as it would have been all parties would have been no worse off as far as broken ties' goes than We now are.

We hear that Charleston is not evacuated and that [Lt. Gen. John Bell] Hood and [Maj. Gen. Nathan Bedford] Forrest have both gained a great victory.[11] I scarcely feel glad. It is a Confederate victory but will only prolong the struggle and do us no good I fear. The troops in Virginia have been drawing rations of spoiled corn meal and nothing else for over a month. They are surely a patriotic band. They must be fed better or they cannot fight.

January 6. The day has been dark and rainy. We have a great deal of rain and severely cold weather. The hands have been shucking and shelling corn. The girls have been quilting a quilt for old Edom. I have been knitting and mending and thinking, thinking.

January 7. Saturday night. The day has been windy, clear and cold. The hands have been sprouting the wheat patches. Laura is sick with a sore throat.

January 8. Sunday night. The weather is cold. Laura is sick. There is no gladness but gloom everywhere. I suppose it is as it should be.

January 9. Monday night. The morning was rainy, the day was dark and cloudy and now it is raining in torrents. I think the roads will become impassible. Mr. Cunningham is working in the blacksmith shop. Everything is to mend, and everything is out of order. There surely is no more destruction in this place than any other.

January 10. Freshet. Last night it rained all night long. I never have heard as much rain fall in so short a time. When We arose this morning We could see but little earth. All was rivers. The rain continued until noon. It thundered and lightened like it was midsummer. The damages to our lands and fences and roads is terrible. Mr. Cunningham is still working on our farming tools. The negroes finished shucking the government corn. I done nothing but knit and fret over the high waters which will for some time prevent me from getting letters from Mr. Harris.

January 11. BUTCHERING. This morning I hear that all the bridges in the neighborhood are gone. Golightly, Antioch and Seay bridges all gone down stream. This morning We butchered the old white sow. She weighed 220 lbs. making in all (first killing 1407) 1627. Meat Nett 1627 in all. Mr. Cunningham left us at noon. I paid him a bunch of thread for two days do to keep alive. The weather is so cold. The negroes have been getting fire wood and hauling the cord wood.

January 13. Today I have had friends to dine with me. The day passed off pleasantly. George Dean, a young soldier, was among my visitors. He has been at the same camp with Mr. Harris and tells me that I have not heard half the hardships they endure. I need not hear any more. Yesterday I had the most miserable ride on horseback which I ever thought of. I went to Bill Smith's to pay off the note. I called upon our new neighbors, the Brewtons who have moved into the Ralph Smith house. I got a fall from my horse during the trip and had to get down two or three times. The roads are almost impassible even on horseback. York swam a mule over the forest yesterday and brought me a letter from Mr. Harris. The hands are getting firewood. The family are all well.

January 15. Sunday. I have spent an unhappy day. I've heard that there will probably be no mail for a good while. The freshet was greater below that here. Broad river is said to have been higher than ever known before. Considerable damage has been done to the railroad. If Mr. Harris was sick or wounded I could not reach him. There is enough of distress in the thought.

George Dean and Ann called this afternoon. They tell me that Col Harris' sawmill is gone, not a vestige of it left. The neighbors are going to build up the Golightly bridge. It should be done by the state, but the state is now very busy preparing for the reception of General Sherman and his troops, a very weighty matter. It is thought that S Ca. will be the scene of the bloodiest battles which have yet taken place. Spartanburg village is now being prepared for the great hospital. Several large buildings are impressed and soon to be fitted for that purpose.

January 16. One of our oxen is sick today. Lord help me if he dies. The hands are repairing the damages of the freshet. The neighbors are building up Golightly bridge. I sent a hand to help though We have more to do at home than will get done. Everybody is calling on everybody for help and everybody is too busy to help anybody. I've never seen nor dreamed of such times. The weather is cold but bright and pleasant. All well but old Judy. No good news, nor gladness, no joy and but little hope.

January 17. Still repairing the damages done by this freshet. The Golightly bridge is done. The weather is fine and our work is going on tolerably well.

January 18. I spent the day at Mr. Allen's. Came home very tired and unwell. Nothing went wrong in my absence. One of our hands went to help Gwin Harris raise his house.

January 19. The evening is cloudy and cold. We saved a little rye today. The girls spooled a piece of cloth. The negroes are wearing wooden bottom shoes. They wear out so soon there is not much economy in using them. I had a tobacco bed sowed. No mail has been received yet since the deluge. I am nearly distracted.

January 20. Negro trial, great trouble. Today some runaway negroes were caught. One of them, Sam who once belonged to Dr. Dean confessed a good deal and implicated others when were accordingly severely whipped without giving time or chance to prove their innocence. Our boy Elifus and Gwin Harris' Pink were both whipped without proof of their guilt. I never will allow another negro of mine punished on suspicion. I understand that on next Monday the court are to go in search of evidence against Elifus. Things are reversed. People are used to be punished when found guilty, now they are punished and have their trial afterwards. Elifus has cause to deplore the absence of his master as well as I. If he had been here it would not have been managed in this way.

January 21. A very rainy day, nothing done but shuck corn. The girls and I have knitted and sewed and mourned the absence of our best friend. I sent to the office—no mail yet. I'm in trouble. The family are suffering with colds. I am suffering with many things. There is no joy, not even tranquility for me.

January 22. Sunday night. Today has been rainy. I went down to Dr. Dean's and inquired the particular's of the negro trial. I found that as my agent he had done what he thought was right, but I can't believe a negro should be whipped til he has been found guilty. Elifus seems to have shared the fate of old dog Gray, but never again will I suffer Barham Foster (who was a juryman in this case) to act in the same capacity on any business of mine.

January 23. Monday night. Today George Dean, Mrs. Dr. Dean, Misses Allen and Miss Ella Henyman spent the day with us. The young people had a merry day. The negroes have been getting fire wood. The weather is cold and cloudy. We fear another Hog has been stolen. I hear that on the way to jail with the runaways, the men in charge of them suffered one of them to escape. I am sorry.

January 24. Tuesday. The weather is again bitter cold. We do little work. Getting wood and making fires is all We do. There is still no mail. It is thought that it will be long before the railroad will be repaired. I must use what patience I can command. Today I sent my corn tax to town. It amounted to 21 bushels.

January 26. Today We have received a mail. The news is very unfavorable for the Confederacy. Many think We are soon to belong again to the United States. I received six letters from Mr. Harris. He is still spared. The weather is bitter cold, cold and bright as an icicle. Our hands have been getting firewood. It is too cold to think of doing anything else. I tried to thread a piece of cloth. It was too cold to do it. I gave it up till a warmer day. Mattie Ray spent the day with me.

January 27. Still cold, cold, bitter cold. We are cutting, hauling, and burning wood. Mr. Moorman came down to make a settlement with me for his daughter Virginia. He tells me that Tennessee has gone back into the United States. Pocataligo has been evacuated and Wilmington has been taken. It was a bloody battle at Wilmington, four thousand Yankees were slain.[12] Gwin Harris came down and We talked about our difficulty. I think I'll leave it alone hereafter. I am distressed about it but there is no help for it. We are talking about trying this law for an adjustment. Today I gave a woman half a bushel of salt to weave 30 yds of plain white cloth.

January 28. Today I had our meat hung up. I went down to Dr. Dean's in the afternoon to try to get some assistance to save ice. If this weather continues I must try to save some. It is the coldest weather I've ever felt. I hear that Beauregard has thrashed Sherman. Too good to be true.[13]

January 29. Sunday night. We are all well. The weather has moderated a little. I have today been notified to send half our road working hands to help repair the railroad. I wish the government would take all we've got and then call out the women and children and see if that would not rouse the people to a sense of their condition.

January 30. Saving ice. The ice is about three inches thick which We are saving. Gwin Harris is helping us for the privilege of using some of the ice.

January 31. The last day of January. A colder January never has visited our clime since I remember. We have nearly filled our smallest ice house. Gwin's wagon and my hands are engaged in the business. Today my wagon broke down on the road with a load of ice. At the same time my buggy was broken down, having been sent to the relief of a party who had broken down a buggy and were left standing in the road. FIRST LAMB. Ben Finch's little negro girl ran away and came here this afternoon. I sent her home. I hope she will not visit us again. I had welcome letters from Mr. Harris today. He has left the camp at Coosawhatchie and halted for the present at a more pleasant place, farther from Yankee cannon and nearer something to eat. I spent this day at Gwin's, or rather, the afternoon. Mary seemed unhappy or cross and I was sorry for her. I feel like if my husband was with me I would be above all sorrow.

February 1. Today I went to the village in the rockaway and drove the mules. I fell out of the rockaway while going and had a narrow escape from breaking bones. I hear that white flags are flying in Columbia and other cities and towns. Peace! Peace! How it will be welcomed. I brought home on the carriage a piece of timber to make an axle tree for our wagon. I also brought home my factory yarn which had been left at Dr. Dean's town house. Factory thread is now selling at $60.00 per bunch. I gave $5.00 for a pound of copperas.

February 2. Friday. Harriett Mitchell, Nila Camp and Annie Dean spent the day with me. We had a pleasant day. The hands are breaking up the stubble land. Our farm work is going on very slowly.

February 3. It has been a rainy day. We have made some plowlines and had some corn shucked. I went out this afternoon in the rain to see about some weaving. I hear that a peace flag has been raised in Spartanburg. Every one seems to think We are to have peace soon and no one seems to care upon what terms.

February 4. To day I've spent from home. When I got home I felt worried and unhappy. Several things had gone wrong during my absence. The weather is quite pleasant.

February 6. I have had our Irish potato seed taken up. There is about ten bushels, enough for our seed. Mr. Cunningham is working on the wagon and buggy. It is sleeting and is quite cold. Shall We have winter all the year?

February 7. This morning We found the earth shrouded in white, not snow, but hail, hard and sleety. Of course little work has been done. Mr. Cunningham has mended our wagon and buggy and left us. He charged me $10.00 per day. When he told me I could hardly believe him. I fully expected to be charged $25.00. There fell a few flakes of soft snow late this afternoon which is the first I've seen this winter. It has generally been too cold to snow. The hail is now melting. We have two lambs! Our sheep are not doing very well. Some are telling me that I fed them too much. Some knowing of them say sheep should never be fed.

February 8. The day has been cold and windy with not enough sunshine to melt the sleet. Willie and I went to Mr. Bragg's this afternoon to see if We could get some shoes which he has been making for us. We found him sick in the bed the shoes not done. As We come home one of the buggy wheels dropped off and We had to walk home through the mud. The family are all rather unwell. Laura is just from town. She says the people are rejoicing over the prospects of peace. The North seems to be getting into difficulties with France and will have other battle fields besides ours to attend to.

February 9. Today I spent at Billy Ray's. I walked there and back on frozen ground. The trees are still bowing beneath their load of sparkling jewelry. There is now a bright full moon in the sky and as I look forth on the clear cold night I can fancy ghosts and witches dancing on the house tops and cutting high capers in the shadowy woods. I had a letter from Mr. Harris. He is still healthy for which blessing I hope to be duly thankful. The negroes have been getting firewood. We have used a great deal this hard winter.

February 11. We builded our coal kiln today. I have been warned to send a hand to work on the coast. I have heard that the government is going to seize all the cotton in the country. I have heard that there is a battle raging at Branchville and that Mr. Harris is there.[14] The weather is still pretty cold. There is still some hail on the ground. I went to Ben Finch's to try to pay off a note. I could not do it. He would have nothing I've got. Creditors once were glad to be paid. Now they flee from a settlement as from a pestilence. Confederate money is trash.

February 12. Sunday night. I've heard that Branchville is in possession of the Yankees and that our commissioners who were sent to Washington to negotiate for peace have returned to us with the intelligence that a sharp sword and stout arm will alone procure peace. It has been one of the most miserable days I've ever spent. There is no ray of light to alleviate the gloom. The family are not well. The weather is still cold. $200.00 per bushel has been offered and refused for salt. Soda is $20.00 per lb. Mercy on us all.

February 14. A heavy snow storm. Order for Coast labor counter commanded. Billy Ray at home on furlough. He brought me a letter and watch from Mr. Harris.

I got 8 bunches of thread for my last crop of cotton. I got an oven lid for $12.00 and oven and lid for $16.00. Our coal kiln is doing well. We have seven lambs.

February 15. Tom Hayden and Ann Mitchell came down in a two horse buggy to spend the night. They are courting in fine style. The day has been too disagreeable to do anything but make fires and sit by them!

February 17. The day has been changeable. The morning bright. The afternoon cloudy with a little rain. The hands hauled fire wood and tended the coal kiln. The Misses Underwood spend the day with us. Our cook is sick and the girls had to cook the dinner. It was a sore trial to them.

A Presentiment. When Mrs. Harris, my esteemed mother-in-law, among numerous objections to her son's alliance with me, mentioned that of insanity being an hereditary affliction with my family, I laughed at the idea of ever being in any danger of it. But the years which have intervened since then have left upon me the impress of the trials and sufferings the in passing bestowed on me. I sometimes have days of misery for which I cannot give, even to myself, a cause. These spells are periodical and today for the first time I have thought perhaps they were the premonitory symptoms of insanity. It is a dark doom to dread. I wonder if the hopelessly insane do suffer much. If it is to be so who can avert the fate? I pity my husband and children more than myself.

I wish I had a better pen. Oh! the war, the war!

February 19. The Yankees are burning Columbia and destroying our railroads.[15] Our army flies before them. Crowds of women and children are coming up on the train every night. People are wild with excitement. Our cause seems lost.

February 20. PLANTED IRISH POTATOES. Had a fight with our girl, Ann, which ended in my tieing and whipping her with the assistance of Mr. Bagwell. Some remarks of the children about the affair have hurt Mr. Bagwell's feelings. He knows nothing about the management of negroes. We are all in a dreadful state of excitement, almost wild. The Yankee army are advancing upon Spartanburg we fear. They are now destroying Alston and Columbia. Mr. Harris, I expect is in Columbia if alive. It has been impossible for me to sit or be still or do any quiet thing to day. I am nearly crazy. Gwin Harris according to previous agreement carried some of bales of cotton to Bivingsville for me to sell or exchange for yarn. He brought it back. The proprietors of the factory are expecting to be burnt out. Distress and anxiety prevails everywhere. My brain aches and throbs and my soul is weary.

February 21. Gardening. Today I done the first work on my garden, planted peas, onions, lettuce, radishes, and various other small affairs. I have set out a few fruit trees and given away a few. The other excitement about the Yankees has somewhat subsided though they are still threatening us.

I am quite unwell having passed two or three anxious and particularly trying days.

February 22. People are in an awful state of excitement. They may, almost, be said to be flying about with streaming hair. They are just ready to believe anything they hear provided it is horrible. I never heard so many false rumors before. Some things are, however, distressingly true. Some wagons loaded with government taxes and bound for Shelby, N Ca. were turned back to Spartanburg today, so we concluded that the latter place is still the safest.[20]

I had a fight with old Will and hurt myself worse than him. It is a painful necessity that I am reduced to the use of a stick but the negroes are becoming so impudent and disrespectful, that I cannot bear it.

The day has been cool and cloudy. The hands have planted Mr. Bagwell an Irish potato patch and commenced sowing oat at the Camp Place. I spent the day with Mr. Bagwell, and in looking over the orchard at Camp place (hereafter the girls say it must be Buffalo Hall). I thought that perhaps there might be some young trees dead and others needed their place. I found only three dead. I feel little inclination to make improvements. I can scarcely keep quiet long enough to do anything. I try not to think, but how can I help it?

February 23. A rainy day. No news from the army except that the enemy have gone in the direction of Shelby N. Ca.[16] I have spent the day in repairing old clothes. Old Willie is quite sick.

February 24. A rainy day. We have drawn our coal and got a poor turn out. Nothing seems to prosper in my hands. No news from Mr. Harris. I have almost last my natural feeling. I don't know who to feel.

February 25. Another rainy day. Nothing done but shuck corn.

February 26. Sunday. I have passed an unhappy day. There seems no pleasure in the present and no hope in the future.

February 27. Monday night. It is raining a little. The weather is quite warm. We have been very busy today weaving, spooling, knotting, sewing, making soap and dyeing cloth. Gwin Harris and his family dined with us. The field hands commenced cleaning up the Buffalo bottom. We hope, thence, to make some corn this year. I paid $4.00 for making a pair of little boy's shoes.

February 28. The weather is once more fair and pleasant. I busied myself in the forenoon with dyeing and warping cloth and in the afternoon I went to Dr. Dean's on some business. I hear no news from Mr. Harris. The dreaded Yankees are between me and him.

March 1. 1st Day of March and but little preparation as yet for a crop. There are no oats of consequence in the ground and but a few furrows plowed in our stubble land. I think there is no man or woman living who has seen a harder winter than this. We have, upon an average, two fair days in a week. Today has been cool cloudy and misty. I have been quite busy dyeing and arranging for making cloth and preparing some thread to make harness. The hands have been cleaning off the banks of Buffalo branch. Ann has come home from the field quite sick. Several of the family are suffering from colds.

March 2. Cloudy rainy weather. The air We breath seems watery. The hands are cutting and making rails to make Mr. Bagwell a turnip patch. Late this afternoon a cavalry soldier came and begged to stay all night. I allowed him to stay but shall do so no more. I asked Gwin and Mary to come and stay all night with me. I have hear things about my lodger since dark which will cause me a sleepless night.

March 3. I spent an anxious night, but lost nothing that I know of by giving the soldier a nights lodging. Dr. Dean and Gwin Harris both think I done very wrong to let him stay. I think so too. There are thousands of soldiers now passing through the district on their way to join Gen. Lee near Richmond. Two have just asked to stay tonight but I sent them away. In the same way my poor husband will be turned away to sleep in the rain and mud. A soldier's life is almost worse than death. Three of our family are sick. The weather is awful. We are living in a cloud, but little work is being done. Laura is at Dr. Dean's. I am so much afraid that some of the cavalry men will steal my fine horse that I have hid him last night and tonight. No news from Mr. Harris.

March 4. Today the sun made its appearance the first-time in over a week. The first flowers of Spring are slowly and cautiously making their appearance. The day has been spent in drying damp clothes and washing and cleaning up. The out door work has been cutting and slitting rails. Hattie Camp is spending the day with us.

March 5. The Sabbath day. I sent to see if there came up with the cars last night any news. None. No news from Mr. Harris in three weeks. How do I feel? Cousin Harriet Allen spent the day. Dr. Dean and Nela [Nila] the afternoon. I feel very milched.

March 6. This has been a suitable day for plowing and We have been trying to get some oats in the ground. Elifus and Edom have put up the coal. It is nearly two weeks since it was drawn and it has been too wet to put up ever since. I have been out this afternoon trying to hire weaving. I find no one to weave for Confederate money. There are hundreds of soldiers passing to and fro. It is a little dangerous for women and children and fine horses to trust themselves on the road. Ann is still sick in bed. She has been so mean lately that I have little sympathy for her. The negroes are all expecting to be set free very soon and it causes them to be very troublesome.

March 7. I have spent the day making candles. The negroes are sowing oats at Buffalo. We churned today—the first time in many months. One of our cows had a calf. It died and We are getting a fine quantity of milk. I was invited to spend the day at Dr. Dean's with Sis and her family but I felt so little like being social that I declined the invitation. I am sick and sore with anxiety for Mr. Harris. I have still no news from him.

March 8. Another rainy day. Laura finished weaving a piece of cloth. The family are all unwell.

March 9. Rainy day. The weather is surpassingly well. Everything is wet inside and out. I have spent this day as busy as a bee and now I can't tell what I've done. So it is with many days. I sold two bushels of oats for $10.00 per bushel to a poor woman who works in the field and makes her own crops. It is contrary to my rules to sell for money anything which man or beast will eat but I was sorry for this widow. I scarcely expect anyone to get so sorry for me.

March 12. It is a beautiful day. Cousin Annie Dean and Jennie Dean spent the day here. I tried to make the day pass pleasantly and I am afraid We escaped the Sabbath.

Chapter 5

Lieutenant Watson's Camp Reminiscences

Born on April 1, 1840, in the rural Bethel community of South Carolina's York County, James Adams Watson was descended from warriors and priests. His great-grandfather, Colonel Samuel Watson, was a hero of the American Revolution while his father, the Reverend Lytle Samuel Watson, pastored Bethel Presbyterian Church. As his native state left the Union, James Adams Watson, a lieutenant in the Twelfth South Carolina Regiment, promised to keep a diary of his role in the conflict. The war's fast pace and Watson's constant movement, however, prevented him from regularly recording his activities. Less than two months after the rebellion's end, Lieutenant Watson, back home from Virginia battlefields, prepared his impressions of life as a Confederate officer.[1] His reminiscences began with the following recollection:

Camp Reminiscences

It was my desire, on entering the service of the Confederate states, to keep a Diary in which to take account of important events—giving their dates, etc. But for various reasons this was found to be impracticable. It is my intention now, whilst events and dates are fresh in my memory, to give a brief monthly synopsis of my entire camp life—only specifying the most important dates. I have given a brief outline of events in which my company and regiment participated.

Bethel, SC
August, 1865   J. A. Watson[2]

August 1861

The first Battle of Manassas[3] had just been fought and a victory won—The Enemy was making grand preparations for another onset—The Governor of South Carolina[4] issued a proclamation calling for four thousand troops to serve during the war. Under that call "The Palmer Guards" was organized at Yorkville[5] on or about the 8th instant[6]—having on its roll nearly one hundred members. The following persons were elected as commissioned Officers—(W. H. McCorkle, Captain; L. M. Grist, 1st Lieutenant; J. T. Parker, 2nd Lieutenant; J. D. Witherspoon, Battalion 2nd Lieutenant). On the 20th instant (a day to be remembered) our Company left for the Camp of Instruction at Lightwood Knox Springs (six miles above Columbia)—arrived there on the evening of the same day. We were mustered into service in a few days by Capt. J. Logan Black[7]

September 1861

The 12th S. C. (Regiment) was organized early in this month. "The Palmer Guards"—on account of the seniority of its Capts commission—was placed on the extreme right and denominated Co "A." The following persons were elected as Field Officers—(R. G. Dunavant, Colonel; Dixon Barnes, Lieutenant Colonel; Cadet Jones, Senior Major). This month was spent primarily in uniforming and equipping the (Regiment) Drills and other military weapons—of course—were of frequent occurrence.[8]

December 1864

We put up Winter Quarters on the line during the first part of this month. About the 12th we took a big trip by way of Dinwiddie [Courthouse][9] down to [Belfield][10] on the Weldon Rail Road about thirty or forty miles from Petersburg. We were gone four or five days—had very cold weather and very hard marching. Taking every thing into consideration it was a very unpleasant visit. The balance of the month was spent in the performance of common Camp duties.

January 1865

The month passed away very quietly. Not much of any thing to do. Lieut. Miller[11] was retired on account of ill health on the 17th. I was promoted to 1st Lieut. A short time afterwards to date from the 17th. All serene on the sight.

February 1865

After the 5th, 6th and 7th we had to march down to the sight—the weather was wet and freezing. There was fighting going on down at

Hatcher's Run[12] at that time. The rest of the month passed off in a very quick manner. We received some substantial momentos from home friends during this month.

March 1865

We had a good many Reviews, Inspections, Drills, etc. during this month. On the 25th we had a considerable skirmish on the Picket line at Jones' Farm[13]—loss in the Company one killed. About the 30th we moved down to Burgess' Mill[14]—the weather was very wet. On the 31st we were actively engaged in the Battle near Burgess' Mill[15]—loss in the Company several wounded. I received a considerable bruise on the left arm, but did not leave the field.

April 1865

On the 1st we were skirmishing on the Picket line near Burgess' Mill— On the 2nd we commenced the retreat—actively engaged in the Battle of Sutherland Station[16]—cut off—couldn't cross the Appomattox River.[17] On the 3rd captured by the Enemy—marched up the River that evening. On the 4th still marching with the 2nd Corps[18]—on the 5th started to Petersburg under a mounted guard commanded by Lieut. Pemberton[19] [a brother of Ex.-Lieut-Gen. J. C. Pemberton of the Confederate Army]—camped at Sutherland Station that night. On the 6th got to Petersburg and took up quarters in the Old Weldon Depot.[20] On the 7th we marched to City Point[21]—were put in the pen there under Negro Guard. On the morning of the 8th we started for Washington City on the U. S. Mail Boat. City Point still under Negro Guard. Had a pleasant ride nowithstanding the unfavorable circumstances under which we were placed. Got to Washington on the morning of 9th [the day of Lee's Surrender]—were marched up in the city to the Provose Marshal's Office—them turned over to the Prison Guard and marched down to the Old Capital Prison. We were quarantined in the second story of that mansion—thirty-odd of us in one room. On the night of the 13th that whole city was illuminated in honor of Lee's Surrender, raising "the old Flag"[22] over Fort Sumter considered by the "Yanks" a grand time. On the night of the 14th at ten o'clock Lincoln was assassinated at Ford's Theater and died at seven o'clock on the 15th—cannons booming, bells tolling all day—all on account of Lincoln. On the 18th "a grand Procession" took place—turn out of the Military— firing cannons, etc. We could witness the whole proceedings from our window. On the 19th Lincoln's remains left the City—another turn out of the military—more shooting of cannons etc. We left Washington on the 22nd for Johnson's Island, Ohio[23]—got to Baltimore that evening—left in a few hours for Harrisburg, Pa.—got there that night—left the next morning for Pittsburgh—travelled all day through the mountains—got there that night—left immediately for Mansfield, Ohio—got there the next morning [the 24th]—[stayed] a few hours and left for Sandusky City[24]—got there in due time and took the Steamer G. W. Reynolds and crossed over to Johnson's Island that evening. Took up quarters in Block 7. Found a good many friends and acquaintances "in the pen." During the whole time I was treated with respect by the Sentinels and the Officers commanding them. Our fare was light of course.

May 1865

This whole month was spent in Prison. I passed off the time by reading, playing draughts,[25] etc. Taking every thing into consideration it might very justly be considered a miserable life. All sincere in Block 7.

June 1865

About the 12th an order was received for the release of the line officers in taking the Oath of Allegiance.[26] I was released to the meanest government in the world—one too against which we had been fighting for four years—this I consider to be the most humiliating act of my life. But it is a forced measure and we have to make the best of it. We went on the Steamer G. W. Reynolds to Sandusky City—took the train for Cleveland—got there that night—it is a large and beautiful city situated on the shore of Lake Erie. Left on the 21st for Pittsburgh Pa—got well pleased with the appearance of things—treated kindly by the citizens, etc. Left in the evening on the Steamer C. W. Thomas for Fortress Monroe[27]—got there the next morning [stayed] a short while and took passage on the Steamer Escort for City Point—got there in due time—took the train and arrived safely at Petersburg the same evening. Left there on the 25th—had a break down in [two]—got to Danville[28] on the 26th—got to Greensboro on the same day and to Charlotte on the 27th—left there on the 28th—got off the train at Robertson's Old Field[29] that evening and arrived safely home on the 29th. This is the end of [my?] camp experiences.

Chapter 6

For My Only Living Daughter

William Joseph Miller, a member of the Twelfth South Carolina Regiment, received his formal education on the battlefield. He was born on August 12, 1845, in the town of Yorkville and enlisted in the Civil War at age fifteen. He saw action in some of the conflict's major engagements, including Second Manassas, Sharpsburg, and Chancellorsville. Miller describes these, and other battles, in the following narrative. The details are vivid. For example, he recalls at the 1862 Clash at Second Manassas, "The wounded [Union soldiers] begged me so pitifully for water that I gave some a little." Later, the teenager tells us about stumbling over corpses. Then, there were surreal moments in which troops became children: "I have often seen whole regiments and brigades snow-balling each other...."

In 1916, more than half a century after General Lee's surrender at Appomattox Court House, Miller prepared this document for his daughter, Barnette. Even at age seventy, Miller's memories bring the horrors of war faced by a young Confederate into clear focus.

My Experience as a Soldier in the Confederate Army. Written at the Request of Barnette, My Only Living Daughter

In 1861 I was going to school at Tirzah A.R.P. Church[1] to Mr. J. Ponkey, a native of Virginia, and a school teacher by profession. He had spent the greater part of his life teaching; has a large school, including young men from adjoining counties. School was out the last of June 1861, and every one was talking of the war between the States then going on. The entire class of which I was a member, and the youngest in the class, was going to volunteer. This, I suppose is the reason that I thought I ought to follow their example. Steve Johnson, a classmate, Mr. Wm. Brown, and Randolph Pierce, all close neighbors, joined the company then being organized at Yorkville[2] by John L. Miller, and Wm. Dunlap of the Neeley's Creek[3] community. This company was made up of men from Western York, and a number from the Eastern part of the county. We were assembled at Yorkville in camp for a few days, and then organized into a company. Mr. J. L. Miller was elected Captain; Wm. Dunlap, First Lieutenant, H. Bigham Second Lieutenant, and Richard Simmons Third Lieutenant. We were then sent to near Columbia to Camp of Instructions called Lightwood Knot Springs.[4] There we found several other companies drilling. That was in July. We remained there nearly three months drilling every day, for both officers and men had to be instructed. We were drilled at first by young men from the State Military School.[5]

I think the election of officers by the companies is a mistake, for we always vote for some favorite, having no regard to the merits of the man as a tactician. Our officers were brave men but very often deficient of other qualifications.

At the camp above mentioned, we were given uniforms and I wish to say that was the only clothing I ever got from the government for the entire four years. What I got after that time was sent me by my parents from home, and these were often badly needed before getting there, owing to their not being able to get them to me. Why I got no more clothes was for the reason that so many of the soldiers had no one at home that could furnish them clothes and the clothing was issued to companies only two or three suits at a time. The most needy got them if possible to get them on. So you can see I spent the next four years of my life working for one set of clothes and $11.00 per month, and rations when they had them for

Confederate Veterans assembled in Rock Hill, S.C. in 1931 to share their memories of the war. (Courtesy Winthrop Archives.)

us. The $11.00 soon depreciated in value at the last to about what would buy stamps, paper and envelopes for writing letters home.

About October 1861, we were sent to the coast of South Carolina near Beaufort. We had been organized into regiments and brigades. Gill Dunovant of Chester County was colonel. D. Barnes Lieutenant and Cad Jones Major, Dunivant soon resigned. Ours was the 12th regiment. The brigade was composed of [the] eleventh, twelfth, thirteenth and fourteenth regiments. Gen. Maxy[6] Gregg was Brigade Commander. We were placed on Hilton Head Island, commanding the entrance to Beaufort harbor. There was a small fort[7] with a few small cannons mounted, and plenty of sweet potato patches, which were enjoyed. There is something in a soldier's life that give him a good appetite, and he indulges it if there is anything he can get. After a month or more the Yankees sent a fleet of boats to take Beaufort, but Hilton Head Island was in the way. However, they soon demolished the fort. Then we had a time getting off the Island. They shot bombs at us that fell in the potato patches and dug enough potatoes for several messes, but they was one time our appetites were not the trouble. We got back to the main land and camped at a village called Pocotaligo. They said the name was derived from an old African driving a pair of oxen which stalled in the sand and another came along and said to the stalled man and oxen to "poke his tail Negro." Anyway, it was a beautiful place to camp, with plenty of potatoes, fish and oysters to eat, but after a short time the enemy came out of the main land too, and we were sent to drive them back, which we did.[8] This was our first time to be shot at and to shoot at men with our rifles. I cannot say that we enjoyed it, but after driving them back to their boats we felt important.

We moved up the coast to a place called Greenpond. At that place I had Typhoid fever. Capt. Miller got me in a private house, there being no hospitals at that time. The name of the family was Harrison, very wealthy people. The father had been Mayor of Charleston at one time, he having lived in the City and also on his farm at times. They were very nice and kind to me. Mr. Randolph Pierce was detailed as nurse for me. I was there a month. After getting so I could eat, one of the girls came to me and asked if I could eat boiled custard and I, of course, said "Yes-mam." She brought in a glass, also a spoon. That was the first time I had ever seen that kind of custard. They had not gotten to boiling custard in the up country at that time. I enjoyed it very much. The old gentleman had four daughters. Each one had a pony to ride and that was their daily exercise. The younger ones would ride where I could see them to gratify me and also to be a diversion which gave me some thing new to think of. Mr. Pierce ate at the table with the family. He said they were nice to him. I had often thought of the debt of gratitude I owe them, but have never been able to show them any kindness. On asking a Charlestonian once of them, he said he knew the family. That the parents were dead and one of the daughters was married and lived in Beaufort. The others he had lost sight of.

I was soon able to return to duty and we were sent to Virginia the first of 1862. Our first camp was near Fredericksburg,[9] near the the Rappahanock River. We remained there until the Seven Days Fight[10] around Richmond.[11] Gen. McClellan[12] was near Richmond with a strong well equipped army. The first day's fight was at Gaines' Mills.[13] We were engaged most of the day. That was our first real fighting. We had the opportunity to show what was in us as soldiers. We did fine as long as we met the enemy in the open, but late in the evening we came on the enemy in breastworks,[14] with plenty of cannon. Then we were checked. That was where the first soldier was killed by my side, a nice young man by the name of Poag. About sunset Gen. T. J. Jackson[15] came on the field with his division and soon had possession of the breastworks. That was the first time I ever saw the famous general. We were delighted to see Jackson's troops come to our aid for we were needing it badly. After wading the creek previous to this time, the enemy on our front having disappeared out of sight, our company was placed in front in skirmish line. That is, one man every five steps apart. We were then sent forward to find the enemy. On going through a thicket of bushes, I came on four Yankees concealed. They sprang up holloring that we surrender. I do not know which was the more excited or surprised (I was out of sight of our own men in the bushes), the four Yankees or myself, but I told them to throw down their guns which they did. I marched them out in the open and was told to take them back and turn them over to the Colonel of the regiment, which I did. By the time night came on we had a pretty good idea of the duties of a soldier viz: To obey orders, and that about sums up the whole of it.

We were engaged the next day at Fraser's Farm,[16] but were supporting others after the battle at Savage Station.[17] Mr. W. W. White and myself walked over part of the battle ground where Gen. Jenkins[18] brigade fought and captured a battery of artillery. Dead Yankees and horses lay thick at that point. We counted fifty-four horses where the artillery was. These sights brought the fact to our minds that it was a serious affair we were engaged in. After several encounters we drove the enemy to the James River under the protection of our gunboats. The day after the last engagement, it rained very hard all day. We had had no shelter up to that time. We had no tents but had just stood and taken the weather like the cattle in this country once did. That evening were given a ration of corn whiskey. Our mess got ours in a quart canteen that had a mouthpiece and also a tube. I had never drunk any whiskey before and thought I would take my ration through the tube. I do not know how much I drank but in a short time I felt so important that if Gen. Lee had said so I could have whipped the Union army myself. I soon lay down and went to sleep and when I awoke I felt as if I ought to be whipped myself. That was the only time we ever drew whiskey. There was some excuse this time, for the troops had been marching and fighting for over a week and out in all kinds of weather without any shelter. Up to this date[,]our rations were sufficient.

After the Seven Days Fight was over there was a reorganization of Lee's army. The second corps was formed with General Jackson as commander and our brigade was placed in this corps. From that time until Gen. Jackson's death[19] we never lost a fight we were in.

In August[,] 1862, after the fighting around Richmond[20] we were sent to Gordansville with Jackson's corps and soon came in contact with the Union troops commanded by Gen. Pope[21] at Cedar Mountain. We had a fight late in the evening, but not a decisive conflict.[22] That night we camped near the battle ground in the weeds, sleeping on the ground all through the woods. At a late hour of the night calvary troops coming back from the front, some of them riding through the woods to get around some artillery standing in the road, rode over men sleeping. They woke up under the impression that it was the enemy, and it was very dark and there was much confusion. I heard that some men ran off for safety for a short time and came back after daylight to be made fun of. Steve Johnson and myself had lain down under a cedar tree with low limbs. We thought in the darkness it was a good place so kept quiet.

In a day or two our corps was sent over Blue Ridge down the Shennandoah Valley, back through Thoroughfare Gap in Gen. Pope's rear, capturing Mannassas Junction[23] on the railroad,[24] which was Gen. Pope's base of supplies. We were on the trip there three or four days and rations gave out. I will say here that we had orders to leave our knapsacks when leaving Cedar Mountain and have never seen them since. These contained all of our extra clothing, so that left us with only the clothing we had on. While in the Valley we were issued two roasting ears to each man, but did not give us any time to cook them. We ate them on the cob raw and it answered the purpose. Before getting to Manassas Junction Steve Johnson gave out like a great many others, and I thought that I would stay with him and help him on, but soon fighting was heard in front and I left my friend to do the best he could for himself as there was trouble in front and I had to go. I must acknowledge that it was thought that Jackson was after Gen. Pope's ration base and if that were a fact, I wished to be there for we had had only raw corn to eat for the past two days. There are several things a soldier fights for.

On the 28th of August [1862] we had Gen. Pope's base of supplies (Mannassas Junction), and plenty to eat of all that was good. There were, beside the army supplies, little stores with dainties to sell. These were owned by men who followed the Yankee army. We fell heir to all. That was the first time I had seen condensed milk but did not try any. Gen. Jackson had a guard placed around the depot where the main quantity of supplies was located. These consisted of crackers, bacon, sugar, coffee, molasses and whiskey. After giving us all that we needed the remainder was burned, as we could not take it with us as our wagon train was left behind. As we were about ready to march away[,] a young friend came to me and said that his canteen was full of molasses and asked what I had in mine. I answered "water." The weather was warm (August 28th). He said to me. "You take my canteen and I will get yours full of molasses." I did so and he came back in a short time with mine full of whiskey. He slipped past the guard, got into the depot, made a hole in the end of the barrel with his knife blade, got the canteen full and slipped out of the building then burning. What he brought back proved to be whiskey, but we soon got rid of it.

We then started over Bull Run Creek but before dark we were in trouble again with the enemy. That was Thursday evening. We reached Bull Run Creek over a bridge going West. Next morning about sunrise we were eating breakfast and a shell from the enemy lit close to us. At once we were ordered into ranks and from that time until dark, not having time to eat dinner, the Yankees kept us busy.[25] The condition was that Gen. Pope[,] having learned that Jackson was in his rear with only his corps and Gen. Lee a day's march from us, turned his entire army of seventy thousand men to wipe us up or capture us. We got in a railroad cut and on its banks we spent the day fighting. I was detailed once during the day to go for water. I had eleven canteens beside my own. That was three gallons. With my gun and other things to carry, I was pretty well loaded and had to hunt water. I came back as soon as I could and when I got back our men had driven the enemy from our front so I had to go over part of the battlefield which had a great many dead and badly wounded lying on the field. Some of both armies. The wounded begged me so pitifully for water that I gave some a little. One was a Yankee badly hurt. I gave him a drink[,] then dragged his gun away and next delivered the canteens to their respective owners when they were hotly engaged. The enemy at that time had sent in fresh troops and they drove us back to the railroad cut. One of our regiments gave away and the Yankees came over in a gap on our right and for a few minutes we were in a bad fix[,] but a regiment of Louisiana troops came up and we soon had a number of prisoners. That was one time I realized that we were in close quarters, but we did all that we could to help out the needy. A young man named James Kincaid, who stood in ranks beside me, was killed and it was not long until John May, who was raised in Ebenezer,[26] was killed near me. These things stir a person's blood and give him strange sensations, but there is something in a man that he will stand and fight it out with his comrades for he could not think of anything else. Finally night came on and ended the strife. We were worn out and lay down on the battle field and slept soundly, expecting to wake in the morning and renew the contest. We had explicit confidence in Gen. Jackson's ability to bring us out victorious. Fortunately, Gen. Lee came on the field that night with the first corps, and we were glad for our command had been fighting two to one. Jackson had on the field 25,000 men and Gen. Pope had 70,000.[27]

Next morning the fight was renewed but with a fair show in numbers.[28] The enemy was badly beaten and fled toward Washington. Then the long march commenced (August 30th, 1862) for Maryland.[29] We had no trouble with the enemy until we crossed the Potomac River, which we waded. It was about knee deep and very wide and rocky. After crossing the River the enemy commenced to trouble us, but these were only skirmishes. Rations were scarce as ours had to be hauled a long way by wagon. Gen. Lee issued an order that we must not disturb any private property. However, it was very difficult to make hungry soldiers respect ripe apples and roasting. So I thought when we went into Maryland I would have some apples. I went to the wagon train where I had a friend and got a horse so as to be able to ride under a tree and soon got my haversack full. However, others had preceded me and got all the lower apples, so I had to climb the tree. The good lady of the house caught me up the tree and she certainly said enough. I got down, got the horse, rode off eating a nice ripe apple and said not a word in reply. I thought we were about even— She had her say and I had a nice lot of fruit.

Soon after we got into Maryland Gen. Jackson's corps was sent back higher up the Potomac River (leaving Gen. Lee and other troops in Maryland) to capture Harper's Ferry,[30] a town of some size and well fortified with 11,000 troops. We waded the river again, capturing the town, troops[31] and a good supply of rations. We soon got word that the enemy had attacked Gen. Lee and that he was hard pressed at a small town named Sharpsburg.[32] We waded the river again and got to Gen. Lee in the morning and were sent into battle at once. It was a severe struggle; all day we were in a tight place. The Union army in great force was in our front and the river [was] at our back, but we were able to hold our own all day. The next day they did not attack us. We stayed there all the following day ready to fight[,] but neither side disturbed the other. I suppose it was a failure to both.[33] The following night we waded the river again—that being the fourth time for our corps.

After getting back into Virginia we felt at home. We went into camp near a large creek. As stated previously, we left our knapsacks near Gordansville, about the 10th of August, 1862, and it was now October 9th, of the same year. We got orders to clean up. The men had only the clothes they had on their persons and had had them on nearly two months. So you can imagine our condition. No washing in two months. We stripped off and got into the creek. We had no soap but we had plenty of cold water and did the best we could washing our clothes. We got through, got out of the creek and hung out our clothes to dry. We sat around on stumps and on the grass, waiting for them to dry so we could put them on again. No one but a Confederate soldier knows what they had to endure—the want of rations and need of clothes. Many were barefooted by this time and foot sore. It was shortly after this time that I had Gangrene in my foot. I lost one toe, half of two others and a bone out of the side of one foot. I was sent to temporary hospital at Winchester, Va., and if it had not been for a noble lady of the town I think we all would have died or perished. She came once a day with lightbread and milk for those in the hospital. The nurses were men detailed for the purpose and these were both ignorant and careless of their duties. The good lady tried to make them do better but only when she was present did it do any good. I know the lady mentioned was one of the saints on earth. I have oftentimes and again thought of the dear old creature.

In December [1862] they sent all of the sick and wounded to Stanton, one hundred miles away, in ambulances. These were something like the old ante bellum carryall. When they got ready to take us the coats and pants of many of the soldiers could not be found. They gave us such as they had. My pants were too large and the coat too small so we were gruesome sights. Some of the men were sick, others wounded. December in the valley of Virginia is a cool month. The drivers of the teams would camp out at night and often leave us to take care of ourselves and some of the men could not walk and I was one of them. We crawled around on our hands and knees. After getting to Stanton, we fared very well compared with our late experience. Stanton was the nearest railroad connection with Richmond. After staying at Stanton a few days we were sent to the hospital at Richmond. Our treatment there was all we could expect. I was fortunate to get in a ward or room attended by Dr. Nye, a young man who once practiced in our neighborhood at home, and he was very kind. I returned to duty in the Spring with a crippled foot that impeded me in walking ever since.

The battle of Chancelorsville[34] was fought in May, 1863, where we lost our trusted commander, Gen. T. J. Jackson,[35] and our corps was never again what it was although we did good service under Gen. A. P. Hill,[36] who had charge of us after Jackson's death.[37] We camped for some time near Fredericksburg. Then the unfortunate battle of Gettysburg,[38] July 2nd and 3rd, when the Union army held the battleground.

Our army again crossed the Potomac River, back to old Virginia. In March 1864 Gen. Grant[39] was placed in command of the Union army. We were camped near the old Wilderness battle ground[40] and fighting commenced in earnest at Spotsylvania Court House.[41] It looked as if we were all to be killed. It was very evident to the private soldiers that the Union army had a commander that would fight to the last.[42] At the above named battle on May 11th and 12th the fighting was fearful and continuous.[43] It seemed a contest between the two armies as to which would go to Richmond first. Finally around Richmond and Petersburg was reached but we were on the inside and the siege commended. Our brigade was placed immediately south of Petersburg where we held the breastworks until March 1865.[44] The fighting then was spasmodic. At times the enemy would attack our line, to be driven off; then the sharp shooters would continue to worry us. Then again it would be very quiet. The two double lines were close. When quiet, we would swap newspapers, tobacco for coffee, with the enemy. It was a very simple process. A Yankee out on the picket line would shake a paper or bundle of coffee and holler at us as to what he had to exchange with us and he would place it on a stump or some elevated place, and go off; then we would go and get it and leave our package for the party to come for. I never knew or heard of either party cheating. We stayed so long in the same place that we built houses of pine poles about ten by twelve feet square, with a mud chimney. Occasionally a Yankee bomb shell would come along and demolish a few of the huts, and the chaplins and servants would have a race for a place of safety. It was great sport to the soldiers to see them running, and often the pickets in front of us would engage in a fight and drive each other back to the breastworks; then return and get the wounded and bury the dead.

Late one evening I learned that a friend out on the picket line had no rations that day. It was often the case as we did not get our rations regularly. I carried his to him and it was dark before I returned. There being no road to return, I meant to take a straight course back. It was very dark and coming through a cornfield, I was stumbling over something and stopped to see what it was. It proved to be that they had buried a number of the enemy and some of our own men by placing them in the middle of the rows and throwing some dirt on the corpses, and the rain had washed it off, so I moved briskly for camp. It was not at all times a gloomy affair. We younger soldiers played ball often and in the winter time we had snow. I have often seen whole regiments and brigades snow balling each other, but finally Gen. Grant extended his line South until he flanked us out of the breastworks.[45] For some time we had strung out until we had only one man every three feet, which made a very weak battle front. Then the retreat toward Appomattox commenced.[46] With the enemy pressing us closely, we crossed the Appomattox River at a small town named Farmville, and we had had no rations for one day. Mr. James Ferguson, the adjutant[47][,] and myself stopped at a house in the town and the good woman was cooking corn meal cakes on top of the stove for the hungry soldiers, and they would take them off the stove half done and march on eating them. We got some and left and when we got to a bridge over the river, it was afire. We got over and then followed the river for about a quarter of a mile or more, going around a very steep hill. Just as we got over, a regiment of the enemy calvary was coming up the opposite side and ordering the soldiers on the road to surrender and come back. We concluded that we were not ready to give up so we started up the hill and they commenced to shoot at us, and continued until we got too far off. I think the only thing that saved us was that we were running up a steep hill and the balls were striking the ground at our feet. Apparently, they did not think of our rising up all the time and moving briskly. Anyway, we did not surrender as others were doing. That night in camp we only had three men in our company and that was the condition to a large extent. Some had gotten behind, some captured, some completely worn out.

I will tell how I became a member of company H. I was at first a member of company B. All of my neighbors and close friends who first joined company B from our community were dead—some from sickness and others killed. Steve Johnson[,] my lifetime friend and classmate, was killed at Gettysburg. There was a man by the name of Moore in company H that was a young lawyer from Rock Hill.[48] He was very anxious to get into company B, so I made the change with him, upon the advice of some friends and relatives in company H.[49]

Soon the enemy had us surrounded. Their cavalry in front and the infantry pressing us closely. Then Gen. Lee Surrendered us all.[50] It was sad to us and very trying on some of the men. I saw strong men shed tears. It was a bitter pill to give up our guns to the enemy. As I said, they had us surrounded by a picket line and kept us three days and we had nothing to eat. After the surrender by Gen. Lee, Mr. McCoy and myself decided that we would see if we could get through the Yankee pickets and get something to eat. In the thicket we found a picket who said he would let us through on condition that we not tell on him. Of course, a man who had had nothing to eat in two days would make that promise. So we got through and went to a camp of Yankees. They gave us all we wished of crackers and pickled pork, and then made room for us around the fire to broil our meat and eat our fill. They also bought what Confederate money we had as a relic to take to their house. We then got back through the line again to our own camp. Then several others followed our example. We were then paroled (I thought mine yet). The paroles were signed by commanding officers.

Then it was for us to get home. Gen. McGowan[51][,] then in command of the brigade (Gen. Gregg was killed at the battle of Fredericksburg) meant to bring us home organized, but he had nothing to fee us on, neither did we have anything to eat and nothing to buy with. He started home with the command and the first day stopped at a farm house. He went to the corn crib and got one ear of corn and gave it to us. We built a fire and shelled the corn in our frying pans and tried to roast it, but it was a failure. Twelve of us then agreed to stay together until we got home and the whole brigade come to the same conclusion. Our plan was to devote the first day trying to get something to eat. We tried until the middle of the evening and no one would give us anything. We came to a Mill and shouldered a bag of about one and a half bushels of meal and gave the miller an order on something and carried the meal off. We did not go far until we saw a small hog in a field. One of the party who had a pistol hid by a large stump and the others drove the hog up to the stump and the man at the place shot it. We tied his feet together and carried him off on a rail; then a little farther on we came to a house where there was an old chicken hen out in the lane. We drove her off some distance and caught her. That night we camped and cooked the meal into corn dodgers; borrowed a pot and cooked the hog and chicken. We then divided the whole equally among the twelve men.

We then made all the time we could going home. Our clothes were rough and ugly, but what were we to do five hundred miles away from home with nothing to eat and no means to buy with. Our supply of food lasted until we got to Greensboro, N.C.[52] There Mr. McCoy's greenbacks and mine that we got for our Confederate money which we sold to the Yankees for relics to take home, were used to get us some flour and that did us to Charlotte,[53] N.C. There I had a kind aunt, Mrs. Eugenia Miller. She gave me supper and enough for the others, which I carried to them. Mr. Jim Ferguson, one of our old mess,[54] was very sick and had to stop. All left him but Mr. A. M. Black and myself. A train of empty cars came to Concord, N.C.[55] where we were, and there were hundreds of other soldiers. They stopped the train and took charge of it. So we got in with the others and rode to Charlotte, running the train backwards. So we three got to Charlotte first and stayed there all night. The next morning when we got to the railroad bridge over the Catawba River, it was burned and all the flats at the ferries had been concealed. A company of Yankee soldiers were there putting in a pontoon bridge. We crossed on it about the middle of the evening; then eight of the company who lived in the Neeley's Creek community, left us and went down the river. A. M. Black, J. G. Noland, Jas. Ferguson and myself came together near Rock Hill.

Then I left them, coming up through Evenezer to the dear old home. Mother was looking for me. I stayed at home the balance of the year, but was busy all the time. The next year, 1866, I found one of the prettiest and best girls in York County and married her.[56]

Going to the war when fifteen years old, I have been looking after my own welfare from that early date. I have made some mistakes and some success. I have tried to live in peace with my God; and with mankind, and can say truthfully that if I have an enemy I am not aware of it, and in conclusion, I will say that I have always been impressed with the nobleness of the women of our Southland.

William Joseph Miller, Co. H.

12th South Carolina Regiment, Confederate Army

Rock Hill, S.C., July 1916

Chapter 7

Trapped on Union Soil

Those caught up in the chaos and societal dislocation were not of only one gender. As this document, deposited in the Winthrop University Archives by history professor Mary Elizabeth Massey indicates, southern women also suffered in the war. In this account, Eugenia Phillips, the wife of a prominent Washington attorney with family ties to Alabama and South Carolina, found herself trapped in the District of Columbia when the war commenced. Imprisoned by Union soldiers as a suspected "spy," Phillips asserted to her guards that her family's only transgression was that they had been "born Southerners and not responsible for that." Ultimately freed because of her husband's political connections, Phillips and her clan became nomads, migrating through the Carolinas to New Orleans. When that city fell to the Union, the family headed back toward South Carolina.

A Southern Woman's Story of Her Imprisonment During the War of 1861 and 1862

Now followed days of increased sorrow, and we found our situation daily more harassing. One morning in August we were all seated in the dining room when quite a noise attracted our ear. Soon a man advanced, followed by a squad of soldiers—all armed. This individual came to me saying "is this Mrs. Phillips." I nodded assent. "Then you are my prisoner and so are all those others." This person proved to be detective Baker[1] well known in those times. My party consisted of my two young daughters,[2] my sister and a visitor, the latter also arrested. No explanation was

93

given, and I requested that we should all go up stairs, where privacy could be felt. He seated us with a squad each, while he opened presses, drawers, desks, boxes—everywhere was searched for treasonable documents. My dresses were turned inside out, pictures pulled down &c. Meanwhile the soldiers of the regular Army looked with disgust and when occasion offered, expressed it in language more eloquent than refined—"at these doings to ladies." My favorite maid an Irish woman of great intelligence happened to be dusting my room when we all entered. To see her surprise was worth seeing. She immediately said angrily "I am an English subject, you dare not touch me." Baker paid no attention to her, but he evidently saw some signs between her and myself. It seems that in a drawer I had kept family letters, which were full of secrets to a mutual friend, and I was wild over the idea of their publicity and determined to make an effort for their destruction. So I caught her eye, directing her to the aforesaid drawer, and in a moment she had them concealed in her dress. But the Spy[3] had also seen it all, and ordered the "English subject" below with a guard over her. I then gave up hope—but it seems she had got into the good graces of the jolly soldiers, and begging them to let her get a drink of water, they acquiesced, but followed her. She flew into the kitchen where the range was in full blast—pitched the letters into the fire—and I was safe. The guard did not see this act. After when the house had been entirely and unsuccessfully gutted—Baker turned his attention to his foreign subject who sat calmly awaiting her fate. "Give me those letters and damn you" was the speech. I have no letters was the response. "Then I shall send you to Fort Lafayette"[4] tearing open her sack Waist and looking in vain for the letters he thought so safe. The spy took vengeance in a great bit of cursing and left evidently disgusted with his want of skill. There being no evidence of rebel documents after a thorough search, also invading Mr. Phillips[5] office. The head detective left his prisoners in the hands of his subordinate. Our house became our prison: our mail was opened before indignant eyes: Men occupied every room, friends were denied admittance, people viewed our well known abode with fear, and we were completely shut out from the outer world. We were kept this way for a week, in order to detect contraband communication, and nothing having been discovered, we were told to prepare for removal in the house of a Mrs. Greenough,[6] a well-known female—who had been found in secret communication with the Confederates, and as she had been watched, it was thought polite to her us together. In vain Mr. Phillips offered our house for the prisoners comfort—he was refused and we were driven around to a house on 16th St.[7] I requested leave to go into my parlor to have some books I valued

put away—a very vulgar man, sat with his legs out of the window han-
dling a precious book. He stared at me, saying "I hope you know me." "I
have not that pleasure but I shall Know you in the Rogues Gallery[8] and
shall live to see you hung." About two months after this, I was written
to come to Richmond to recognize this man. His name was Applegate,
he was found to be a Federalist Spy and hung, and I was not sorry one
bit. We reached the house designated, were all put into one filthy room
in the attic—a bed soiled and innocent of any covering, rude soldiers put
over us, and surroundings appalling to dainty folk. What our crime was
we were not able to ascertain—only that General Cameron[9] and Senator
Seward[10] thought the country endangered with such dangerous women at
large. Our gaoler, a very common man, took a great fancy to my eldest
daughter which gave me great concern, as his kindness was evidently sug-
gested through his coarse notice of the girl. He would send messages up
to our prison, entirely too familiar, so I soon took measures to cool his ambition—which discover(ed) he commenced a system of cruelties and insults
very alarming to our inmates. We were watched day and night; soldiers at
our door, everywhere along the stairs and passages; and altho' I tried my
best to disarm the young ones fear, still I became myself much depressed
and thought of how I should seek some one to carry a note to Mr. Phillips,
telling him of the persecution and consequent alarm felt. In this state of
dejection one day we heard a noise as if some one was trying to slip a note
under our closed door. We had been warned to avoid all communication
outside of the legitimate source—that is not sent by the Provost Marshall.[11]
The note got thro' the crack, we saw it with emotion, but I did not allow
it to be touched—fearing it was a bid to compromise us. This happened
near our dinner hour, when a guard escorted us below, watching every
mouthful. I dallied in the rear, when a whisper from one of the guards
arrested my attention. "Lady (he said) I am but a poor soldier, a Union
man—but my heart is full of horror to see how Capt. Sheldon (the gaoler)
treats such ladies. If you will trust me and write a note to your husband,
I will take it tonight—but you must not speak of the war." I looked at the
man to study his face, which struck me as being full of honesty and feeling. He begged me to be very careful—to give him no money, no notice of
any kind, as he is watched. I was duly excited of course, but had decided
to trust this soldier, his name was Hepburn, which I recall with gratitude.
When we returned to our prison, I locked the door, whispered the news
that help had come, and bade them keep hopeful, that I intended trusting
this man and writing a note, telling of our dangerous condition. I wrote
the note to my Husband; it said "That we were submitting to the daily

insults, that every day Sheldon became more insolent, that we see Mr. Stanton[12] (who was a friend of Mr. Phillips, and about to enter in a law partnership with him) was necessary, and help solicited." We waited in great excitement for the next day to come, and determined if Stanton came to us, to expose this wretch "Sheldon" who had exceeded his authority over us. We retire full of hope and I had a curious dream which I interpreted in our favor. I dreamt we were (prisoners) all walking in a garden when quantities of snakes appeared from under the brushwood coming towards us in fiery attitudes. They passed us all, but attacked Mrs. Greenought and her daughter. When I awoke I shouted "Liberty. We shall be out today." The children looked astonished, re-iterated my certainty of release. The hours passed as usual, when about mid-day we were excited over the ringing of the door-bell below—a most unusual thing. I screamed, "Have they come; we are free" and in a moment Mr. Stanton with Judge Advocate Hey[13] entered our prison. We were introduced by Mr. Stanton, who seemed to weep copious crocodile tears. When all were seated, Judge Hey said "Ladies, General McClellan[14] (then in command) has sent me to tell you that he does not want war upon women; that he wishes to know why you are prisoners: that he had heard nothing about the matter and that you are to be released to-day." A shout of delight greeted the joyful news and I then told Judge Hey that all I knew about our sins of commission centered in the fact that we were "born Southerners and not responsible for that." Of course, this news was received only good humoredly, and we were told to prepare for our release. But we had some complaints, and succeeded in getting bold Sheldon relieved from his, too responsible position. Well these gentlemen walked home with us, our house very near. Mr. Phillips was all delight and taking Stanton by the hand he said "Stanton What can I do for you after receiving this favor." "Yes Phillips (said this patriot) you may well call it a favor as none but yourself could have tempted me into that den of infamy" pointing to the White House where ruled Lincoln. I mentioned this in evidence of the character of this cruel man. It made a great impression on me, when succeeding events made it history and insincerity. But we returned home only to be watched by spies, which condition of life being unsupportable, Mr. Phillips concluded to get from Gen. Scott[15] permission to leave and go South—the permission was readily granted and we made preparations for a sad departure. We were sacrificed all our household goods, even the wrapping of the newspapers were not allowed. But this did not prevent some very loyal Federal Officers to provide me with traitors notes for Jeff Davis, which I carefully concealed and delivered. But I have never mentioned any names concerned in such dangerous business. I see these Officers constantly, but never allude to this interesting episode of our lives. We left Washington in a Flag of Truce Boat—and behaved like fiends when we heard the Confederate guns of welcome to their persecuted people.

Just prior to the incident in May and June of 1861, turmoil and depression scattered about the Capital where Phillip Phillips was a Congressman from Alabama with a lucrative law practice in Washington. As the question of slavery was becoming more of a problem, officials in Washington were becoming more aware of Mr. Phillips' "Union proclivities." Southern officials in Washington were beginning to leave because of Southern secession. Each Senator was presented a day to deliver his farewell speech. Because the Phillipses had made numerable friends within the Congress, they were heartbroken to see so many leaving. Everyone gathered to hear the speeches only to return home with heartache. Mr. Phillips was upset because he did not want to leave the Capital, so he inquired about his chances of remaining in Washington. There were few friends of the Phillipses left in Washington.

In the absence of the southern friends, there were constant rumors concerning the Phillipses. Mr. Phillips told his family that they had to remain calm at all times and to have less communication with the people from the south. Friends became fearful about visiting the Phillipses. No one suspected Mr. Phillips' integrity or loyalty while he was under Federal administration, and even though he was against secession, whenever there was a question of fighting he would go with his section. As Confederate prisoners arrived in the Capital, the Phillipses were allowed to aid them. Female spies entered the Phillipses home pretending to be in need of aid. The Phillipses were suspected of giving to the Confederate forces information on the advancements of the Union.

One weekend, news reached the Phillipses of a Federal Army's defeat. The family became very concerned. Now, they were even more aware of the dangerous situation. Orders were given for all lights in the house to be extinguished, and no one was to be admitted; however, many of their friends were allowed to enter. The cook was given orders to provide food to the visitors and wounded soldiers. Mrs. Phillips made them aware of the fact that a southern family had taken care of them, and they should never forget that fact.

After the arrest and imprisonment, they were released. A boat took them to Richmond where the family was heartily welcomed. Mrs. Phillips delivered papers to Jefferson Davis the next day after they arrived in Richmond. After visiting the city, the family left for New Orleans. Mr. Phillips had chosen to continue his law practice there. The family was saddened by having to leave Washington. The adjustment was great for them. They were still aware of the bad effects of the war. The Phillipses managed to go through the Winter of 1862 with relative safety.

Chapter 8

Augustus Franks, German Confederate

The Civil War not only pitted brother against brother, American against American, but also immigrant against immigrant. A large number of these primarily west European "old immigrants" came to America in the two decades preceding the conflict and caused the population to swell to 31,443,100 people by the time of South Carolina's secession. In the South, the two largest groups of these immigrants were the Irish and the Germans. While the Irish distributed themselves fairly evenly, an overwhelming number of the Germans settled in Texas. As that state seceded in early 1861, the Germans rallied to the cause, supplying the Confederate army with numerous officers and over a dozen companies comprised entirely of Germans. Typical of these southern sympathizers was Augustus Franks.

Franks was born August 25, 1825, in Bavaria and later served as a sergeant in the Bavarian military. The Franks family migrated to the United States in the 1850s and settled in Marshall, Texas. Despite his previous higher rank, Augustus Franks was a private in the South's army. Although his discharge date is unknown, Franks did survive the war and fathered four children by the time of his death on October 29, 1873. Much is known of Franks' military service because of the letters he wrote home, mainly to his wife Babette. Dated from October 1861 to August 1863, the letters describe with emotion a wide range of war aspects. His ethnicity, apparently, did not dampen his loyalty to the South. Ill, he wrote Babette, "I pray to God every hour ... that I may be able again to kill those infernal Northern devils who disgrace with their hideous presence of the streets of the city [Nashville] whose residences are inhabited and ornamented by females having Roman and Spartan education and nobleness and grandeur of character and manners."

In camp, near Hopkinsville,[1]
Jan. 5, 1862

Dear Wife!

Although I only wrote to you yesterday, I am writing again today for all around me looks dead and sad that I am seeking refuge with you. It is Sunday and rained all day—no thought given to cooking. Nobody wants to go after wood, [but] it would not burn anyhow. A piece of cold veal cooked yesterday must serve as dinner and supper. Tonight I have to do what is called the night watch, and for four hours I'll have to splash around in the rain and deepest mud of this camp.

Bruckmuller[2] heard through Tony Beal[3] that his child has died. The poor fellow sits in a corner and does not reply to questions or consolations. He wants to ask for his discharge from the army. There is little doubt he will receive it, especially since he suffers from hemorrhoids and chills ... has never been able to do much service. And ... because only two drummers[4] [are needed]. Bruckmuller believes that the band ... can get along all right.

Between Teller[5] and myself there exisists a state of war for several days. For several days ... he did not want to do any work, and I gave him a good piece of my mind in which I did not use dainty words ... that he believed I alone could fetch all the wood and water. He has nothing at all to do in this world ... except whistle a tune on his flute several times during the day. So far I cannot make anyone in my tent talk to me, and be cause I don't 'now what else to write to you, I'll go and see what the boys in the other tents are doing.

Miss A.H.[6] then told how ... kissed and cried violently when you ... her ... and you, dear Babette,[7] know ... not to write a word of this. You complain not to know what you should write, [so] why don't you tell me who visits you and I ... word that Frances[8] is so big already and that she resembles you so much. That I love Eugenia[9] more than Frances is a [lie?]—I never made a difference there.

It is getting dark, so I must stop writing.

We still have not yet received any money.

I wish spring was here. This weather is unbearable. In the last three nights, [I] have been neither warm nor dry. It takes a rugged nature to stand this. In all my outgoing letters, with the exception of one, I have always forgotten to write to please send me, if possible, two pairs of underpants of red flannel like my shirts. These would be best.

It is not possible to continue writing in this weather with rain, wind, and darkness.

auf Wiedersehn,

Your husband,

Augustus

Addressed to Mrs. A. Babette Franks, Marshall, Texas[10]

Hopkinsville, Ky.
6th of Feb., 1862

My dear wife!

It is only a few hours that I closed my other letter and I believe I expressed my opinion therein that the army will for some time be immovable. Yesterday evening I was in town to see Dan Dopplmayer[11] whose case of pneumonia is no further dangerous, though he will not be fit for duty for several weeks. When I came near to our camp (Texas Village), I heard uncommon shouting and I thought that something must be the matter. A _____ was in camp and brought the order to cook two days rations and march at daybreak the next morning. Where to proceed? Toward Louisville? Up to the Ohio? No ... Clarksville and Fort Donelson![12] Judge of my dismay, dear Babette! If I hate anything it is to retreat a step, although we go from Clarksville again forward to Fort [Donelson]....

Well night came and with it the most tremendous storm that lasted all night. We have not had a clear day in weeks and the condition of the roads.... The order must be countermanded, but this morning winds cleared away the clouds and the order to ... off the brigade was executed. The tents were dripping with water, taken down with so much trouble and ... builded houses. The regiment has left some time ago except ours,

Captain Alexander's company,[13] and two companies from all other regiments with the necessary cavalry and artillery. We form the rear guard. The Lincolnites (Unionists) are so anxious to see Hopkinsville, we may pinch their noses yet a little before we leave this place. We'll follow the army the day afterward, and a fine road we'll have to march on after it was cut up by several thousand ... cavalry, artillery, and 600 or 700 transport wagons. Why this retrograde movement ... a hundred times? We don't know the answer. The Lincolnites are marching on us with overwhelming numbers. Some say Flagel's brigade[14] will occupy this place ... and ours by disease decimated brigade will be sent to Fort Donelson to reinforce General Lay's brigade[15] which is not strong enough yet to _____ the pressing Lincolnites. _____ guess is that General Beauregard[16] is changing the positions of the whole army in general since he took command at Columbus.[17] Well I don't care how, but surely it don't look like going forward.

Listen, says Doctor Ganstan,[18] sitting in our tent. He looks sort of scared, and said he don't only want a victory but sends utmost prayers up to Heaven that we be victorious. Great God, he says again, I can't _____ a minute!

That ever since ten o'clock this morning the enigma of the above is that I write this letter under a cannon. There is the road of cannons in the direction of Columbus and Fort Donelson. We hear it so distinctly that we can count every _____tonation. It is now 2:00 P.M., and my estimation is that since 10:00 A.M., 25,000 were fired. It must be a great battle, and I am inclined to think it takes place at Columbus. Mark that day, dear Babette—the sixth of February, 1862. The tidings of a battle fought on that day will surely reach you soon.

And we all here, armed with the best guns and men eager as ever for fight and cannot participate in this beyond all doubt glorious and victorious battle.

I close this letter here with the intention to finish and mail it when we arrive at our destination—Clarksville, Fort Donelson, _____ddyville.

                                              Hopkinsville
                                              7th Feb., '82

My dearest wife!

Just now I learned that General Clark[19] took a strong position fifteen miles from here, and there is no telling when I shall be able to write to you again, although I shall do so at the very first opportunity. But in the midst of the woods and during the preparations for defensive war there will be very little chance for writing and....

The above is only a rumor. I hardly believe our army will stop before reaching Clarksville, but nevertheless, I [had] better mail this letter while I can.

A fight yesterday ... Fort Donelson. The reports are so contradictory and unreliable that I ... say the result is not known. We all believe that our troops came out victorious.

Good bye, dear, dear, Babette. I expect hard times for a while. Address your letters as you have done before, to Clarksville, and write as often as possible.

All our sick got off today, well enough for circumstances. Mayer[20] got sixty dollars today, and that enabled him to hire a carriage to go to Clarksville.

Kiss my dear, dear darlings and give my very best to my friends.

Your _____,

Augustus

Nashville
April [15], 1862

My dear wife!

By the time I write this I only see enough ... write you a, perhaps unintelligible, letter. Since I got my eyes poisoned the doctors told me not to write or read anything, but I can't obey such a command. I am bound to have to talk with you, my dearest, through the medium of writing.

Besides the inflammation of my eyes, I have been very sick for about ten days so that I couldn't leave the bed. I knew very well, and Doctor Becker[21] himself thought, that I never will get well as long as I have to lie in the hospital. If you ever have got one of the seven letters which, with the kind help of Mr. W. Clark,[22] I tried to smuggle through the federal lines, you know the causes of my present, miserable state of health—the exhalation of mortified wounds poisoned my eyes. Four days and nights [of] fatigue, fighting, and exposure on the tramp to and on the battlefield at Fort Donelson gave my constitution a hard and bad lick.

During the time of my sickness, not a day passed away without being visited and assidously cared for by several ladies of Nashville who would come upstairs to my room and, with their own delicate hands, adjust my couch and administer to me all those little attentions which do a sick person more good than all the medicines of the world. These young and beautiful ladies, my dear Babette, visit daily our sick and wounded soldiers, [and] come in their carriages filled with the choicest delicacies the city can produce. These ladies belong exclusively to the first, richest, [and] noblest families of Nashville, and I do not think that....

I pray to God every hour ... that I may be able again to kill those infernal Northern devils who disgrace with their hideous presence the streets of the city whose residences are inhabited and ornamented by females having Roman and Spartan education and nobleness and grandeur of character and manners.

It was the seventeenth day of March, just a month after these terrible days of Donelson, when Miss Susan Clark, one of the young ladies who came to visit me daily to see after my wants, told me that Doctor Becker expressed his opinion about me to her _____ that a change of locality and a few weeks in a private house would speedily restore my health. Miss Susan therefore offered to me the hospitality of her father's house. I told Miss Susan that being a prisoner of war I couldn't leave the hospital; but to my great astonishment she told me that General Buell[23] allowed certain wounded Rebel soldiers to be taken to private houses by their being put under parole and by making the Magnanimous Protector responsible for the safety of their progress. I accepted this kind offer, chiefly when Miss Clark told me that her father intends to take every Texan, wounded or sick, his house. Already she had made plans and preparations to remove Mr. McCracken, Conrad Fisher,[and] Charles N.[24] to her father's mansion, while she intended to bring me to her brother-in-law's house, Mr. Cliff's house.[25] His house [is] in the center of the city and in close proximity to a famed eye doctor's house, while Mr. Clark's house, or better—mansion, is situated a mile from the city on the Franklin[?] Turnpike Road.[26] The reason of Mr.[Clark's] and mainly of the lady Clark's particular predilection for the Texans. I will tell you in my next letter, my dear and dearest Babette.

I am in a beautiful room [with] a library and a fine piano at my disposition [and] a table not to be found in the finest hotel. And yet if I could see you, my dear Babette, and Eugenia and Frances, I wouldn't give a fiddlestick for all this.

McDowels Military Prison,[27]
St. Louis
May 20, 1862

Dear wife!

"Success to the South! Independence and happiness to the land where Eugenia and Frances one day shall sing in immortal songs the heroic deeds of the men of 1861–62," I said to Brentano.[28] After I had done with my secession speech, and raising my glass of wine and telling the crowd to do the same I said, "Hurrah for Jefferson Davis and the independence of the South!" I did not holler. I was perfectly sober, only agitated and excited by passion and love for all what is down _____ South. Brentano assured me that the saloon is exclusively frequented by our friends and that he did not betray me. I had since been entirely convinced. It was sometime after I had quit talking that some of the friends came to my table, informing me that a Patroville[29] was at the door, but I could leave yet safely by the backway. I refused to do that believing that in my capacity of a paroled soldier and prisoner of war I had only sworn not to fight against the Northern government as long as not exchanged. It never entered my thought that expressing my sympathy for the land wherein my children are born and for which I fought and always will fight could be considered a crime even by the most despotical government of the world. But this remonstrance of mine was of no avail. The officer of the guard answered to every expostulation of mine, "I arrest you by the order of the Provost Marshall, General Farrar."[30] I had to go, and after some minutes I saw myself an inmate of the Hotel Lynch (Military Prison).[31] The next day I was transferred to McDowels M.P., and since the twenty-sixth of April I had two conversations with the Provost Marshall. He can't help to believe that I came in a *criminal* intention to St. Louis. My home being in Texas, it looks to him suspicious a man going from Nashville takes the route by St. Louis. He threatened me yesterday to send me to my regiment [in] Chicago. I said that's all I want. I long to see again and join my companions of arms. I am sure that they can never prove that I acted in whatever a slight capacity of a spy. It's not my nature.

Chapter 9

My Dear Elodie

War's cannons cannot silence human love. In these letters, Confederate Captain N. H. R. Dawson corresponds with his fiancée, Elodie. He serves early in the war in the Carolinas, Georgia, Alabama, and Virginia while his beloved volunteers her talents on the home front in Selma, Alabama. The horrors of war are evident. For example, Dawson writes of the death of a comrade "killed yesterday in his tent, having his head shot off by a 24 lb. ball." Still, he longs for Elodie and concludes "may God bless and keep you, and grant us an early and happy meeting."

To Capt. N. H. R. Dawson

Wednesday Morning, 16th

This morning I was awakened by a note from my brotherinlaw Kellogg informing me that he was a *prisoner* on board the Southern Republic and on his way to Montgomery,[1] and also informed me of the death of my Brother Sam,[2] killed in the Battle at Corinth.[3] We have telegraphed to New Orleans hoping to hear this sad news untrue. I had little thought another day would bring with it two such trials and sorrows. Mr. K[ellogg] has been with our army for 6 weeks and said while Gen'l Johnston lived he had no trouble and was with *our side* during the Battle but[,] I suppose[,] did not participate.[4] I went to see him but the boat had gone, but Mr. Hagood saw him and gave me all the particulars of his conversation with him.[5] I fear we can do but little for him, and will be obliged to wait for time to prove him a friend to our cause. I am greatly distressed on my poor Sister's account and deeply regret he ever came to hear of, or see us, but I trust in One who can and will aid us in all our troubles. I see the bill has passed as you thought.[6] I cannot write more this morning, but will soon, with

love yours[,] Elodie

Yorktown, April 19, 1862

Though surrounded by difficulties and danger, expecting every moment to hear the call to arms, I cannot refrain from writing you briefly[,] my dear Elodie. We arrived here yesterday evening after a march of ninety miles from Fredericksburg[,Virginia]. I have not time to tell you some of the trials and incidents of the march. I am quite well fortunately, and hope for the best, tho we are to have hard and hot work. We are on the eve of a grand battle, which will go far to the end of the war.

I have thought much of you this morning, the anniversary of our engagement, and cannot but deem it a fortunate day, therefore believe that we are yet to have some days of happiness. My mind is much up to leave the service, after the expiration of my regiment, which will be within forty days after the expiration of our di[vision's?] term of service, say June.

There is heavy skirmishing on our lines daily. Last night there was a continual cannonade [, and t]he day before[,] a heavy skirmish, in which we defeated the enemy. My love for you[,] my dear Elodie [,] is paramount to everything else. I am now boundup in a _____ of [?] and against all my wishes and hopes am compelled to remain here, the disappointment being increased by the fact that I have disappointed you in fixing the date of my return. This[,] of course you know[,] is not my fault, but it is a great misfortune, one which I lament exceedingly. I have no time now, however, my dear Elodie, for regrets. I must look to the future for a brighter day. You have been mine one year today, and I hope in a few months that all of our hopes will be realized. I have kissed your likeness frequently this morning, and will keep it ever near my heart. I will write you as often as possible, but you must be content with short letters.

I hope to hear from you today by Mr. Shortridge or Mr. Kidd.[7] Remember me to your sisters and with much love, I remain, my dear Elodie,

ever sincerely yours[,]

N. H. R. Dawson

Write me to Yorktown.

Yorktown[,] Va. April 21, 1862[8]

I have seen Gen. Whiting[9] this morning, and he agrees with me, that the Conscription bill does not retain officers.[10] I have th[ere]fore declined a reelection as captain, which the men all desire me to accept. Duty to myself, and duty to you; and an unwillingness to remain here, in my present position, induce me to do this. The regiment will be reorganized, in a few days, [t]hen I will be released. I will wait a reasonable time, on the battle, now pending, and if I [survive?] it, will leave soon afterwards for Ala[bama] where I hope, my dear Elodie, to have all of my anticipations of happiness realized in our early marriage.

Capt. King and several other officers will take this course.[11] I may go into the service again, if I can get a good place, but this will depend very much on circumstances, which the future will develop.

I received, on the 19th, after sending my letter to be mailed, your affectionate letter of the 6th inst[ance]. As I thought of you all day, on account of its being the anniversary of our marriage, the receipt of your letter was doubly welcome. I wrote you on the 18th from Williamsburg[,Virginia.] Reginald came to see me on the 19th,[12] and I rode over to Yorktown and dined with him, seeing Mr. Peques and Col. Morgan, besides many other friends.[13] The place is very old and dilapidated, but the site is very pretty, and it commands a beautiful view of York river, and of Gloucester point, on the opposite shore. The old fortifications thrown up by Cornwallis have been enlarged, and greatly strengthened, and all that science and art can do has been done to make them formidable.[14] Reginald's regiment is in the works, and he showed me over all of them. Our lines extend across the peninsula, and their riflemen keep up a constant fire upon our pickets, who lie in rifle pits four hundred yards beyond our breastworks. An occasional cannonnade is also kept up, and we have lost a few men from this firing. Burwell Blount, of M[o?]hill[,] was killed yesterday in his tent, having his head shot off by a 24 lb. ball. He was the son of Co. F. S. Blount.[15] We were ordered out on Saturday night, on account of heavy firing. It proved to be a false alarm. I never heard such volleys of musketry in my life. It was terrible.

Col.Winston[16] thinks the battle here will decide the fate of the war. I do not feel so hopeful. There has been a good deal of heavy firing all the morning.

An order has just been received to hold the election for officers this evening. I look forward with much hope, my dear Elodie, to our meeting. I anticipate much happiness, even from under the dark clouds, which overshadow us at this time.

I had intended only to write you a short note, and must now close. Good bye, my dearest. May God bless and keep you, and grant us an early and happy meeting. With much love, I remain,

Ever affectionately and devotedly,

N. H. R. Dawson

Chapter 10

A Grand C.S.A. Victory

Even southerners who found themselves cut off from their native region cheered the Confederacy—at least in the war's early months. An example of this patriotism was displayed by Mary Pringle Mitchell (1831–1901). Living just outside New Haven, Connecticut, with her husband, Donald Grant Mitchell, Mary wrote her South Carolina relatives a steady stream of correspondence which, by late 1862, had lost much of its earlier optimism. Tragedy had befallen her family with the death of her brother Charles and Mary Pringle. Hundreds of miles from home, she desperately searched for small glimmers of hope that her beloved Confederate States could achieve independence.[1]

5 August 1862

My Mother and Sister dear

I do not, can not beg to comfort you, for God only can. My head and heart nearly burst when I heard of our noble Charlie's[2] death, altho I have grown to rejoice for & envy the good who are taken from this world of tears & fears. Why then, should we mourn? not for the dead, but for the living, who must toil on—*None* of us would design such a glorious change as our Brother's faith & trust & peace & holy calm now given him. Our own Angel's infant faith, our noble William's calmness & guileless Charlie's happy trust are pictures of death & the Hereafter that we poor sojourners covet! I feel that life now is not worth the living—God grant that all with you brightens in proportion to the darkness that overhangs us. Today we had *nearly* decided to emigrate to Canada or to France, but a certificate of exemption from this wicked drafting given by our sincere friend & Doctor, has determined us to linger a little longer until we might get off with his sacrifice until Mr. M[3] can learn of some chance of finding board elsewhere. As to my husband's being drawn into this hateful unchristian war, that is out of any question. I should sooner have him die in jail, than help in such a cause and God knows his heart is too pure & christian to be so sacrificed.

I can not tell you how much I thank you all for the touching details of our noble young soldier's happy death bed which I read and re-read with streaming eyes and sent to E[4]—I have written to Maria[5] alas & by her to tell me something of Julius,[6] as she may hear through N.O. A thousand thanks to dear Brother for his photograph which gives me pleasure & comfort and the standing one of our Angel is *charming*, indeed, Mr. M says it is the best yet. Oh! how I long to have you criticize the different ones we have, but I dare not trust them to such hazardous mail conveyances as we now have to be thankful for. Do thank Miss L for her carte de visit[7] too. Tell her my poor heart blesses her every time I look upon it. The letter with these three came yesterday with the sad ones about our brave soldier's death! Oh God! how hard to think of him as dead, no don't let us call him as pure & good dead? but talk of him & think of him as in his Happier Home gone to join our other dear & blessed ones as each of us yearn to do. My head swims & my hands tremble so, since this news & the general anxiety I suffer in these days that I can hardly write coherently. I have written your report to JJP. Tell JP Jr that his father made us a visit a short time ago & was rejoicing over his safe arrival in the C.S.A. You miss so many of my letters that I am afraid I write the same over very often. Did you get the one telling Amos B that A.P.H's business was growing that he goes his errands everyday ? with his baggage made & is industrious [illegible]. E wrote some time ago. Tell Bick Mama's photograph has not come yet, but I hope it is not lost in his letter of 15th came those of 2d & 3d July & good Mrs. B's report through Mrs. Voll came together. Write dearest whenever you can, you do not know how I watch & yearn for letters.

Tell the Pritichards & Stock—that their sisters are within three miles of me & I went to see them, a few days since & they are well but longing for news of their family.

Do give my warmest love to good Ella & Fanny, & tell them that even in these wicked N.S. there are some warm hearts who do sorrow & feel for them.

Ever loving yours—

I[8] do not send you E's letter for fear of their committing him in these days of terror & sure arrests to Fort Warren,[9] but be assured they & his heart are all that you could wish my dear Parents. The morning your letters about our beloved Brother's death came, I said to a friend in answer to her kind enquiries of you all, that until this wicked war but few white men ventured to stay a night where so many of the best of the land are now living—aged and dying! I had no sooner said this than I went hoping to the P.O. & alas! There I found the too sad confirmation of my talk, awaiting me. Continue to write often, for should we emigrate, a true friend would forward letters to us. Tell Papa I am watching most eagerly for his photograph & Bick's *must* come too, but I dare not ask what involves cost when I know how your [illegible] must suffer I hope in the event of reverse & confiscation that E or our little Prince might reserve the land for you all. J.J.P. tells us that Mr. E of Boston has saved the Hilton Head estate for its heirs. As our blessed mother writes "God enlist all things."

I send a slip as a specimen of the N.S. *patriotism*. Ah! our worthy neighbors would not find an exemption in a [illegible] or in old Spain, if Beau or Jackson were invading & pillaging their Homes! We are drifting fast into war & mobs at the North & my ambition is too great even to losing our cherished little home where until now all has been so bright & hopeful. The poor blacks how I pity them! God forgive me for the revenge and vindictiveness that the devilish spirit of your aggressors lead me into feeling. May a merciful God continue to help & save you all until your aim is accomplished.

Always in vision of hope,

My little ones are all well—Baby Don[10] a splendid specimen of bright & happy childhood. What a blessing he has been to my poor heart, a constant comfort & streak of sunshine in so much darkness. Love & blessing to all who may yet think kindly of me & mine. Where & how are the Alstons?

13 August

Tell Papa I am watching
for his carte de visite

My dearest Mother

I wrote to you on the 5th by J.B.L. but my poor heart bleeds so, and yearns so towards you all, that I find my self writing weekly, besides by every charity offer that is made me. My fears & anxieties were torturing enough before, but oh! God! This last blow makes life harder yet. Our beloved Charlie had fun often here, with us, than any of our brothers, and whenever I turn & walk there is something to bring him pleasantly & lovingly to my thoughts in the house, in the garden, on the lawn, in town, and thank God! in our little church too! Yes at God's altar he and I kneeled & partook of Christ's Holy Sacrament. I knew *well* all his virtues & all his perfections, and loved him dearly for them all. We, who are left, recall the charm of his life & envy him the blessing of his death. Bick promised me his photograph some time since, & I hope he kept it safely for me. Tell me some of the Boston names in his class & I will write to Mrs. Appleton to get me a copy of the group Bick speaks of, but I ought to know something about the picture, perhaps you might find the name of the artist or one you have in his class book & then with a description & date of the picture. I might write to the artist. Ah! these photographs quiet & cheer our sad hearts wonderfully.

The journals inform of the wicked despotism that now rules the North, but my hope is that it is all for the good of the CSA & my ambition is to say goodbye to the N.S. & find a home some where else where there is some humanity & christianity.

You will be glad to know that I have heard of one or two of the kind hearts, who take care of the Confederate's grave & I sent her message to them that there are sometimes as many as fourteen bouquets in the grave at a time & flowers are to be planted upon it.

Poor Mama is most anxious to hear from Julius, as she has not heard for a long while. I have begged a mutual friend who hears from N.O. to inquire where he might be. There is so much indignation felt in Mississippi against N.O. that there is no communication between Natchez & the City; but this friend's brother is in Mississippi & she heard of him through N.O. & they know Julius.

E writes often he & I try to comfort each other and to find something to hope on but it is hard work in these dark days. Louis Napoleon is now my strong hold & your best friend I am sure.

Do tell me if you are supplied with shoes & gloves & how the Army is clothed & if well provisioned. The few extracts from Southern papers interest me more than the rest of the journals put together & I know full well now that what is not called a victory always means a N.S. defeat & a grand C.S.A. victory. But Heavens! what do even victories cost in blood! Do give me all news of our noble boys & may God protect & guard them from all danger. Pray yours ever lovingly,

FM

August 20, 1862
Mrs. Wm B. Pringle

Tell me dearest ones if you
receive this & send if possible
the names of the noble heroes
who fell in the heat of battle—MPM

My dear Mother,

Indirectly, I have heard from you up to June 20—two months ago—
up to that time I believe you were all well, you as well as usual I trust the
same good has been continued to us. How I gloried and yet troubled over
the James Island victory[11] I did not know how many of our brave boys
may have fallen there, and I trembled for them while my heart swelled
with pride for gallant old Charleston and her sons. The bravest sight of
all the war! If So Carolina started the war she has at least done her duty
nobly in it. I see now that Stevens'[12] Division has gone from James Island
to reinforce McClellan and I hope that for a time at least Charleston and
the old house and home will be allowed to rest—But not one soldier I suppose; they must have gone on to reinforce the great gathering of the Southern Army at Richmond and to very hot work I am afraid—for though our
success so far has been glorious it must have been at very heavy cost—I
shared in all your victories though I cannot be of them—You see "I am still
here" mortified and disgusted that I am not with you all—I don't know when
I am most anxious to be with you, when I hear of your trials & sacrifices
or when I am proud of your successes—. But though I gnash my teeth at
my evil star in being here I know I am right, so far, to have stayed. I have
not been able yet to unravel the tangled meshes that business here has
inevitably got me into—what was mainly kept me has been those old City
slip cases in which we have, after seven years, achieved a victory—but the
fruits of victory are almost as hard to reach as the victory itself—We have
got judgements against the City but now she has been trying to resist the
payment of them. Every month, almost every week we have been deluded
with the hope of settlement and still the payment has been delayed. You
know too well what duties I have to others and I can't possibly afford to
lose this fruit of my seven years' labor, without failing in some of those
duties; and situated as those are near to whom I am in duty bound I cannot hesitate, that I must stay here until I can get out all that I have. If I
were to leave now I should have but a poor chance of getting any part of
my fee—For judgements against the City cannot be sold for anything like

their value. Very soon I hope however they will be paid in Bonds of the city which I can dispose of, and then I shall be free to pick up whatever I can—

Month after Month too I have been looking for peace; but it seems still very far off. Perhaps after all when I do join you I shall be more needed than I have been yet—I have to check myself sometimes, wishing that the way may hold on until I can be "doing my duty" as you say. There are many ways of doing one's duty. Ill luck has thrown a duty on me that is hard to stand but I hope it will soon be over—this part of it.

Physically I am perfectly well, and I suffer no annoyant of any kind, there are so many here of my way of thinking—Tell Aunt Brewton Arthur and family are well. Has she heard that they have a little daughter some four months old? Capt. & Mrs. B are very well & flourishing exceedingly—Tell their friends of them.

You have all been very kind and thoughtful about writing—I think no one here has been so often heard from home as I have—And I suppose a great many letters have gone where they can tell no tales. The last I wrote to you is at the bottom of the Pacific as many of yours to me are doubtless at the bottom of the Atlantic. It was in the trunk of a friend who narrowly escaped with his life in the recent burning of the "Golden Gate"[13] our largest passenger steamer. I was very sorry that my letter had gone down, because I should like to have had it reach you—Who knows what fate this may have?

I have been speculating much often what has become of the negroes and the crop on Santee. I know that Papa made them stick to the old place a long time, and if they held on until the affair at James Island they were all right but I saw by one of our telegraphic dispatches that some Federal gun boats had gone up the Waccamaw and Santee Rivers some months ago; and I feared that Richfield would have to be abandoned, at least temporarily I hope it may not have been so—If you have a chance to write again tell me about this and tell me how Papa is getting on financially— And about Julius, what has become of him and his corps in the taking of New Orleans? How gallantly Vicksburg has held out! When you write to me direct, under enclosure to the firm W.P. & F Atty at Law. The letters will then seem to be a mere business letter. Goodbye with much love to all—I can't tell you how much—I am very affectionately—

EP

I have not heard any letters since those of 4 July with the sad tidings of beloved Charles, but hope you have received mine. I sent this as of much value than one of mine.

This goes via Bal—& Richmond, Virg. & send a reply through same channel, more lovingly than I found this letter was too heavy for Baltimore so will send to J.B.L.

12 September

Please always mention my
brave and noble brothers
who are left—

My dearest Mother

More than a month now since I have a line from any of you my beloved ones. God only knows what you all may be suffering. Woudst that we could help or comfort you in some way. Oh! how my heart & prayers have followed our gallant soldiers in the recent battles, and how God has followed and blessed them too, dear Mama. All glory be to Him! for the brilliant successes of C.S.A. & may it continue to the end which I trust is, *now* near by, but alas! which will have been uppercased by the blood and lives of the purest & best of men. The N.S. now begins to feel the war as *justice* requires that she should. Many & many a Mother's & wife's heart now feels that a flag is *not* worth the price they have paid for it! My poor friend Mrs. F is now lamenting the sacrifice of her only Brother, feeling most bitterly that his home demanded his love more than his flag. In all my sorrow & anxieties she is a true friend & in her grief feels more comfort in my sympathy, than in any other.

Poor M—again her heart strings have torn—A.H. writes me that one of her blooming boys is taken from her. Is it our Angel's favorite? Do give her my heartiest sympathy & warmest love, the Almighty saw fit to afflict the good as well as the bad of his unhappy America.

A letter from E tells me that one for you was lost in the Golden Gate & a letter from Maria yesterday speaks of a recent letter from J.J., she and children were well making a visit to the Isle of Wight for sea air, she sends much love & most earnest sympathy to all.

John (G?) P. is in N.Y. & enclosed was the just and appropriate obituary on our beloved Charles which he cut from some Charleston papers. Tell me who wrote it.

The children are all well and good. Minnie & Liz[14] are much grown & ought to be going to school, but I can not bring myself to sending them away and school & so shut my eyes to their ignorance hoping for some change when the war ends. Baby goes by the name of Stonewall now & I often tell his Papa I had him christened too soon; one child closeby has been baptized Mary Beauregard and another Jeff Davis, children too of N.S. soldiers!! There may be 20 million North but ten of the twenty are at heart with the South, but are *afraid* to talk. Thank God a change of feeling *is beginning*. Jackson would be received today with cheers even by his enemies. How I watch his movements & pray God to bless him always. You would be surprised to see how the admiration of the C.S.A. generals forces truth & justice even into the abolition journals. I heard one person say we shall soon have a Dictator & "I hope it will be Jackson!"

Ah dearest Mother & sisters God grant us Peace soon and may those who are left gather a few crumbs of happiness from the crumbling remains of prosperity.

Do tell me how dear Papa is. I tremble for the effect of so much excitement upon him.

I am afraid you receive but few of my letters Husband & children all write in heartiest love sympathy with you lovingly—

26 August 1862

My darling Mother

My heart and thoughts and prayers unceasingly with you all that is some relief to write, hoping that somehow my poor epistles may reach you and keep us kindly in mind now that our Messenger of Love is away, but only gone as a Soldier and even happier messenger than before a grander angel to save us from falling into the wickedness of the times. And how our heart bond grows! our noble Charles makes the heavenly home & family all the more inviting to the wayfarer.

I envy my beloved sisters their beautiful faith and truth all the more because I feel more and more that this awful war has driven out any good that may have been in my nature & give rise to much malice and vindictiveness.

My children comfort & cheer me as nothing else can. My baby Don is seated on the table as I write, laughing & clapping his hands but my poor heart sinks as I look at him & feel & feel that I may never have the happiness of having him see those I love best. God only knows how this war will end. The desperations and malice of the U.S. frighten me almost to despair; but God grant that the C.S.A. may be able to hold out until the suffering of the world will force their selfish timidity to give way to their honest sympathies. Our friends of the U.S. are beginning to realise everyday that soldiers who have to be bought are not worth the half of those who have their whole hearts in the struggle.

Do write me everything that you suffer for imagination is even more torturing to me than fact & poor Edward too begs to know everything, suspense is agony. E is to be envied even in his exile, as being out of reach of compulsion & as holding a refuge, may be, for the future, in a country that will be first to throw off Federal rule. I wish all of you & all of us were only there now.

Heaven grant that our dear old City is strong enough to resist the frightful armaments that [illegible] for destination. Can you tell me anything of Lise N. she has not acknowledged my last letter & I hope she may now be in the C.S.A. Do remember me lovingly gratefully to all sympathies & inquiries till then. Altho I am in the enemy's country my heart & best wishes are always with *them*.

I answer my darling sister in this general way as I know that there is more chance of a letter addressed to a Mother reaching its destination in these days of our vigilance.

God bless help & protect all with and around you always, Husband, & children all join with lovingly—

6 November 1862

My dear Brother[15]

I and my two boys come to thank you for yours of 17th Aug which came to me on Saturday 1st Nov & made my poor heart throb with gratitude, for its words of comfort, confidence, and cheer. May God help and protect you all from your cruel and vindictive persecutors, and reward you, and punish them as their fiendish deeds deserve.

I forwarded your enclosure immediately. You will be glad to hear that E is flourishing and watching for the happy time that will allow him to join those who have all his sympathy, and for whom he now labors most indefatigably. A gentleman, who has recently seen him says his property is now worth at least $250,000! so our good Brother's hopes are bright now with the prospect of giving a good account of his stewardship. Tell Mama he proposed in his last letter that this family should migrate, and I am *delighted* with the suggestion & Mr. M too thinks favorable of the plan & we have it under serious consideration. As E says his long residence & position there will enable him to give us a good start & our being there might be of service to him & release him all the sooner. And again dear Brother, in the event of unhappy success of Lincoln's wicked intentions, our going there might be the beginning of a place of refuge for those who are dearest to us, or on the other hand in the event of the much hoped for success of the C.S. we should quickly find ourselves knocking at his door.

I am trying to pressure Mr. M to go, and take a book. There are some kind friends in N.O. outcasts like me from the C.S. & I could always have one of them to stay with me, in his absence or they would forward all letters should I go suddenly. I fear many of my recent letters have been captured, and I have written every ten days and sent several letters from E—also one for Mrs. K telling her of her Mother's death, in March last! Do ask Mama to enclose by way of trial, a letter to Burton H. Harrison[16]—Richmond as I find letters come very promptly, by the underground R.R. so directed.

Heaven grant that the political revolution in the N.S. may work some good and that reason and humanity and christianity may take the plan of radicalism and abolitionism—The triumph of the Democrats is in fact a victory to the C.S. inasmuch as it is a national disapproval of the present incumbents and incumbrances. I have heard many a Democrat express a willingness for separation, and a third for reconstruction under your president! but I maintain that J. D. *would not* accept of the U. S. however earnestly pressed upon him. God grant that your independence *is* now well nigh established without the help of any people, or any outside party, only by your own strong will, valor, *nobleness* and an all wise Providence, whose aid your people & your Govt, your soldiers, all charmingly recognise. God bless each and all as my asking prays He should.

This long letter will show you how much I value yours; you don't know with how much pride I have read it to Northern friends as from the Pro: Marshall of C. Warmest love to you & yours all from us all....

Chapter 11

Our Banner Is Waving

James Morrison Stitt's letters are written on stationery which features the Confederacy's flag, the Stars and Bars, with three bars, red, white, red, and a blue field featuring a circle of eleven white stars. The top margin of the paper highlights the following poem:

> Above us our banner is waving—
> The hope of the brave and the free:
> We must watch, must guard, and defend it
> Till the minions of tyranny flee.

In these two letters, Stitt, born on November 2, 1835, writes his mother, Lucinda Caroline Ezell Stitt, and his sister, Mary Jane Stitt.

Letter One

Camp Lee Richmond Va.[1]
October 10, 1862

Dear Mother[,] [It] has bin some time sence I have riten you or all of you a leter and I suppose you know why it was by this time. [When] I rote last I had the janders[2] at Petersburg.[3] [The] Regment[4] left in a few days afterwards and left me there with 10 or 12 more of our company[.] [We] stayed in camp some two weeks. [When] the camp was order[ed] to brake and all that [were] able to go to our regments and all who were not to the hospitable[5] at petersburg. [I] was not yet will but dud not like

120

to go to the hospitable and and[6] went to the Regment Camped at the Benton bridge between Druarys bluf[7] and Richmond[.] The next day we left to reinforce Jaxson[8] and I was detached as gard to the baggage train which suted me vary well for I could not have marched far &[9] we had the privilige of riding but the bregade[10] got on the train at Richmond and rode as far as rapdam station[11] which took us a week to make the trip that far but I [fared][12] well in the way of getting something to eat on the rode which strenthend me up[.] [So] by the time we got up the rigiment I felt prety stout[.]

[The] day after we caut up with the bregade it started to marching and i[13] was then in ranks with them[.] [I] stood it fine for a few days but at last I began to fail in my legs and got worse every day till my knees and ankels would hardly work a told[14] but I folered on. [I] would drap out through the day but always come up at nigh utill we got to Maryland near fedrick city[15] when I was taken very sick one night[.] [and] [The] next day the doctor told me to go to the hospitable at fedrick and gave us surtificates as it was not known that the regment was going near there & that was the only chance of getting to a hospitable[.] [But] before we started the bregade was ordered to fedrick and we Pinch Sprat & John Squires[16,17] with me ware[18] put in the rear & our guns & nap sacks, put in the ambulance[.] [but] [When] within 2 or 3 miles of fedrick then Jaxsons hedquarters [The] bregade was ordered back some 20 miles on the patomack[19] to blow up a brige & we ware left in the woods in charge of one of our lutenents[20] where we stayed 2 days when we herd that the yankeys[21] ware [advancing] that way and our lutenent thought it best to leave & go to the other side of town[.] [but] [By] the time we got to fedrick the enemy had it about surrounded so [the] lutenent put us in the hospitable and went to find his way out as best he could to our regment[.] [Whether] he got through or not we have not herd. [The] next day the yankeys came up on all sides and we were ther prisners.[22] [They] then took our guns & catrige boxes from us & let us remain as before onley we ware under gard[.] [On] Friday the 12th we [were] taken and [Sunday] we [were] put [into] an old hotell[23] [some] 450 that were sick at the hospitable[.] [All] of that numbere that [were] able were put [into] it[,] crowded so that had hardly rome to lie down[.] [but] [The] sec'cs ladeys[24] fed us well with everything that was good[.] [The] government rations [were] only 5 [?] crackers a day[.] [We were] helt here untill [Wednesday] when we were sent to Batimore[25] by railrod[.] [When] we got there it was 9 or 10 oclck in the night but it was not long before the [secessionists] had as much for us to eat as we could eat of the best of eatables &

Top: Civil War re-enactors seek to recreate the scenes documented in this book. Here, re-enactors fire on the enemy at Sharpsburg (Antietam), Maryland. (Courtesy Scott and Glinda Coleman.) *Bottom:* Re-enactors defend their fortifications at the Battle of Secessionville in South Carolina. (Courtesy Scott and Glinda Coleman.)

enough left to fill our haver sacks which [lasted] us [some] 2 or 3 days[.] next moning we [were] crowded into a boat & after 2 days & one nigh travel we landed at fort deleware[26] a [place] that I never shall forget[.] [We] were treated as dogs[,] half fed and[27] half-starved for water[.] [I] never did suffer for bred and water in my life as I did there[.]

[Our] money could by nothing ther without a big discount[.] [We] could get only 10cts for a dollar & hard to get that but for silver or gold we could get things as cheap as they [ever were.] [If] I could have had 40 or so dollars in gold or silver I could have made 7 or 8 hundred dollars[.] [I] could by a lofe of bred, & for 25 cts. eat what I wanted & sell the balance for 4 dollars. [If] I thought that I would ever be taken prisner again I would insist for [some] of your gold[,] for a prisner [fares badly] without money but i hope never to be taken again[.]

[Well] as I have said our [fare] was bad at fort delaweare but we are on [Confederate] soil once more where we can [fare] well[.] [We] are parrolled, 9800 that [were] there and sent to [the] Richmond fortifications[.] [Here] we will stay until we are exchanged[.] [Most] or more than 2 thirds of the men at fort delaware [were] sick men taken on the roads and Fredrick City[.] [I] have not herd from our regment [since] we left it and am anxious to here from it. [I] saw one man from the 48 wich is in the same brigade[.] [He] says that it was in the fight[.] [He] was taken in the [fight] & could not tell much about it[.]

[Write] soon and direct your leters in care of Capt. Cannon[28] in cheharge of the paroled solders. Camp Lee near Richmond, Va. [I] want to here from you all[. I] sent a copy in this leter to back yours by[.] J M Stitt

Letter Two

Camp near Weldon NC[29]
Friday February the 12th 1864

Dear sister I take the present opportunity of writing you a few lines to let you know we are all well[.] [Since] writing last we have had several [trips] one to newborn[30][.] [We] left our camp here on thirsday week[,] took the train for [Goldsboro,] lay over there until cars came Saturday morning early then took the train for kinston got there about daylight drew 4 days rashings[31] & started our march for newburn. [We] marched some 15 or 20 miles[,] struck camp by daylight[,] [were] on the road again[,] crossing the trent river[32] on pontoons & that night took up camp some 12 or 14 miles from newborn having marched [hole in page] 20 miles[.] [&] [about] 2 o'clock munday morning [we were] on the road again & soon after sunrise [were] in line of batle some 4 miles from newborn. [There] was 3 bregades that crosed the Trent with ours[:] barters & Kimpers Virginians[33] together with a strong force of calvary & artillery[.] Gen. Barter being the oldest brigadier was in command of the 3 bregades. [The] other forces [Corse's, Clingman's & Hoke's][34] bregades having gon down the dover road[35] the direct road from kinston to newborne[. They] captured between 400 & 500 prisners comisaris[36] clothing & so forth[.] [We] captured only 6 killing [three.] [Well] as I have said we were in line of battle until Tuesday about sunset had no fightes only between our pickets & the yankeys sharp shooters acros the river. [They] killed a leutenent in the 24[37] & wounded 2 pirvate when [were] ordered to kendle large fires along the line (which we [were] not allowed to have the two nights before) & then retreated back for kinston[.] [We] marched that night some 12 miles through mud & [hole in paper] from shoo mouth to wast deep[,] the wagons [and] artulery having tramped the bottoms out of the roads & night being dark as egypt. [We] struck camp about 2 & took up march about 7 in the morning [and] marched about 23 miles making 35 miles in 24 hours. [The next day we] reached kinston where we lay until Saturday. I suppose it was the largest army we ever had there[.] [It] was said to be 12 or 15,000 troops round kinston[,] 6 bregades though some of the old bregades did not look larger than our rigment[.] [There were] some 5 or 6 deserters taken with the yankeys prisners that [were] tried & shot[38][.] [Well] Saturday night we took the train for weldon & Sunday got safely into our quarters once more[.] [Weary] & worn we considered this one of the hardest trips of the war & [were] vary much rejarsed[39] at the idea of being snugley shet up in quarters in antisipation of a good rest with skined feet & swelld legs[.] [So] sunday night we went to bed early in order to get a good night sleep but about 2 oclock munday morning [we] had marching orders to cook our rashings & be ready to march by 6[.] [At six we] marched to the railroad but getting no transportation returned to camp & stayed till evening then took the train for petersburg[.] [The] yankey having made a raid down on blackwater at ivor station[40] but when we got to petersburg they had gon[e.] [We] got there about 11 oclock munday night & left about 9 Wednesday & came back here to our quarters[.] [The Twenty-fourth] & ours [were] the onleys ones that got to petersburg[.]

[Well] this is about all the nuse[41] which I suppose you have herd through the papers before this time[.] [Prices] in petersburg are still going up corn 18 dollar turkeys 12$ eggs 50 cts a piese bacon 5 & 6 dollars per pound. [There] is a prospect of our boys getting their furlows. [They] will probably come in this evening[.] Capt. Andry[42] has one on the way[.] [I] will send this by one of them so if you will excuse what I have ritten I will say no more[.] [Write] soon & tell Dovey[,] Nancy & Jeffey[43] to write[.] [I] am always glad to get letters from any of you[.] [If] you need any money you can get it of mine as i said before [by] selling something that will bring it[,] corn or hay[,] not more though than you kneed. [So] no more at present but remain your true friend & brother[,] J. M. Stitt[44]

Chapter 12

Thirteen Hundred Miles from Any Place

As 1862 ended, the South's fortunes looked bright—even to hospitalized South Carolinian William W. White. President Abraham Lincoln agonized over the inability of his generals—especially George McClellan—to mount sustained offensives against the Confederacy. Replacing the hesitant McClellan with the overly eager General Ambrose Burnside, Lincoln would soon be disappointed again, this time at the Battle of Fredericksburg. In this brief letter White wrote his cousin, Thomas, whom he addresses as "Plug Ugly."

Camp Wigfall,
Thirteen Hundred Miles from Any Place
December, the one, 1862 and awful cold

Good Morning "Plug Ugly,"

Your loving Epistle, in which you vented all your spleen, and heaped upon me all the base cognomens of which your mummy-head was master, reached me through the politeness of Mr. James Scott.[1] It should not have been answered at all, had it not been for the slurs which you attempted to cast upon my hitherto, spotless character for which I have determined that you suffer the power and elegance with which I wield my pen. Now, I had hoped and prayed that when I entered the army in defense of my country, that our operations would then be ended, never again to be revived. But it seems in that I am disappointed, for no sooner did you learn my whereabouts, than you favored me with one of your soul-stirring, love-reviving, _____-splitting productions. [It was] couched in such ambiguous language that any other a wise man like myself, would never have deciphered it. You commenced, by dealing out ridicule, as you thought of overwhelming power, which would in an instant crush its intended victim and thereby gain a complete rectory. I am proud to inform you that your weakly missiles fell far short of the mark, and now rebound with three-fold force and strike the assailant a stunning blow which I hope will have the desired effect of silencing your feeble battery. While on the other hand, the target at whom those chaffy words were intended, still stands unharmed and ready to meet a thousand such enemies. But you, Thomas, like all *long eared* animals would not stick to one side, but croped the fence and wound up your tirade, by a heart-rending and sympathetic appeal for us to reopen our correspondence. After considering all things, I am willing to do [so] provided you will promise me that will not let the people in the neighborhood of your school, know that I am acquainted with you. Do you promise? I know you will say yes.

Now, Cousin Thomas as we have made friends, we should cast aside all recollections of the past endeavor to live in place for the future. I will, therefore, bring my nonsense [to a close], and hasten on as my time is short. To give you a detailed account of my ups and downs since I left Georgia, would require more time than is alloted to me at present. I've had a hard time, though I have been in no fight and aren't hungry to be in one. Still, I have been exposed to a long and dreary winter of sleet and snow, and that too in plain view of the yanks. However, they were on one side of the Potomac[2] and we on the other, which was fortunate. Had it been otherwise, someone would have been hurt. Notwithstanding our hardships, I consider that we have done well [as] we have had plenty to eat during the whole time. As to general war news, I guess you hear more than I do, for I have not seen a newspaper in thirteen years. Therefore, I cannot tell you anything new. You need not blame me for not writing to you, for I have written inquiring of your notorious place of abode, but could hear nothing of you until about four weeks ago. I received a letter from Mrs. Collins[3] informing me that you [was] teaching school at Red Rock.[4] Another thing, there is a little, blue-eyed beauty in Georgia, who writes to me very week and it consumes nearly all of my spare moments to answer her sweet and interesting letters. I expect to see you again in about fifty years provided I should live that long, and then I will tell you enough lies to last you one season. What has become of Uncle[5] Burrell and Ira?[6] I wrote a letter to each of them yet I have never received a line in reply. Give my respects to the Kenefr's family,[7] to all inquiring friends, and my wool-dyed, double and twisted love to the girls' around Red Rock. Answer soon and direct to

General Hood's Brigade   William W. White
Care of Captain J. B. O'Neill   Fredericksburg
Camp A18th Regent G.U.   Virginia

Nothing more at present as the drums is beating for dress parade.

Your Devoted Cousin William

Chapter 13

Not Just a Man's War

This chapter focuses on southern women who witnessed the rupture of the Union. One woman, Ella Gertrude Clanton Thomas, lamented, "Our country is invaded—our homes are in danger—we are deprived or they are attempting to deprive us of that glorious liberty for which our fathers fought and bled and shall we tamely submit to this? Never!" A mother wrote her warrior son: "I have been very busy since you left preparing winter clothes for you all." Another woman compliments a Confederate unit's appearance but then adds, "It made me feel unpleasant to think how few of the many there would perhaps return...."

Ella Gertrude Clanton Thomas kept a journal most of her life and upon the outbreak of the war in 1861 she wrote these words:

Our country is invaded—our homes are in danger—we are deprived or they are attempting to deprive us of that glorious liberty for which our fathers fought and bled and shall we tamely submit to this? Never! My husband will go—my brother Jimmie will leave in the same Co. so will Jack (Mr. Thomas' younger brother) and I am proud to see them exhibit the noble, manly spirit which prompts them to go. It proves that southern blood has not degenerated in consequence of the life of luxury and ease we have been living. "He is thrice armed who hath his quarrel just" and surely ours is a just cause—We are only asking for self government and freedom to decide our own destiny.[1]

When it was time for Ella's husband to leave, she thought only of him:

...and when my Husband turned to me to say goodbye I could only cling to him (in) speechless agony—After kissing again and again the children and bidding the weeping servants farewell, he mounted his horse, in a perfect torrent of rain and rode off to the camp. I knew that I would see him again and when the procession came up the street an hour afterwards, the Hussars escorted by the fire brigade and numerous carriages filled with ladies, I nerved myself to stand by the window and wave my handkerchief to Mr. Thomas, but it would not do. The tears came thick and fast and I could see no more—My every thought was for my husband....[2]

Undoubtably Mr. Thomas' thoughts were with his wife and all the hardships she would face, but he also probably thought that men must be men, and fight for freedom and protect the weaker sex.

Ella Thomas writes:

Every letter to Richmond costs ten cents. A serious drawback it must be to many a poor soldier in hearing from his family. The 10 cts which pays for his letter perhaps deprives his children of bread. Yet what a luxury to hear from the loved ones at home![3]

Often letters were lost in the war zone even though they meant so much to the men. Letters were ruined because the men would literally wear out the words on the page from reading them so often. Sometimes the letters were drowned in the rain or burned for warmth. Everything was used to write on and not an inch was spared.

Women helped to support the war effort in every way they could, even if it meant giving up their earthly possessions. Ella Thomas wrote:

Some of our women are emulating the example of our Revolutionary mothers. We read of one lady giving her jewels valued at 1200 dollars, of another giving her diamonds worth 600 dollars, the latter of Columbus, Ga. The order is given for sand bags, uniforms and the busy fingers of our women are engaged in the task of love and in an incredibly short space of time, the order is filled.[4]

The money raised was not used for themselves and their children, but for the men. South Carolinian Kiah Sadler wrote to his family about raising money:

For regards to the ladies raising money for the clothing the soldiers tell them, "Go ahead," for the weather will soon begin to get cold, the nights are cold now. Tell them as soon as they raise the money and cloth to send on for our measures. As for the cloth, let it be coarse and warm, not costly.[5]

His mother, Mary Sadler, wrote back:

...I have been very busy since you left preparing winter clothes for you all (.) I went down to the weavers the other day to see my weeb (.) It is very pretty (.) I will get it home next week (.) I will make your pants and vest. Your coat will have to be made when you come home.[6]

Ella Thomas visited Empire House on Whitehall Street in Atlanta, Georgia. Sadly she wrote in her journal of her encounter with death:

The night before we visited there (Empire House) three men had died. The wife of one of them arrived the next afternoon but he had been buried before she reached there. She was a plain respectable looking woman, the mother of three children, the youngest of whom was six weeks old. She was giving way to no burst of sorrow. She could not indulge in the luxury of grief but I know what a desolate heart she must bear under the calm exterior and knowing the value of genuine sympathy I seated myself by her and told her how sorry I was for her—"That I too had a husband in the army." Her lips quivered and shaking her head she replied, "You'll lose him I reckon." A few moments after she wished to know "how long my old man had been in the Army?" I never thought the homely old expression could convey so much pathos.

Not all men died in hospitals where the women could conveniently find their bodies and know their tragic fate. In a memorial to Lena T. Copeland, the preacher remembers a time of utter strength and determination in this woman:

During the Civil War, she, a young woman, assumed the responsible offices of her bothers when they had answered their country's call to arms, arranging her widowed mother's affairs intelligently and profitably. There is one memorable incident we would record as well as many others already known that testifies to her readyness to cooper with any emergency, however trying. When her brother, Mr. B. Frank Hollingsworth fell pierced by a fatal ball at Savage Station, being buried with other comrades slain in the field of battle, she went to Virginia to where he had been buried on the field of honor, recovered his mangled body, wrapt only in his blanket, uncovered his face so that there would be no mistaken identity—with the aid of faithful comrades placed his cherished form in a coffin and brought him back home to rest with his kindred far from the scenes of strife in the quiet churchyard at old Sardis—where she is now reposing close by.[7]

Chapter 14

In the Midst of Life,
We Are in the Midst of War

Written by the Wilks brothers of Chester County, South Carolina, these letters graphically illustrate the range of feelings that Confederate soldiers must have felt as they prepared to engage the enemy. As the war drags on, the confidence and excitement of anticipation give way to loneliness and nostalgia for the life left back home.[1]

Camp Whatley
Culpeper County Va.
Dec. 4, 1862

Dear Alice,

Your letter of 8th Septem. (September) was received on yesterday. It was directed to Wihohester and we have never been to that place as yet. We were in Augusta County, near Staunton for awhile. We left Augusta on yesterday two weeks ago and came on to this place. We went down the Valley of Va (Virginia) through Rockingham County, and crossed the Blue Ridge Mountains at Swifts Gap into Green County, thence by Standardville, Madison C.H. and Orange C.H. to this county. We are camped near Rapidan River at present and about eight miles from the place where the Battle of Cedar Run Mountain[2] was fought. I liked the country about Staunton very well and was well pleased with the ladies. I formed the acquaintance of some very interesting ladies and found them highly accomplished and intelligent.

I was treated very well by the citizens. But we had to leave good old Augusta County, its many clever people and fair ladies to come to this point. Augusta County you will find on the map in the Valley of Virginia, the Valley of Va. lies between the Blue Ridge and the Alleghany Mountains. At Madison C.H. a fellow soldier and I took supper at a house where there were some nice ladies, and we enjoyed ourselves. We have had some quite weather and it is quite cold at present. We got back on yesterday from an expedition over toward the Potamac. We went out on Monday. I learned that there were about seven prisoners and about fifteen horses captured from the Yankees and two Yankees killed. Our party lost one horse killed, and I believe it was supposed have been killed by the Confederates. I learned that Ely Hardin is about here though I have not seen him yet. Some of his legion was with us on the Expedition we made.

You say that Miss Sarah's School was out. If Pa will not send you, it would be well for you to go to School. Do not neglect your books, for a highly cultivated mind constitutes a principal part of happiness. Do not think that dressing fine is everything. Of course every one should dress well, but that should not be made too great an object. I can not say how long we will remain here or where we will go should we leave here. Tell Louis and Kit that Eli and John are well and were with us on the expedition we made. Provisions are somewhat scarce about here. We draw flour, beef and salt for our rations, but we buy things when we can get them.— Tell Ma I would like to have another pair of socks (woolen) and a pair of glooves. Give my respects to all the family and friends generally. Write again and the news.

Your Affectionate Brother

W. Thomas Wilks

Camp Rapidan
Christmas Eve. Dec. 24th 1862

My Dear Sister

Your letter was rec'd days since, and I would have answered before but I've been kept so continuously moving that I could not with any satisfaction. Tomorrow is Christmas, a day which in the halcyon days of Boyhood, I hailed with the wildest demonstations of joy, those happy days of Christmas Which are past and gone an still remembered. The Rabbit hunts and various other innocent sports in which we were accustomed to revel and brought most vividly to my mine. In imagination I can picture the old red hills of Chester, where I've romped and played in happier days. We are far way for home engaged in battling for the independence of our country and when the loud thunder of war is hushed and our countrys flag triumphant, then our hearts will swell with pride, because we'll have the proud consciousness that we are numbered with the Champions of liberty. A great and most bloody battle has been fought at Fredricksburg[3], resulting in a glorious victory for our army. We did not loos as many men as our enemies, but sufficient to cast gloom and grief around many happy friends.

We were near an heard the sound of the cannon distinctly, but it was not our lot to be engaged as we had other important points to guard. We have a noble and a gallant Band of Veterans to command. We give the Yankeys little rest. At the hour midnight when they think we are far way, Marion[4] like, with a yell, sufficient to awake the demons of perdition, we are charging these camp with flashing swords, and woe to the Yankey who offers resistance. But, no brave soldiers will strike an enemy when he surrenders. At our picket post I often talk to the Yankeys and they have so far behaved like gentleman and soldiers. One soldier will sympathese with another even if he be an enemy.

We all have very hard trying times but I feel as enthusiatic now as the day war commenced. This time we are all tired of the war, but I'm willing to know it to be the universal sentement of the Army to fight. Aye, to the last volly and man, to the last ditch and mountain. Our land has ben comsomed with blood, battles have been fought which have been comsomed with the blood, battles have been fought which have startled the world, but the war still rages with unparallaled fury. They will never conquer us. Tell Frank and Levi I wish them a good rabbit hunt tomorrow. Tell the rest Pa an Ma and all our relations and friends I wish them merry Christmas(.) Yes I do wish them all much pleasure(.) Tell them I'm much more happy than might be expected. Yes no here harnessed and equipped in my countrys cause. I'm happy, proud that I am a Confederate soldier who wouldn't be a soldier. I glory in (the) title of an humble Private, in my heart is the cause. When the day of battle comes I do not quake and trimble like a poltron,[5] but am proud to follow the headlong brave, to victory or death that is death parting breath, and where else would a Southern Soldier wish to die than on the proud encrimsoned field of glory. Our Brigade has become a terror to the Yankeys, Genl. Hampton[6] a perfect General always leads the charge, and whoes a soared where is not.—He is a native S. Carolinian, and is worshipped by his men, noble magnanimous and fearlelssly brave. Give all my love. Tell them I would like to shake their hands tomorrow. Tell Lou I go on picket tomorrow. Soon, write again. And I'll try and write you better letter.

Yours

E.C. Wilkes

Amherst Co. Va.
April 9, 1863

Dear Alice,

Perhaps you may have looked for an answer to you letter ere this, as your letter was written sometime ago. I received your letter nearly a week ago—on my return from Bookbridge County. John W is still in Rockbridge at least he was there when I left last Thursday. I am tolerably well. Eli is well also. We are having weather along now though the nights are cold and frosty. This is a tolerably good country here, though I do not like it as well as the other side of the Blue Ridge Mountains. There are some clever peoples about here and some tolerably good looking ladies. Before we came here(,) there had been no Regiments in this section hence soldiers are something new, of course they have been accustomed to soldiers who went from this section.

I hear that we are to move from here soon in the direction of Prince Edward or Halifax county, but I cannot say for sure where we will go, for all I know we may go back to the Valley. We are not getting a great deal of horse feed now, but we are getting our own rations of meat & flour that the law allows, but I eat a good many of my meals in the country. I have formed some acquaintances. I have become acquainted with several ladies named Waller. They are some what quality people, though intelligent & clever.

Tell Ma that I got the clothes and they fit very well except around the waist is rather tight when buttoned. It is a good suit, however. Give my respects to all the family. If you see Rody give her my respects & ask her why she does not write. I have received a line from her that I remember since I came to Va. Write soon & invariably direct to Richmond.—

Your aff-brother

W. Thomas Wilks

Culpeper Co. Va.
Jan. 19, 1863

Dear Alice,

Again I will try to write you a letter. I received your letter some time ago and was glad to get it. I am in tolerably good health at present and may this letter find you enjoying the same blessing. The health of our Regiment is tolerably good at present though there is still some sickeness among the men. Our camp has been moved twice of late and now we are only about five miles from our old camp near the Rapidan. The weather is quite cold at present and for all I know it may remain so for a while. We have been remarkly blessed with good weather. I hope the cold weather may be soon over and that we shall soon hear the singing of the birds and see the green buds putting forth. Spring will come at the appointed time and will be hailed with pleasure. It is now the middle of winter: there is no snow on the ground, but the weather.

I hear talk of peace occasionally, but I don't know whine we will have peace. I am sure that peace will be hailed with the greatest joy. May it come soon(.) I do not know whether we will remain in this section long or not for I do not know what move will be made. Eli and John are well. George too, I believe is well. I can not say when I will get to come home. I hope the war may be soon over and that we may be permitted to return home. We are damped at present about seven or eight miles from Culpeper C.H., But I have not been to the C.H. as yet. I go out into the country and am treated very kind by the people.

I like Virginia and think a great deal of the people. The country has suffered a great deal on account of war. The Yankies were all through this part of the state and committed a great many depredations. In fact the country is well nigh *eat out*. I have heard of some deaths in Chester District and some weddings. Truely in the midst of life we are in the midst of death. Hence we should at all times ready to meet its awful summons. Be careful that you are not too fascinated with the worldliest gaiety and false glory. But place your most ernest affections upon the things that are incorruptable and that faididst not away. This world is only worthy of a limited amount of our affections.—Cultivate the mind and be sure that you read the Bible.—Tell Rody if you see her to write to me. Tell little Alice howdy, and Emma too. Give my love to all the family and write soon. I do not get a great many letters. My hands are getting cold (for the weather is cold) and I will close.—Your Affectionate Brother,

W. Thos. Wilk

Chapter 15

The Ground Where I Lay

Even though warfare is chaotic by its very nature, there are moments when a participant can pause and reflect upon his thoughts and record them on paper. Perhaps playing a role in the brutal drama of combat can be sorted through by a careful compilation of a journal or diary. Thomas Belue, a Confederate soldier from Union, South Carolina, used a sixty page journal which he carried with him throughout his service to document his experiences in the Civil War. In a small fragile diary measuring four and three quarters inches by three inches, Belue preserved for us his memories of what Historian Shelby Foote has called a war "as big as life."[1]

(Note: The original document contained a peculiar feature: Every mention of a number was enclosed in brackets. For example, the second sentence read, "Wednesday the [fifteenth] left Richmond for Stanton." To improve readability and prevent confusion regarding the use of brackets, we have eliminated those brackets here.)

July 14, 1863, left Howards Grove Hospital[2] [and] came to soldiers home in Richmond [Virginia]. Wednesday the fifteenth left Richmond for Stanton.[3] Arrived at Stanton at eleven o'clock p.m. [and] spent the remainder of the night in the car. Passed through town Thursday the sixteenth to Camp Ewell,[4] two miles from Stanton on the Winchester pike road. Spent Friday the seventeenth in preparing to march to Winchester.[5] Saturday the eighteenth left Camp Ewell to go to Winchester under the command of Major H. H. Smith[6] and [Captain] W. Willis.[7] Marched eleven miles and camped. Marched Sunday the nineteenth to Harrison-burg[8] twenty five miles from Stanton. [D]rew rations for two days and camped. Monday the twentieth marched twelve miles and camped on a farm. Tuesday the twenty first marched to Mt. Jackson[9] fifty miles from Stanton forty-two from Winchester. [D]rew three days rations and spent the night. Wednesday the twenty-second marched eight miles and was turned back. This point being one mile below Edenburg.[10] [M]arched to Mount Jackson and camped on the same ground of the [preceding] night. Thursday the twenty-third came seven miles to New Market,[11] at thru place at squad of [convalescents] turned to the left

Thomas Belue, a Confederate soldier from Union, S.C., compiled a sixty page journal during the war. (Courtesy Winthrop Archives.)

across the [Shenandoah] Mountains[12] to Spereville[13][?], myself not being well was sent by [Captain] Willis to report to a hospital on the road to Stanton. [C]ame [four] miles above New Market toward Harrisonburg[,] spent the night with Mr. March[14] who treated [very] kindly without charge. Friday the twenty-fourth left Mr. March to go to Harrisonburg to report to the hospital it being [eighteen] miles from New Market[.] [T]aken dinner at a gentleman's house I did not learn, also without charge. [C]ame to Harrisonburg a little before sunset[,] reported to the General Hospital[.] [H]ad fever a severe cough and pain in the head. [A]t the time was received into the first ward [and] fever continued [untill] about the [middle] of the day [Saturday] the twenty-fifth at which time I began to feel better, the [cough] continues but with less pain. Sunday the twenty-seventh was nightmare. Tuesday the twenty-eighth was not so well. Wednesday the twenty-ninth better again able to be up and about. Thursday and Friday the thirtieth and thirty-first [enjoyed] tolerable good health. Harrisonburg has good many nice buildings [and] is the county site of Rockingham county.[15] [H]as mountains on the east and west. Peak mt. on the east Shenandoah and others on the west close by. Saturday the first of August, 1863 applied for a discharge from the Hospital got it, and transportation to Stanton by stage[.] [S]pent the night under a _____ at a camp close by Stanton. [R]emained there [untill] Monday the third of August got transportation to and taken the cars came to Gordonsville[16] and from there to the [Rapidan][17] Station [learned] that the Regt. would cross the [Rapidan] River at the Summerville ford[18] that evening seven miles below [Rapidan] section. [W]ent two or three miles and spent the night under another tree. [S]tarted early Tuesday the fourth taken a snack of [breakfast] for $1.00. [A]rrived at the regt. at ten or eleven o'clock near [Summerville] ford. [I]n camp regt. went on [picket] at [Summerville] ford in the evening. Received order early [Wednesday] the fifth to be ready to march. Marched at ten or [eleven] o'clock down the road toward Frederickburg[19] some eight or ten miles and camped[,] this place being some ten or twelve miles from the [battlefield] of [Chancellorsville].[20] Remained in this camp without anything of note the sixth and seventh. On the eighth moved [and] camped some half mile. The weather is very warm. The ninth had had co. drills in the morning and Battalion drills in the evening, such the time passed for some days. Sixteenth regt. went on picket at Noah Church[21] on the Fredericksburg road to [guard] against a [calvary] raid[,] two co. being on post at a time the remainder of the regt. being in readiness. [W]e remained here [untill] the evening of the eighteenth being relieved by the 2nd S.C. Regt. we returned to camp. The twenty-first the day [appointed] by the President for humiliation, posting and prayer. The day I think was generally [kept]. [H]ard [excellent] preaching and fervent prayers by different chaplains of different Regt. [Received] orders in the evening to be ready to move the next morning at seven o'clock. Twenty-second marched at the time named[,] moved southwest in the direction of Hanover Junction.[22] [Marched] twelve miles halted in a pine old field at twelve o'clock p.m. at which place we remained [untill] next morning. The twenty-third marched at the dawn of day came seven miles and camped on the neighborhood of [G]ood [H]ope [C]hurch[23] twelve miles from Fredericks Hall[24] depot which is on the Central Railroad.[25] This is rumored to be a [permanent] camp for a while if the enemy makes no advance. [B]eing properly camped co. Regt. and Brigade drilles commences. [A]lso co. inspection everyday and Brigade inspection occasionally. [S]o passed the remainder of the month. Sept. the first and I assisted Lieut. Stern[26] to make out the co. [payroll]. Sept. the third [Battalion] drill at nine o'clock a.m. Brigade drill at four p.m. All is usual up to the seventh when we got orders to cook three days rations and be ready to march at four o'clock the next morning. The eighth marched at the time ordered some fifteen miles to Beaverdam Station[27] or the Central Railroad. [M]arched some five miles down the road and camped. Marched at seven o'clock next morning the ninth eighteen miles down to Hanover Junction were we arrived about twelve o'clock. [W]as to take the train to Richmond at six o'clock but [did not] get off. [M]arched on two miles and camped to take the train next morning. All was [suspicious] to know where we were going but none was able to learn that fact. The tenth marched back to the junction. [L]eft on the train for about ten o'clock arrived at Richmond about one o'clock[,] distance twenty-eight miles. [M]oved over near the Petersburg[28] depot and remained there [untill] ten o'clock at night, was ordered on the train and arrived at Petersburg at two o'clock a.m. distance twenty-two miles. Marched to Weldon[29] depot halted on the pavement where we spent the remainder of the night on the hard brick[,] the most of us without anything else under us using our baggage for pillows. [F]or [myself] I had an unbroken nap from three [untill] day-light all ignorant as to any certain point that we are going. [S]ome think to Charleston other to [Chattanooga] Tenn. Sept. the eleventh taken the train about eight o'clock a.m. for Weldon[30] N.C. [,] reached Weldon about three o' clock p.m. [L]eft this place at five o'clock p.m. for Wilmington, N.C.,[31] reached this place after the nights travel at nine o'clock a.m.[,] distance of 162 miles. [S]pent the remainder of the day the twelfth and night in cabins built for soldiers winter-quarters. The thirteenth marched out to the [wharf] and crossed the River Cape Fear[32] on a steam boat. [G]ot on the train at eleven o'clock leading to Manchester[?]S.C.[33] reached Florence[34] about ten o'clock a.m. the fourteenth distance 107 miles. [T]aken the N.E. [Railroad] at this place for Charleston at twelve o'clock[,] arrived at Charleston at twelve o'clock at night [,] got off the train marched into Chapel Street and spent the remainder of the night taking (distance from Flor. to Chars. 193 miles) a nap on the pavement. [M]oved at five o'clock a.m. the fifteenth across the Ashley River[35] to the [Savannah] depot. [D]rew three days rations of bacon and crackers which was a very welcome draw our rations having giveout 24 hours previous. Left [Savannah] depot at Charleston for Savannah about one o'clock p.m. [R]eached Savannah Ga. at nine p.m. distance 102 miles. [L]eft Savannah at ten p.m. for Macon Ga.,[36] reached this place at three o'clock p.m. on the sixteenth distance 190 miles. Leaving Macon about five p.m. on the N.W. road[,] arrived at Atlanta about two o'clock a.m. the seventeenth[,] remained in the cars [untill] day. Change cars at this place for the first [since] leaving Charleston[,] distance from Macon to Atlanta 102 miles. Left Atlanta at seven o'clock p.m. on the Atlanta and Western road leading to [Chattanooga] Tennessee. Reached Dalton Ga.[37] about four o'clock distance 100 miles. [G]ot off the cars and camped in a piece of woods close by. [D]rew and cooked a days rations and slept a good nights sleep as we travel the entire way [crowded] in and on top of freight boxes and platform cars thereby our chances was bad to sleep. [W]e learn hear that the enemy is falling back to [Chattanooga] which is 38 miles from this place. Sept. the eighteenth got order about seven o'clock a.m. to get ready to [move]. [Moved] forthwith back to the depot[,] got on the train expecting to start every [minute] but [did not] start about about sundown. [W]ent twelve miles and got off the cars and camped close by. The Yankee [picket] being at this place one week ago. Got order directly after camping to be ready to move at daylight. [T]he nineteenth marched at seven o'clock on towards Ringgold Station.[38] Passed Ringgold about one mile and camped in area of battle. [A]bout the middle of the day heard cannon in the morning [occasionally] on before us towards Chattanooga. [I]n the evening the firing increased as if a general [engagement] had taken place, it seemingly is six or eight miles ahead of us, we think it the beginning of a big battle. [D]rew three days rations and was preparing to cook when the drum beat to fall in[,] left a detail to cook rations[,] it was now about dark. [M]arch back to Ringgold and took a sort of country road in the direction of the cannonardering. [M]arched about ten miles and camped just across the [Chickamauga][39] Creek, where we reached some time after midnight. [R]emained here [untill] and hour or two by sun of the morning the twentieth. [W]as ordered to move forward, marched a mile or two and halted in a peace of woods being by the [picket] firing and [occasionally] cannon. [A]bout ten o'clock the battle was farly cemmence, after an hour or so we was ordered up, in a short time we was under the fire and became ingaged. We continued to advance and kept up a regular at the enemy giving way, we [persuing] crossing several lines of breastworks, drove them back a mile or more to a hill where the enemy had a strong position. [F]ighting a while I received a wound through the hip[,] in a few minutes another on top of the head[,] our line soon fell back. [Being unable to get back I was left under the fire of the enemy where I remained [untill] about midnight. [D]uring the evening two other Brigades came up just on the ground where I lay and ingaged the enemy most desperately[,] my only shelter being a small tree. At night our men began to pass about me getting off the wounded and told me the enemy had left the hill and gone. [B]ut all of the men was after their own Brigade and Regt. and I could get none of them to take me back. Late in the night one of our Brigade came by me of the 8th S.C. Regt. I called him to me and asked him to have me taken away from there. He said that my co. was close by and he would let them know where I was. In a few [minutes] one of our litterbearers came to me and he too went to let the co. know. In a short time Sergt. G. S. Spears.[40] Sergt. B. F. Jones[41] and Lt. Goudelock[42] and I think one other of our co., but [can not] now [recollect][,] came to me with a litter and taken me back to the co. and lay me down on the litter by the fire[,] to hear lay [untill] next morning. Lieut. Stern and Sergt. Jones made [inquiring] of the couler bearer and if I had been taken back, he told them that I had. I was a couler gard was the cause of my not being looked after by the co. Early on the morning of the twenty-first I was taken by the litter bearer back about a mile where there was a field hospital and layed down on my blanket where I lay [untill] a while before sundown without any attention, and by hard beggin I got them to put me in a big waggon and was taken some two or three miles futher back to another hospital[,] reaching this place after dark, here a Dr. dress my wounds for the first. They had got and taken a peace of bone from my head. This hospital was principally Alabamian[?][43] I tried to get them to take me to Kershaw's Brigades Hospital but could not. I had no person to wait on me only those that would do so voluntarily, which a Mr. Randatt[44] a Alabamian that was detailed to wait on the wounded of his co., give me what attention he could which was but little as everyone seemed to have that he could do. I remained here the twenty-second, the twenty-third and part of the twenty-fourth laying in the hot sun part of the time only as I could get them to hang my blanket over me to shade me. The twenty-fourth I was then back a mile to another hospital in the woods, on a little straw where my wound was dressed on the morning of the twenty-fifth, the second time. Hear I lay on a rocky hillside with but little attention in my way. Fortunately the weather was dry and favorable except nights we suffered some with cold as we had no one to make a fire for us and the dews was tolerable heavy, about this time. The glands of my neck became swollen and painful. I remained at this place [untill] the evening of the twenty-ninth when I was put in a road waggon and halled over a very rough road to Ringgold a distance of eight or ten mile. [L]ay on the platform at the depot [untill] three o'clock a.m. The thrtieeth when I was put in a box-car and came to Atlanta a little before sundown, a while after dark we left Atlanta for LaGrange, Ga.[45] distance of 70 miles and was received in the Oliver Hospital Ward E.[46] This place is well attended in every respect. The ladies visit it regular and bring a variety of nice eatables for the wounded and sick[?][47] [greatest] respect and sympathy for the inmates. We reached this about two o'clock a.m. the first of [October]. The sixth had a furlough recommended, got it the seventh and started home at one o'clock p.m.[,] reached Atlanta about an hour by sun[,] left Atlanta at dark for Augusta,[48] 171 miles distant. [R]eached Augusta and daylight a.m. the eighth. [G]ot on the S.C. train and reached Columbia, S.C. at night. Spent the night at the way side hospital distance 143 miles. Left Columbia for home. [E]leven o'clock a.m. [G]ot to fathers about two o'clock p.m. the tenth. My wife. Brother and sister reached father the ninth from search of me at the hospital at LaGrange, Ga. which I had left. My wounds seemed doing very well when I got home, but got worse which [kept] me pretty much confined for two or three weeks, after which I mended very fast. Thus I enjoyed the comforts of home.

Chapter 16

There Is a Place We May Meet

By the spring of 1864, the coldness of war is evident in J. C. Faucette's letter to his friend, Kiah Sadler. Faucette reports on a small skirmish: "Did not do much after all: killed a few negroes and captured one piece of artillery and horses." Even at this late stage of the conflict, after three years of combat, "all our soldiers are in the highest spirits." Contrast that optimism with Faucette's observation. "Our lives I hope dear Kiah will be spared." Similarly, another of York County's sons, Joseph Alexander Thomas, dreams of his 300-acre farm. He confides, "I do long to see you all, but in all probability that never will be in this world, but if not, there is a place we may meet to part no more." And the war continued to separate these men from their loved ones for another year.

Weldon, N.C. 5th April 1864

Dear Kiah,

Your last favor came duly to hand.[1] I have deferred answering a long time. The fact is, I have not had a good opportunity of writing letters til very recently! Since I last wrote you I have been on a visit home.[2] My brothers were furloughed at the same time.[3] I made application on this ground and was successful. I need not say I enjoyed my leave of absence. My older brother had been in General Lee's army from the beginning of the war. The younger with the 31st at Charleston and other places.[4] I left

145

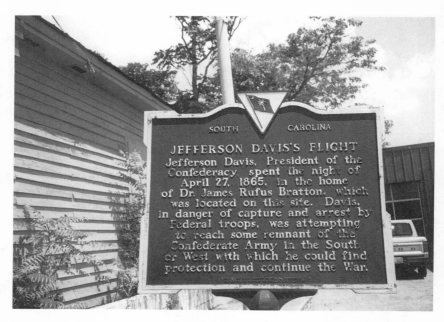

SOUTH   CAROLINA

JEFFERSON DAVIS'S FLIGHT
Jefferson Davis, President of the
Confederacy, spent the night of
April 27, 1865, in the home
of Dr. James Rufus Bratton, which
was located on this site. Davis,
in danger of capture and arrest by
Federal troops, was attempting
to reach some remnant of the
Confederate Army in the South
or West with which he could find
protection and continue the War.

Fleeing Union troops, President Jefferson Davis spent a night in Yorkville, S.C., as the curtain went down on the Lost Cause. (Courtesy Scott Hollis.)

home Feb. 29th and arrived at camp the next day. The troop I left at Weldon[5] had gone on the Suffolk trip as they call it.[6] I set out to join my command—found the brigade away down in the Chowan Country.[7] We remained there a number of days getting bacon, forage, etc. We then came up to Franklin Va.,[8] the present terminus of the Seaboard R R Road. Thence we tacked and went thundering down on Suffolk to the great astonishment of the men; Yanks and citizens.[9] Did not do much after all: killed a few negroes and captured one piece of artillery and horses. This was March the 9th. The 31st we were quietly resting in our quarters at this place.[10] On one day I marched thirty odd miles. The whole brigade with wagon train and all the artillery marched on the 7th twenty eight miles by noon, to decieve the enemy. Too hard entirely. Since our return I have been unusually busy filling out the regiment with arms and accontrements and fixing my papers for making out quarterly returns. I am about at leisure once more.

Capt. Chambers has been unwell and unusually busy since our return.[11] I gave him your little note: he had not written you when I last saw him. The weather has been very inclement of late: so much rain will produce a lull in military operations.[12] But it is the universal belief a "hot time" awaits us. All our soldiers are in the highest spirits.[13] May our arms be crowned with complete success. Now is the time for all Christians to call upon the Lord God of hosts "for help and deliverence." I trust that great good will result from our churches and people fasting and praying. Oh! Do you not look forward with ecstacies to the happy time when our heavenly Father will say "It is enough; stay thy hands"; When peace and liberty are ours; when we will be permitted to meet all together once again, no more to [part], from the friends we love so dear. Our lives I hope dear Kiah, will be spared. Let us continue to trust our blessed Redeemer. I am often reminded of the times we once had in our social prayer meetings. I miss them very much. Charlie[14] and myself however, try to benefit each other—often go to the woods to converse with one another and with our God. By the way he and Elins[15] are on furlough. Joel and Clark send their good wishes.[16] I must stop—too dark to proceed. Will add a P. S. in the morning. Good night.

J. C. Faucette

P. S. Wednesday morning of 6th April 1864

Our regiment numbers at present 932. Yesterday 925 expressed for Gov. Vance to come and address us.[17] I think he will certainly be reelected.[18] Capt. Durham, the present 2 blasts of the 49th is raising a battalion out of the brigade: he is to be Major.[19] It is to be a sharp shooter corps.[20] I think of joining it.[21] Joel and Clark will get into it, I think.[22] I do not want a commission, will accept a position on the "non-command staff."[23]

I continue to correspond with my lady friend: almost ready to fall in love occasionly. How is it with you. If you are spared till the termination of the war, do you expect, like most all the young men, to get married right off.[24] Let me hear from you soon. Excuse all the imperfections.

I am truly your friend,

J. C. Faucette

26 April 1864, James Island,
Legares Point, near Charleston, S.C.

Dear Sister and Family All: I seat myself to drop you all a few lines to let you no I am well, still hoping these lines through the kind blessings of God may reach you and find you all well. I have wrote to you but have not received an answer as yet. I got a letter from home last week. They were all well and spoke of Jane Pursley[25] getting a letter from some of you and that you were looking for Samuel[26] home sick. I hope he is home before this time for camps is the last place to be sick. I have no news of interest at this time only that there is a great stir among the troops at this time preparing for the great struggle before Richmond.[27] The eighteenth regiment is in the City now, has returned from Florida. I have not seen any of them yet. I have been looking for Warren Pursley[28] to come over and see us but none has come yet. We are kept very close at this time, no papers, nor furlows granted here and we are expecting to go to the West or Virginia soon, but let come what may I will try to be satisfied. We are fareing very badly here as to provisions and shoose and close. 'Tis a shame to the Confederacy. I am looking for a box from home this week. I have not eat one bite of Confederate bread since I came here. We get grits or rice but not half enough of that, a little meat about one fourth of a pound per day for three or four days and then one or two days none, but it makes you laugh to hear the wild expressions of the hardy soldiers about meal time and the time to go on picket which is every other night, and fatigue every other day or two. Working on the batterys men do not feel like work on such diet as we get, but if we do get to stay here a month longer, we will fare well as the Island is covered with blackberries. Dear Sister and neaces and family, I do long to see you all, but in all probability that never will be in this world, but if not, there is a place we may meet to part no more. If we are prepared for that place happy are we. You all have seen trouble in this life which is even severe, but nothing to the gnawings of conscience in the world of Eternal Despair. O, may it be our happy lot to shun the road of vice and folly and be prepared to enjoy a home in the heaven where Saints immortal dwell! O, let the love of God inspire each of our hearts to do his will! Tell the boys I have long looked for a letter from them, and you may think I am scare of paper which is so, I am afraid you can hardly read this, but I will try to have a letter supply next time. Everything is very, very dear here, and those in the city are actually suffering at this time. 'Tis hard to think of children crying for bread, and it can't be got for them. The new issue[29] has not made the matter much better if any here, but wickedness is increasing daily. Sin abounds to the lowest degree. May virtue arise once again in our land that those fiends may hide themselves! Write to me all the news of the crops, as this is said to be a time of bad appearance, and how you all are manageing to make a living as it has come to be the lot of poor women to be the farmers, but they can serve God and their Country as well at that as anything else. So farewell to all. Live for God and Heaven. Joseph A. Thomas to Narcissus Bryant and Family All.

Chapter 17

The Lost Cause's Last Rites

Present with General Robert E. Lee in Virginia at the war's conclusion was the Reverend James Spratt White, member of a prominent upper South Carolina family. By March 1865, White had heard about Columbia's fate. He writes his sister that "I am glad that Sherman's army did not pass through York District." There was not much to rejoice about, however, after four tragic years of war. The Confederacy was in its death throes and the Presbyterian minister-soldier vented his anger at the deterioration in discipline among southern troops. White alleges that "Wheeler's Calvary" is terrorizing the war-weary civilian population. He laments, "We were not prepared for this promiscuous plundering of our homes at the hands of *Confederate soldiers.*" Thus, the pastor prepares for the South's last rites.

Our final passages come from the diary of Captain Julius Mills, a member of F Company, 23rd South Carolina Volunteers. Mills hailed from the same county as the long dead Captain Obadiah Hardin and Mills, a prisoner of war, senses the pending death of the Confederacy.

I got the money ($100) enclosed in your last letter. It will be very useful. Your letter of the 27th inst., has also reached me.

Camp _____ Richmond
March 8th, 1865

My Dear Sister,

I have had the pleasure this morning of reading three letters from my friends down South—one from yourself[1] of the 3rd inst., another from Aunt Mary[2] of the same date, and the third from Ada[3] at Statesville, written on the 2nd inst. This was an unusual entertainment, and one which I would rejoice to have imparted more frequently. Write as often as you can, for we know not how soon our communications will be again intercepted by the enemy.

The attention of our soldiers in the army is not turned so much to the cruel treatment visited upon our people by Sherman's forces (this was expected), as to the strange and unanticipated conduct of "Wheeler's Calvary" which may be very properly be _____ "the Robber's Ban." We were not prepared for this promiscuous plundering of our homes at the hands of *Confederate soldiers*. We would not say a single word against their action if it was authorized by our government for its safety and protection. If these persons—whoever they may be—were doing all in their power to whip and defeat Sherman, our soldiers would bear the afflictions cheerfully and without a murmur, but as there is every reason to believe that they are not earnestly and energetically engaged in the service of our common country, we most decidedly enter our protest against their unwarranted and barbarous operations. If I mistake not the character of our soldiers here this "Wheeler's Calvary" will oft, if possible, meet with the punishment it so richly deserves. I can not think they belong to Wheeler's forces, and if not, they bring eternal disgrace upon the good soldiers of his command.

Of course, I am glad to hear that Sherman's army, did not pass through York District.[4] We can not be too humble and thankful for this merciful deliverance from the hand of our enemies. We _____ the chastisement as much as those upon whom the blow fell. Let it make us the more willing to assist them who have suffered such heavy losses. Our property is saved, theirs is destroyed, and we are no better than they.

Our army is still quiet—the enemy making no important movements. It is raining today, the wet weather will render the roads almost impassable for a long time, and of course, military operations must be suspended. I sincerely hope and pray that Sherman will be driven back. If this be done, Grant will not be able [to] accomplish anything towards the capture of Richmond. Our army is strongly fortified, and it will be a difficult matter

As the conflict ended, African Americans were among the Union soldiers who occupied Yorkville, S.C. (Courtesy Historical Center of York County.)

to drive us back from our line of entrenchments. Our soldiers are in good spirits and ready to meet them.

Tell Hutch,[5] if "Wheeler's Calvary"[6] attempt to take our homes or anything else without proper authority, to defend it to the last. If you have an opportunity please send me one of those army jackets—I will need it this summer. Tell Aunt Mary I will answer her letter in a few days. I am glad to hear that our people are loyal to the south. It encourages our soldiers at the front. When you write me always mention the families in our neighborhood which are represented in our company. I have written several letters this month—hope you will receive them all. Did you burn the letters at home directed to me? You acted prudently in destroying those I have written from the army. It makes my heart sad to think of the destructive fire in Columbia.

Capt. Alston and Janice Spratt are both well.—

Gen. Lee has issued an order requiring strict observance of Sunday the 10th inst. as a day of fasting, humiliation and prayer.[7]

Remember me kindly to all friends.

Your affectionate Brother,

J. S. White

The following are excerpts from Captain Julius Mills'
diary.

April, Saturday, 1st, 1865. Five Forks. A beautiful April fool. Captured with the greater portion of Pickets command in front of Sheridan
this evening. A *terrible* blunder. Col. Culp, Capts. White, Evans, Cooper,
Swinton, Woodruff, Lts. Wise (of my Co.) Neal, Weals, Huggins, and
many others of our Brig. with us. I was taken to the rear and remained
over till morning. Nothing to eat—was alone—miserable feelings. Very
wet and cold.

Monday, 3rd. We arrived at City Point this afternoon and were
rationed for the first time. It could not be had elsewhere for so great a
number. I made the acquaintance of Capt. Lattimer of the 11th Regulars
who treated me kindly and to whom I am greatly obliged. Indeed he was
most timely in his offerings. He is a South Carolinian-Edgefield—lived
near Beach Island.

April, Sunday, 9th, 1865. We were called out this morning to be sent
elsewhere to Johnson's Island we hear. We took a beautiful car. We passed
through Baltimore at about 4 o'clock. The streets were crowded. Many a
smile of sympathy for us greeted us from the ladies. Oh, Maryland, Maryland! How you suffer. The Guard was doubled, and everyone seen offering
sympathy was arrested. Ladies as well as men were arrested (four or five
ladies).

Saturday, 15th. President Lincoln and Secretary of State Seward of
the United States were assassinated last night! Yes, in this the nineteenth
century has been committed a tragedy of history. How will it effect the
country is the question! The deed was committed last night in Washington by Wilkes Booth. All are anxious for the news of its further develop-
ment. Col. Hill announced the above and asked no demonstration on our
part. Of course we would not, when a dozen pieces of Artillery bears upon
us! I spend the time with Lelia now—8 o'clock. [Lelia is a girl who is mentioned throughout the portion of the diary belonging to the Stringfellows.]

Wednesday, 19th. Nothing new today. Reflection comes up. I read.
The mind's eye can nowhere find anything more dazzling, no more dark
than *in man*; it can fix itself upon nothing which is more awful, more
complex, more mysterious or more infinite. There is one spectacle grander
than the sea, that is the sky—there is one spectacle grander than the sky,

that is the interior of the *Soul*. Penetrate it when he reflects, look at what is behind, look at that obscurity. There are combats of giants as in Homer.

Wednesday, 26th. The day was calm and warm. Nothing new. The "Amnesty Oath" is still exciting many of our officers. For decency sake we ought to wait the action of Genl. Joe Johnson with his army. What right have we to act before our Gov. is defunct? None! I am surprised that any officers of rank are offering to take it—Col. Hennington died yesterday, was sick but a few days. He was of the 8th South Carolina. The honor paid a deceased President was paid Lincoln today.

Saturday, 29th. News of Genl. Johnson's surrender. How humiliating! The crises is upon us. What is our duty? I am much perplexed. The idea of the Oath of the Allegiance to the U. S. is horrible. But it is before us. The cause of the South is lost. We must sustain ourselves. We must watch our feelings—be men. Refer to Shakespeare's Troilus and Crisida 1-3 "In the reproof of chance lies the true proof of men" etc. It is 8 o'clock. A party at chess—another at cribbage and all reading. I turned to Lelia. No remedy for a mind diseased.

May, Monday, 1, 1865. Things taking there natural courses. Many, many are applying for the Amnesty. I applied today. The day has been cool. The question of the Amnesty appears thus: Our Gov't is a failure. It is defeated. Our country is overrun. We have no army. The oath will have to be taken by all citizens. Then why remain in prison for some months when the ultimatum is the same. Thus I concluded.

Thursday, 4th. No news, $100,000 reward offered for Prest. Davis. The questions of banishment and seclusion from society discussed. We owe a duty to our comrades in the army which the states must discharge to them. We must not seclude. Our hearts learn to love, and entertain mercy and charity towards his species *individually*, grows patient and tolerant at the weakness of others when he feels his own. I desire to be more useful to the poor, to labor for them. If permitted I will and shall labor for the good. Divine service tonight by Mr. Gerideau.[8]

July 1, 1865. Millwood—Saturday finds me at home. I came hone at once. Spent the first night in the dearest spot to me now.

Here I shall stay. Oh, God, make me to know my obligations to thee, and fill me with gratitude. They will be Done. So endeth my War Diary.[9]

Conclusion

In the spring of 1865, the Richmond *Whig* announced on its front page the demise of the Confederacy. The obituary revealed that the "child" was aged four years and had died at the home of its "parents," President Jefferson Davis and his wife, Varina. The newspaper, searching deep into the scarred soul of the South for humor and insight, reported that the "child's" cause of death was suffocation. There would be no funeral.[1]

Why, then, did southerners fight a cause which ultimately would result in the ruins of Columbia and the deaths of courageous soldiers such as Chester County's Captain Hardin? What motivated immigrants like Augustus Franks to view the Confederacy as *their* nation, their "child"? Why did men—boys, really—such as William Joseph Miller forfeit their youth in order to serve in uniform? How could women, like Ella Gertrude Clanton Thomas, not grasp that the South was not on the side of liberty? And ministers, like James Spratt White, seemed unable to realize that the Confederacy had suffocated in its addiction to slavery.

Perhaps we can find some answers in Thucydides' timeless *History of the Peloponnesian War*. Among the causes of the clash between Athens and Sparta were jealousy, ambition, fear, interest, and sectional rivalry. The two city-states were fundamentally different, as Thucydides suggests, and we see imperialism (Sparta) battling democracy (Athens). Of course, this war ends with a triumph by the aggressive defenders of imperialism, Sparta.[2]

Our Civil War, nonetheless, was characterized by many of the same divisions. By 1860, the South perceived itself as losing national political influence. The election of Abraham Lincoln, to a section which feared any chief executive who would not energetically embrace slavery, proved the power of the industrial north. An agricultural region, which had believed itself under attack since the protective tariffs of the 1820s and

Rose Hill Cemetery in York, S.C., is the site of a solemn gray monument honoring "Our Confederate Dead." (Courtesy Scott Hollis.)

1830s and a series of slave insurrections, saw its economic and political interests threatened by Lincoln's ascendancy. The tensions which had swelled for decades burst into conflict when South Carolina's leaders, the heirs to John C. Calhoun, argued that their interpretation of the constitution allowed their state to secede.[3]

Thus, men and women such as the ones found on the pages of this book ambitiously set out in 1860 and 1861 to create a new nation, a Confederacy in which states would be protected against centralized, suffocating control. White southerners could argue that they were the true disciples of the Founding Fathers. "Independence" was an almost sacred word to these individuals. Obadiah Hardin, William Joseph Miller, Eugenia Phillips, Augustus Franks, N. H.R. Dawson, William W. White, Ella Gertrude Clanton Thomas, James Morrison Stitt, Thomas Belue, J. C. Faucette, Kiah Sadler, James Spratt White, Julius Mills and their thousands of compatriots felt threatened by their neighbors to the north. It was in their interests—and within their constitutional guarantees—to raise their weapons, if need be, to protect their homes from attack by northern troops, they rationalized. Thus, the birth of the Confederate States of America occurred but the "child" was fatally flawed. By the time, four years later, that the "child" suffocated on its misguided quest for independence the section—and its proud people—had become "bathed in blood."

A Note on Sources

The soul of this book is a series of manuscripts deposited in Winthrop University's Department of Archives and Special Collections. Among these primary sources are:

Augustus Franks Correspondence
David Hope Sadler Family Papers
Diary of Julius Mills
Diary of Thomas Belue
Hardin-Wilkes Collection
Harris Family Journals
Hudson Family Papers
James Adams Watson's Camp Reminiscences
John Thompson Letters
Joseph Alexander Thomas Papers
Mary Elizabeth Massey Papers
Mary Pringle Mitchell Papers
White Family Papers
Wilks Family Papers
William Joseph Miller Collection

Periodicals of the war era were consulted. These included the *Charleston Mercury*, Richmond *Whig*, Columbia *Examiner*, and *Harper's Weekly*. The *Official Records of the War Rebellion* (Washington, 1891–1899) and the accompanying *Atlas* (Washington, 1891–1895) were indispensable, as was South Carolina's *Roll of the Dead* (Columbia, 1995). Research aids for individuals involved in the war were Jon L. Wakelyn's *Biographical Dictionary of the Confederacy* (Westport, 1977) and Stewart Sifakis' *Who Was Who in the Civil War* (New York, 1988).

Secondary sources of special use to the authors included Shelby Foote's *The Civil War: A Narrative* (New York, 1958–1974), James McPherson's *Battle Cry of Freedom* (Oxford, 1985), David Randall's *The Civil War and Reconstruction* (Lexington, 1969), Bruce Cotton's *The Coming Fury* (Garden City, 1961), Herman Hattaway and Archer Jones' *How the North: A Military History of the Civil War* (Urbana, 1987), Paul D. Escott's *After Secession: Jefferson Davis and the Failure of Confederate Nationalism* (Baton Rouge, 1979), John G. Barrett's *Sherman's March through the Carolinas* (Chapel Hill, 1956), Joseph T. Glatthaar's *The March to the Sea and Beyond: Sherman's Troops in the Savannah and Carolinas Campaigns* (New York, 1985), John F. Marszalek's *Sherman: A Soldier's Passion for Order* (New York, 1992), Burke Davis' *The Long Surrender* (New York, 1985), Reid Mitchell's *Civil War Soldiers* (New York, 1988), Thomas L. Connelly's *The Marble Man: Robert E. Lee and His Image in American Society* (Baton Rouge, 1977), Douglas Southall Freeman's *R. E. Lee* (New York, 1934–1935), Emory M. Thomas' *Robert E. Lee: A Biography* (New York, 1995) and Rod Gragg's *The Illustrated Confederate Reader* (New York, 1984).

Palmetto State publications examined included Chalmers Gaston Davidson's *The Last Foray* (Columbia, 1971), Joshua Hilary Hudson's *Sketches and Remininscenses* (Columbia, 1903), Alston E. Wilkes' *Echoes and Etchings* (Columbia, 1910), the Catawba Regional Planning Council's *Historic Sites Survey* (Rock Hill, 1976), Mary C. Sims Oliphant's *The History of South Carolina* (Chicago, 1970), Louise Pettus and Ron Chepesiuk's *The Palmetto Story* (Columbia, 1983), J. Edward Lee's *Yorkville to York* (Dallas, 1998), Anne P. Collins' *A Goodly Heritage: History of Chester County South Carolina* (Columbia, 1986), and Walter Edgar's *South Carolina: A History* (Columbia, 1998).

Notes

PREFACE

1. William T. Sherman to Henry W. Halleck, *Official Records of the War of Rebellion* (Washington 1891–95), 1 ser., XLIV, 799; in his memoirs, Sherman argued, "I had every reason to expect bold and strong resistance" (New York, 1875), 254; for a complete study of General Sherman's offensive, see Joseph F. Glatthaar, *The March to the Sea and Beyond* (New York, 1985).

2. *Charleston Mercury*, December 21, 1860; a special edition of the newspaper was published within an hour of the secession convention's decision, *Charleston Mercury*, December 20, 1860.

3. Sherman, *Memoirs*, 2:280–87.

4. Glatthaar, *March to the Sea*, 143–46.

5. Report of Gen. Sherman, in Report of Committee on Conduct of the War, suppl. to Gen. Rep. no. 142, 38 Cong., 2 sess., vol. 1, 286–87; see J. F. Rhodes' article "Who Burned Columbia?" in *American Historical Review*, VII, 485–93.

6. Mary C. Simms Oliphant, *The History of South Carolina* (Chicago, 1970), 279–80; Rock Hill (S.C.) *Herald*, May 11, 1998.

CHAPTER 1

1. Public Records Office of Northern Ireland, Belfast; National Archives, Washington, Register of St. John's (now Stella Maris) Catholic Church, Sullivan's Island. The editors appreciate the assistance of Dale Phillips, Park Ranger, with the Fort Sumter National Monument, who supplied the baptismal record.

John Thompson Letters (T1585), Public Records Office of Northern Ireland. The editors acknowledge the kind permission of the Office to publish these letters. They form a part of a modest collection of papers relating to S.C. history. Subjects include emigration, British siege operations at Charleston in 1780, trade between Ireland and S.C. and life in America.

Bernard Click. *A Guide to Manuscripts Relating to America in Great Britain and Ireland* (Westport, 1979): John W. Raimo, *A Guide to Manuscripts Relating to America in Great Britain and Ireland*, rev. ed. (Westport, 1982).

2. Published accounts vary as to the number of men under the command of Major Robert Anderson. One source, John G. Nicolay, *The Outbreak of Rebellion* (New

York, 1881), gives eight officers and 60 enlisted men. Another source, George Fort Milton, *Conflict: The American Civil War* (New York, 1941), 26, gives nine officers and 74 enlisted men.

3. All words underlined in the letters have been italicized.

4. One source states that, in addition to Anderson, his officers and soldiers, there were eight musicians and 43 non-combatant workmen. Nicolay, *Outbreak of Rebellion*, 63.

5. The Confederate force was estimated to total approximately 7,000 men, with 42 mortars and guns. Milton, *Conflict: The American Civil War*, 26.

6. Fort Hamilton was built in 1831 on the narrows opposite Fort Wadsworth, Staten Island. Today it is a residential section of the Brooklyn borough of New York. Leon F. Seltzer, ed., *The Columbia Lippincott Gazetteer of the World* (New York, 1966), 629.

7. The first answering round was actually fired at about 7:30 A.M. Mark Maye Boatner, III, *The Civil War Dictionary* (New York, 1959), 300.

8. One account states that heat from the fire was so great that more than ninety barrels of powder were emptied into the sea. Only four were saved, and they were all eventually used. Walter Gaston Shotwell, *The Civil War in America* (New York, 1923), 85.

9. Louis Trezevant Wigfall was born to a planter family on April 21, 1816, in Edgefield District. As a young man, Wigfall fought political duels with Thomas Bird and Preston Brooks, and as a result, he moved to Marshall, Texas, in 1848. Here he served as a Democrat in the state senate and the U. S. Senate. An ardent champion of secession, he was one of the authors of the Southern Address which was signed on Dec. 14, 1860, and urged secession and the organization of the Confederacy. He arrived in Charleston for the bombardment and to push for the surrender of Fort Sumter. He went to Fort Sumter without the approval of the Confederate authorities. On Oct. 21, 1861, he was commissioned a brigadier general in the Confederate army but resigned on Feb. 18, 1862, to gain a seat in the Confederate States Senate. Jon Wakelyn, *Biographical Dictionary of the Confederacy* (Westport, 1977), 437–38.

10. When the fiftieth round of a planned 100 round salute was fired, an accidental explosion of powder occurred. A private named Hough became the first federal soldier to be killed in the Civil War. Boatner, *The Civil War Dictionary*, 300.

CHAPTER 2

1. Fitzhugh Lee, *The Confederate Soldier in the Civil War* (Fairfax, Va., 1977), 8; *Chester, S.C. News*, February 24, 1965; Hardin-Wilkes Collection, Winthrop University Archives, Rock Hill, S.C.; Hardin-Douglas Family Bible.

2. Hardin-Douglas Family Bible; the best general history of Chester County is Anne P. Collins' *A Goodly Heritage: History of Chester County South Carolina* (Columbia, 1986).

3. Hardin-Wilkes Collection, Winthrop University Archives, Rock Hill, S.C.

4. *Ibid.*

5. *Ibid.*

6. *Ibid.*

7. *Ibid.*

8. Reports of J. E. B. Stuart, December 21, 23, 1861, *Official Records*, V, 490–94; report of George A. McCall, December 28, 1861, *Official Records*, V, 474–76; report

of E.O.C. Ord, December 21, 1861, *Official Records*, V, 477–80; as the *Official Records* indicate, Hardin's regiment suffered eighteen killed and forty-five wounded at Dranesville; among the killed was Hardin's twenty-one year old brother, Thomas. See Hardin-Wilkes Family Bible and *Roll of the Dead* (Columbia, 1995).

CHAPTER 3

1. Hardin-Wilkes Collection, Department of Archives and Special Collections, Dacus Library, Winthrop University, Rock Hill, S.C.
2. Captain Hardin's courageous actions at Dranesville are clearly documented in the preceding chapter.

CHAPTER 4

1. Located north across the Cooper River from Charleston.
2. This refers to the battles of Wilderness (May 5–7) and Spotsylvania Court House (May 7–20).
3. James Island, the site of Fort Johnson, faces the southern bank of Charleston Bay.
4. Copperas, a metal used in tanning and making ink.
5. Under the new command of General John B. Hood, a flury of Confederate offenses were launched around Atlanta in late July, including the Battle of Atlanta on July 22. In several instances the Confederates held the upper hand early in the battle. Perhaps news of one of these apparent "victories" reached Emily Harris before the Union gained the advantage.
6. Union forces captured Atlanta on September 2.
7. By 1963 resistance to the draft and desertion began to grow worse in the South, and by the following year, dissatisfaction with the war and defiance of authority had become widespread.
8. Sherman had reached the outskirts of Savannah by December 16.
9. The town was located about 35 miles north and just west of Savannah.
10. The city was not evacuated until February 8.
11. Actually, the Confederate forces were defeated in a series of engagements from September 1864 to January 10, 1865.
12. Confederate troops were forced to abandon Pocotaligo on the 15th of January.
13. The rumor was false and on the 28th of January Sherman was moving from Beaufort, S.C., to Pocotaligo, S.C.
14. The Confederate forces abandoned Branchville without a major fight.
15. General Sherman occupied Columbia on February 17. Fires broke out the next morning, causing much of the business area to be burned.
16. Shelby, North Carolina, is located about thirty miles north of Spartanburg.

CHAPTER 5

1. James Adams Watson, "Camp Reminiscences," Winthrop University Archives, Rock Hill, S.C.
2. *Ibid.*
3. This is also known as the First Battle of Bull Run fought in July 1861. The Confederates were the victors.
4. Francis Wilkinson Pickens (1805–1869) was elected governor of South Carolina

in December of 1860. He demanded federal surrender of the Charleston Harbor forts and subsequently directed the firing of the shots on Fort Sumter, which opened the Civil War.

5. Yorkville was the name of the town we now know as York. Yorkville was Watson's hometown.

6. This word means "now passing"; current; present; as, the 10th instant (that is, the 10th day of the month, now passing).

7. He was an officer of the Confederate Army and was probably located in South Carolina or North Carolina.

8. At this point, Watson's journal will begin editing in December of 1864.

9. This courthouse is located 15 miles southwest of Petersburg. This site was the battleground for many Civil War skirmishes.

10. This town was located on the Petersburg and Weldon Railroad near the North Carolina–Virginia border.

11. He was a member of Watson's Regiment.

12. The 3rd Battle of Hatcher's Run was fought February 5–7, 1865, with a Union victory under the direction of Col. William Gregg.

13. This was probably an old deserted farm at one time owned by Jones. It is located three miles south of Petersburg.

14. This is located on Hatcher's Run. It was evidently a site for many skirmishes during the Civil War.

15. There were three battles at Hatcher's Run and each one most likely involved Burgess' Mill—also called Burgess' Farm.

16. This battle took place on April 2, 1865. Sutherland Station is located on the Southside Railroad.

17. This river runs through Virginia into the James River. The Appomattox Courthouse is located near the river where Lee made his final surrender to Grant.

18. This is another regiment of the Confederate Army captured along with Watson's regiment. They are marching under guard together to prison.

19. Most of the information found on Pembertons of the Civil War was under J. C. Pemberton (mentioned in the text). J. C. Pemberton was a general of the Confederate Army and his brother a lieutenant in the Union Army. Their family was from the North.

20. This depot was located in Petersburg along the Weldon Railway line. The town Weldon is in northeast North Carolina.

21. This town is located on the James River about ten miles north of Petersburg.

22. This would mean, of course, the Union flag which was raised in honor of a Union victory.

23. A Union prison camp in Sandusky Bay of Lake Erie. Around 3,000 Confederate officers were held prisoner on the island at the end of the war.

24. Located just below Johnson's Island on the bank of Erie.

25. This is the British name for checkers.

26. This is also known as the "Civil War Amnesty" which stated that persons (Confederates) who would swear to support the Union would receive pardons. The purpose was to give southern state governments a basis for reestablishing themselves.

27. A Confederate fort located on the Virginia coast near the Chesapeake Bay area.

28. This is a small town located in the central-most southern area of Virginia—almost on the North Carolina line.

29. Evidently this was a field or area named by Watson or his family. It is probably located between Fort Mill and Yorkville just off the South Carolina Railroad.

CHAPTER 6

1. Tirzah A.R.P. Church still stands today. It is located in the town of Tirzah, South Carolina, on highway 161 east of York, S.C.

2. Yorkville became York in 1915; see J. Edward Lee's *Yorkville to York* (Dallas; 1998.)

3. Neeley's Creek is to the southeast of present-day Rock Hill, S.C.

4. No information on this military camp could be obtained. Also, no Lightwood Knot Springs can be found on Civil War era maps of the Columbia, South Carolina, area.

5. Undoubtedly a reference to what is today known as the Citadel, the only state-supported military institution South Carolina has ever had. Created in 1842, the Citadel and its sister school, the Arsenal, were known collectively as the South Carolina Military Academy. In the late 19th century, it began to be called simply the Citadel.

6. General Maxey Gregg was born August 1, 1814, in Columbia, South Carolina. At the war's start, he was a colonel of the 1st Regiment of South Carolina Volunteers. Gregg was promoted to brigadier general on December 14, 1861. He participated in the battles of Malvern Hill, Cedar Mountain, the Second Manassas, Harpers Ferry, Sharpsburg (Antietam), Shepherdstown, as well as others. Gregg was noted for his courageous efforts. Maxey Gregg became a symbol of courage for the Confederate cause following his death.

7. Undoubtedly Fort Walker, the only military outpost on Hilton Head Island at the time.

8. No report on a specific battle here could be obtained. These were probably just a series of skirmishes which were unreported in Civil War history books. However, it was found that the federal army did establish a base on Hilton Head Island during the first week of December, 1861.

9. The famous battle of Fredericksburg was fought on December 13, 1862. It involved an attempt by the Union army, under the direction of General Ambrose Burnside, to take the town. However, despite outnumbering General Robert E. Lee's Confederate army 120,000 men to 80,000, the invasion attempt was repelled. The Union army lost over 12,000 of their troops in the battle (one significant casualty for the Southern army was General Maxey Gregg). William Miller did not participate in this battle due to his hospitalization.

10. The Seven Day Fight (also referred to as the Seven Days Battles, the Seven Days Campaign, or the Seven Days Campaign Before Richmond) was a week-long succession of battles involving a Union attempt to take Richmond during the time period between June 25 and July 1, 1862. The Seven Days Battles were those of Mechanicsville, Gaines Mill, Savage's Station, Frayser's Farm, and Malvern Hill. William Miller participated in all of these battles (which will be described in detail later). This particular Northern attempt to take Richmond ended in failure.

11. Richmond, the capital of Virginia and the Confederacy.

12. General George Brinton McClellan (the "Little Mac") was born on December 3, 1826. He died a natural death on October 29, 1885. At the outbreak of the Civil War, McClellan was commissioned as major general of the Ohio volunteer forces. Then the national government appointed him major general in the Regular Army, in command of the Department of Ohio. After the Union defeat in the first battle of Bull Run (July 1864), President Abraham Lincoln called McClellan to Washington and placed him in command of the forces being concentrated around the capital. McClellan then proceeded to form the famed Army of the Potomac (at the age of 34). McClellan's

armies fought at Yorktown, Richmond (the Seven Days Fight), the Second Bull Run (Manassas), Harpers Ferry, and Sharpsburg (Antietam). After the draw at Sharpsburg, Lincoln relieved McClellan of his command. That was the end of his military career. However, McClellan's political career was just beginning. He was the 1864 Democratic Party presidential nominee, losing the election to Lincoln by an electoral count of 212 to 21. McClellan also served as governor of New Jersey from 1878 to 1881.

13. The battle of Gaines' Mill was fought on June 27, 1862. On the previous day, June 26, Confederate General Robert E. Lee attacked the right wing of General George McClellan's Army of the Potomac at Mechanicsville, Va. At this battle of Mechanicsville (which Miller obviously did not participate in), the fighting was at a virtual standstill. However, on June 27, Lee's forces broke through a Union corps commanded by Brigadier General Fitz-John Porter at Gaines' Mill. This action forced McClellan's army to retreat back towards the James River.

14. *The American Heritage Dictionary* defines the term "breastwork" as "a temporary fortification, usually breast-high" (89).

15. General Thomas Jonathan ("Stonewall") Jackson was born January 21, 1824, in Clarksburg, West Virginia. He was a professor of military tactics at Virginia Military Institute when the Civil War broke out. Jackson was appointed brigadier general under General Joseph E. Johnston on June 17, 1861. He earned his nickname as a result of his heroic efforts at the battle of First Manassas (the First Bull Run). On October 7, 1861, he was promoted to major general in command of the Shenandoah Valley and northwest Virginia. After saving General Lee's army at Sharpsburg, Jackson was promoted to lieutenant general (October 10, 1862) and was given command of the 2nd corps of the Army of Northern Virginia. Miller's company served under Jackson's jurisdiction. Jackson-commanded armies fought at Staunton, Fort Royal, Winchester, the Second Manassas, Harpers Ferry, Sharpsburg (Antietam), Fredericksburg and Chancellorsville. Jackson died during the battle of Chancellorsville (his death will be explained in detail later). When Miller first spotted Jackson, the general was just returning from his spectacularly successful Valley campaign.

16. The battle of Frayser's Farm was fought on June 30, 1862. It has also been referred to as the battle of White Oak Swamp, Glendale, Nelson's Crossroads, Charles City Crossroads, New Market Road, Willis' Church or Turkey Bridge. It involved the attempt by Lee's forces to cut off McClellan's retreat from the battles at Mechanicsville, Gaines' Mill, and Savage's Station (a battle which Miller mentions later in this same sentence). Lee tried to attack the Union Army from the north by going through the boggy White Oak Swamp. McClellan realized the Confederate's plan in time and effectively halted this offensive so that most of his army could get away. By the night of June 30, McClellan had his army positioned safely upon Malvern Hill north of the James River. At Frayser's Farm, Lee lost a golden opportunity to split the Army of the Potomac in two and destroy it; McClellan was lucky to escape with his army in as good a shape as it was.

17. The battle of Savage's Station was fought on June 29, 1862, the day before the battle at Frayser's Farm. The Army of the Potomac, under McClellan's direction, was retreating from its defeats at Mechanicsville and Gaines' Mill. Lee's Confederate army was in hot pursuit. A Confederate attack at Savage's Railroad Station was disorganized and failed to result in a major Southern victory, thus McClellan's army continued its retreat (eventually reaching Malvern Hill).

18. General Micah Jenkins was born December 1, 1835 on Edisto Island, South Carolina. He was the founder of King's Mountain Military School in Yorkville, South Carolina in 1855 (when Miller was ten years old). Jenkins taught at his school until the outbreak of the war. He fought at the battles of First Manassas, Williamsburg,

Seven Pines, the Seven Days Battles, Second Manassas, Fredericksburg, Suffolk (Va.), Gettysburg, Chickamauga, and the Wilderness. Jenkins was promoted to Brigadier General on July 22, 1862 (immediately after the Seven Days Battles). He was killed by one of his own men during the Battle of the Wilderness—an accident suffered similarly by Stonewall Jackson a year earlier at almost exactly the same location.

19. This covered a time period from July 1, 1862, until Jackson's death on May 10, 1863. It involved eight major battles.

20. A reference to the Seven Days Battles.

21. Major General John Pope was born March 16, 1822, in Louisville, Kentucky. In May of 1861 he was appointed brigadier general of Union volunteers and was assigned to command of the Army of the Mississippi. Pope was promoted to major general of volunteers in April of 1862. He was then promoted to brigadier general of the regular army in June of 1862. The Union army commanded by Pope was defeated by Lee's Confederate forces at the Second Bull Run (Manassas) on August 29th and 30th, 1862. He blamed this defeat on fellow generals Fitz-John Porter and George McClellan (historians are divided as to whose fault it really was). On September 5, 1862, Lincoln ordered that Pope be relieved of his command. He held only minor posts after this, although he was promoted to major general in 1882.

22. The battle of Cedar Mountain was fought on August 9, 1862. It occurred as a result of Union General John Pope's southward movement in an attempt to hook up with McClellan's Army of the Potomac; obviously, the Confederate army wanted to prevent this. In this particular battle, Jackson's forces defeated a Union corps commanded by General Nathaniel P. Banks. This severely delayed Pope's linking with McClellan's army. Cedar Mountain was a clear victory for the South; the Union had 2,381 casualties while the Confederates had but 265.

23. Junction was not so much a battle as it was a complete takeover. Jackson's forces destroyed this supply depot of Pope's Union army on August 26, 1862. The Confederate army caught Pope's army off guard; they were resting on the Rappahannock River as a result of information that McClennan's army was evacuating its position on the James River. They were unaware of Jackson's movements. The Southern army occupied Manassas Junction for three days (August 26–28th, 1862). As a result of the supply depot's destruction, Pope turned to pursue Jackson. The Manassas Junction takeover served as a prelude to the Second Battle of Bull Run (Manassas).

24. The railroad served by Manassas Junction was the Orange and Alexandria Railroad.

25. The battle about to be described is the Second Bull Run (or Manassas) fought on August 29th and 30th, 1862. Union General John Pope sought out and found "Stonewall" Jackson's troops near Groveton, Virginia (Pope's chase was a result of Jackson's destruction of Manassas Junction). The initial Union drive against the Confederate forces failed; Southern General James Longstreet had come up to reinforce Jackson and turn the tide of this first day's battle. On the second day of Bull Run (August 30), Longstreet's forces outflanked Pope's and the Confederates scored a major victory. As a result of this defeat, President Lincoln had Pope removed from his command.

26. Today, the area of Ebenezer, South Carolina, is incorporated into the city of Rock Hill.

27. Research shows that this estimation of Jackson's and Pope's strength on this first day of battle is more or less correct. Research also shows that it was a corps commanded by Longstreet, not Lee, which came to Jackson's aid.

28. Research shows the actual number of fighting men at Bull Run was 75,000 for the North and 48,500 for the South. It was not exactly a "fair show in numbers," but it didn't matter—the South won a convincing victory anyway.

29. This march to Maryland represented the first Confederate invasion of the north. Soon, Miller would fight his first major battle outside the state of Virginia.

30. Harpers Ferry, in West Virginia, fell to Jackson's Confederate troops with little resistance. Meanwhile, other Confederate forces were positioning themselves at Sharpsburg, Maryland, with McClellan's Army of the Potomac in hot pursuit.

31. Sources other than Miller indicate that as many as 12,000 Union troops were either killed or captured at Harpers Ferry.

32. The battle of the Civil War—more soldiers died on this day than any other day of the war. Union troops commanded by George McClellan attacked and were driving on Lee's Confederate army until the battle of Sharpsburg (or Antietam Creek) was fought on September 17, 1862. Reinforcements by Jackson's and A. P. Hill's corps stemmed the Northern tide (Miller was in Jackson's corps). This very bloody battle featured 12,469 Union casualties and 13,724 Confederate losses.

33. Antietam was not a failure to the North. While the battle itself was technically a draw, Antietam was a clear moral victory for the Union. The day after the fighting ended, Lee's army retreated back into Virginia and ended their short-lived "invasion" of the north (although they would try again—the next time into Pennsylvania). This Southern failure to gain a foothold in the north was seen by many as a victory for the Union. Abraham Lincoln used the Sharpsburg battle as a springboard for issuing his preliminary Emancipation Proclamation on September 22, 1862. Many historians believe that the Southern failure to win at Antietam resulted in Great Britain's decision not to give direct aid to the Confederacy. Thus, in many ways, the battle of Antietam was a turning point in the war and deserves much more significance than Miller gives it.

34. The battle of Chancellorsville (which was Miller's first battle following his return from hospitalization at Staunton) was fought between May 1st and 4th, 1863. Although grossly outnumbered, brilliant maneuvering by Lee allowed his forces to rout the Army of the Potomac (now under the direction of General Joseph Hooker). The Union army retreated back across the Rappahannock River. They had 17,287 casualties in this battle; the South suffered 12,764. However, this victory was a costly one for the Confederacy—General Thomas J. ("Stonewall") Jackson was accidentally shot by one of his own men on May 2. He died on May 10th.

35. There is a misconception about the way in which Jackson dies. It is true that he was shot by one of his own men on May 2nd, 1863. However, this was not in itself a mortal wound. Jackson actually died as a result of pneumonia contracted during the amputation of his right arm on May 10th, 1863.

36. General Ambrose Power Hill was born on November 9, 1825, in Culpeper County, Virginia. Hill resigned from the United States Army in March of 1861 and joined the Confederate Army as a colonel of the 13th regiment of Virginia Volunteers. On February 26, 1862, following the battle of First Manassas, he was promoted to brigadier general. Three months later, Hill became a major general. He was a hero in the Peninsular Campaign of 1862 in Virginia. After the battles of Fredericksburg and Chancellorsville, Hill was promoted to lieutenant general and given command of the 3rd corps of the Army of Northern Virginia (May 20th, 1863). Hill participated in the battles of Bristoe Station, Gettysburg, the Wilderness, and Petersburg. Because of illness (both physical and mental) in his later years, his military performance was uneven. Hill was killed while trying to reach his troops near Petersburg, Virginia, on April 2, 1865.

37. This is somewhat of a mistake. General A. P. Hill was wounded shortly after Jackson; thus command of Miller's corps fell to Jeb Stuart.

38. The battle of Gettysburg (considered by many to be the turning point of the

war) was fought between July 1 and July 4, 1863, at Gettysburg, Pennsylvania. After initial successes (due to A. P. Hill's advance forces), Lee's Confederate charge breaks down and eventually falls to defeat at the hands of the Army of the Potomac—now commanded by General George Meade. Eventually, Lee was forced into an all-out retreat (back to Virginia). The North (who started with 85,000 troops) suffered 23,049 casualties. The South (who began with 65,000 men) reported 20,451 casualties. This battle has been regarded by historians as the South's last hope for victory.

39. General Ulysses Simpson Grant was born on April 27, 1822, in Point Pleasant, Ohio. At the start of the Civil War, he was named colonel of the 21st regiment of Illinois Volunteers. In 1861, Grant was promoted to brigadier general. He became famous as a result of his victories at Forts Henry and Donelson (in Tennessee), Shiloh, Tennessee; and Vicksburg, Mississippi. On March 12, 1864, President Lincoln promoted Grant to lieutenant general and placed him in command of the Army of the Potomac. Grant became to the North what Lee was to the South. It was Grant who forced Lee's Confederate Army into surrender at Appomattox (April 9, 1865). Grant was promoted to full general in 1866. He later served two scandal-ridden terms as president of the United States (1869–1877).

40. The battle of the Wilderness (which Miller obviously did not participate in) was fought on May 5th and 6th, 1864. The battle of the Wilderness represented the first time that Grant and Lee faced each other on the battlefield. However, this first battle was indecisive. It involved trench warfare in which neither side could move the other out.

41. The battle of Spotsylvania Court House was fought between May 8th and 21st, 1864. Grant's Union army resumed the offensive following the draw in the Wilderness. Grant's and Lee's armies raced from the Wilderness battle site to Spotsylvania Court House—a distance of about ten miles. Lee's army won the race and managed to hold off Grant's advance men. For the next two weeks, both sides attempted to score a major breakthrough, yet each attempted offensive failed. The fighting at Spotsylvania Court House was often fierce. This place was important to both armies because roads went through it to Chancellorsville, Wilderness Tavern, and Fredericksburg. Finally, on May 21st, Grant left his Spotsylvania front and attempted to flank Lee at the North Anna River on May 24th. Grant's attempt to outflank Lee ended in failure. Eventually, however, Grant would catch Lee and force him to surrender.

42. Grant believed in total, all-out warfare. He strove only for victory, regardless of how many of his men died in the attempt. He was severely criticized for his military tactics. Many northern newspapers referred to Grant as "the Butcher" and called for his dismissal. However, Lincoln refused to fire Grant; he was the only general the Union had that could win consistently.

43. Many Civil War historians refer to May 12th as the day of the "Bloody Angle of Spotsylvania." This battle within a battle occurred when corps of Federal troops led by Major General Winfield Scott Hancock charged at a Confederate line commanded by General Richard S. Ewell. The federals almost scored a major breakthrough. However, after hours of fighting, the Confederate army managed to repair its broken line at a spot now referred to as the "Bloody Angle of Spotsylvania."

44. On June 18, 1864, Lee's troops arrived in Petersburg. Shortly thereafter, Grant opened up his siege of Petersburg. This siege lasted nearly eleven months. Finally, on April 2nd of 1865, Grant broke through the breastworks at Petersburg. Thus, Petersburg (as well as the Confederate capital at Richmond) fell to the Union army. The North reported only 4140 casualties during the siege—the South's total is unknown, but it is estimated that they lost over half of their original 18,500 man fighting force.

45. General Lee said of this maneuver, "The line has been stretched until it is broken." (E.B. Long and Barbara Long, *The Civil War, Day by Day: An Almanac, 1861–65*, Garden City, N.Y., 1971, 663.)

46. After Petersburg, Lee led his army westward across Virginia in an attempt to reach Lynchburg, where he hoped he could regroup his forces. Lee took his troops to Amelia Courthouse, Sayler's Creek, Farmville, and, finally, Appomattox Courthouse.

47. *The American Heritage Dictionary* defines "adjutant" as "a military officer who is an administrative assistant to a commander."

48. The city of Rock Hill cannot be found on an 1860 map of South Carolina. Rock Hill was established as a community, with the building of its first post office, on April 17, 1852. It was not officially incorporated into a town until 1870 (after the Civil War).

49. Company H was "Stonewall" Jackson's company.

50. The official surrender took place on April 9, 1865.

51. General Sam McGowan was born on October 9, 1819, in Laurens County, South Carolina. He assisted P. T. Beauregard in the capture of Fort Sumter and served as aide-de-camp to Milledge L. Bonham during the First Bull Run (Manassas). After that battle, he was sent to Virginia to serve as colonel of the 14th South Carolina Regiment. McGowan was wounded at the Second Bull Run (Manassas) in August of 1862. However, he recovered sufficiently enough to succeed General Maxey Gregg as brigade commander during the battle of Fredericksburg (in which Gregg was killed). McGowan was promoted to brigadier general on April 23, 1863. As such, he directed the battles of Chancellorsville, the Wilderness, and Spotsylvania (among others). He surrendered, along with Lee, at Appomattox.

52. Greensboro, North Carolina, is located about 175 miles directly northeast of Miller's destination of Yorkville, South Carolina.

53. This is obviously a mistake made by Miller, as later reading will show. Miller's aunt must have lived somewhere else in North Carolina.

54. A "mess" can be described as a group of people who eat together.

55. Concord, North Carolina, is located about seventy miles directly northeast of Yorkville.

56. William Miller married the former Miss Margaret Josephine Reddey, who was a sister of Captain W. Lyle Reddey. The exact wedding date is not known. No information could be obtained on either Miss Reddey or her brother (their names were written in on the typescript). The Millers had four children: Dr. J. R. Miller, Mr. W. W. Miller, Mrs. Annie N. Black (Mrs. Norman), and Mrs. Barnette M. Spencer (Mrs. J. H.). It was Barnette Miller who talked her father into writing about his Civil War experiences. All of the Millers' children are now deceased.

CHAPTER 7

1. Lafayette Baker was born on October 13, 1826, and he died on July 3, 1863. He was Chief of the United States Secret Service. Baker gained employment as a detective, special provost marshall of the War Department in 1862, and brigadier-general in 1865. He searched out traitors, plotters, and bounty-jumpers during the Civil War. Baker disregarded the constitutional guarantees during his arrests and searches. *Dictionary of American Biography* (New York: 1928, vol. 1, 522).

2. One of the daughters is identified as Caroline. The other daughter is not identified. Mary Elizabeth Massey *Bonnet Brigades* (New York: 1966), 90–91.

3. Probably Detective Baker.

4. Fort Lafayette is located in the New York Harbor. Political prisoners, transfer of prisoners, and the return of prisoners took place here during the Civil War. *War of the Rebellion: Official Records of the Union and Confederate Armies* (Washington: 1899). Series 2.

5. Mr. Phillip Phillips is the husband of Eugenia Phillips. At this time he had been a congressman from Alabama and a prominent lawyer in Washington. *Bonnet Brigades* (New York: 1966), 93.

6. This is Mrs. Rose O'Neal Greenhow. She was placed under arrest with some other women on August 23, 1862, after being placed under surveillance for approximately one month. She supplied the Confederate forces with information she had gathered from her friends and from prisoners. *Bonnet Brigades* (New York: 1966), 90–91.

7. The prisoners were kept in a house on this street in Washington.

8. This is a collection of photographs of criminals maintained in police files and used for making identifications. *The American Heritage Dictionary of the English Language* (Boston: 1969), 1125.

9. General Simon Cameron was born on March 9, 1799, and died on June 26, 1889. He was a senator, secretary of war, and a diplomat. Cameron served in President Abraham Lincoln's administrations. He was a man of power and of influence during the Civil War. *Dictionary of American Biography* (New York: 1929), vol. 3, 437–39.

10. Senator William Henry Seward was born on May 16, 1801, and died on October 10, 1872. He was a statesman and held the office of secretary of state during the four years of the Civil War. Seward believed in exercising his authorities. *Dictionary of American Biography* (New York: 1935), vol. XVI, 615–20.

11. This is Lafayette Baker.

12. Edwin McMasters Stanton was born on December 19, 1814, and died on December 24, 1869. He was at one time the attorney-general and secretary of war of the United States. Stanton was a man of dignified reputation. He practiced civil and constitutional law; he served in President Lincoln's administration. Stanton was the successor of Simon Cameron. *Dictionary of American Biography* (New York: 1935), vol. XVI, 517–21.

13. No information available.

14. General George McClellan was born in 1826 and died in 1885. McClellan was the successor to Winfield Scott in the previously named position. He also commanded the Army of the Potomac. He lacked knowledge and inclination but was a good organizer. *A Concise Encyclopedia of the Civil War* (New York: 1965), 145.

15. A Mexican War hero, General Winfield Scott was born in 1786 and died in 1866. He was the Union general-in-chief known as "Old Fuss and Feathers." For twenty years, Scott had a distinguished military career. *Ibid.*

CHAPTER 8

1. Hopkinsville, Kentucky. Kenneth J. Jackson, ed., *Atlas of American History* (New York: 1978) 151–53. Unless otherwise stated, any further geographic information is taken from this exact source.

2. Bruckmuller probably was a member of a Confederate Army band, of which Augustus Franks was also a member. Bruckmuller's exact role is unknown.

3. Identity unknown.

4. Throughout this collection, there are references to the existence of a military band and the membership of August Franks in this group. His exact position in the band is unknown, but his participation in the band seems secondary to his duties as a solder.

5. Identity unknown.

6. Identity unknown.

7. Babette was Franks' wife, Mrs. Barbara Muntz Franks.

8. Frances was Franks' daughter and second child. She was born January 6, 1861, and her entire name was Frances Seraphine.

9. Eugenia was the first born daughter of Franks. November 5, 1859, was her given birthdate.

10. Marshall, Texas, was home for the Franks' family. This city is located in the eastern part of the state near the Arkansas/Louisiana border. Jackson, *Atlas*, 169.

11. Identity unknown.

12. Clarksville, Tennessee, is located in the northwest part of the state, near the Kentucky border. Fort Donelson was located in the same area of Tennessee. February 14–16, 1862 was the sight of a great battle which ended in an unconditional surrender by the Confederates to General Ulysses Grant. Geer, *Campaigns*, pp. 92–103.

13. Identity unknown.

14. Identity unknown.

15. Although numerous sources were investigated, this general's identity remains unknown. In some cases, however, the titles of general, colonel, or major were applied to persons of prestige or power within a community although they were not official officers. Perhaps this could be the case with General Lay. Clement Eaton, *A History of the Southern Confederacy* (New York: 1954), 82.

16. Pierre Gustave Toutant Beauregard was a Confederate general from Louisiana. Ezra J. Warner, *Generals in Grey: Lives of the Confederate Commanders* (Baton Rouge, 1959).

17. Columbus, Kentucky.

18. Identity unknown.

19. General Charles Clark was a Confederate general from Mississippi.

20. Identity unknown.

21. Identity unknown.

22. The Clark family appears to have been a well-to-do Nashville family that befriended Confederate soldiers, including Augustus Franks. Mr. W. Clark is an abbreviation of William Clark, the patriarch of this family. To show his deep appreciation, Franks named his first son, born August 24, 1863, William Clark Franks. Two of Clark's daughters, Sally and Susan, also helped Franks while he recuperated from his war wounds.

23. Major General Don Carlos Buell participated in the Union forces during the Civil War, and saw battle experience in the Tennessee (Nashville) region. Ezra J. Warner, *Generals in Blue: Lives of the Union Commanders* (Baton Rouge, 1964).

24. Identities unknown.

25. Mr. Cliff was the brother-in-law of Miss Susan Clark, and he also resided in Nashville.

26. This probably refers to a road leading south from Nashville to Franklin, Tennessee.

27. This military prison was more commonly known as Gratiot Street Prison in St. Louis, Missouri. Francis Trevelyan Miller, ed., *The Photographic History of the Civil War, Part Seven: Prisons and Hospitals* (New York: 1957), 62.

28. Identity unknown.

29. This term probably refers to an individual with some authority possibly within the Union forces, but an exhaustive search of various sources provided no positive identification.

30. Lieutenant Colonel Benard Gains Farrar was provost-marshal-general of

the Department of Mississippi. The provost marshals were the police force of the Union Army. Miller, *Photographic History*, 187-212.

31. Identity unknown.

CHAPTER 9

1. The Southern Republic must have been a boat. Further on in the letter, Elodie says that she "went to see him but the boat had gone."

2. Sam is obviously Elodie's brother, but there is no way to identify him without a last name.

3. The Battle of Corinth was fought from about April 7 until April 10, 1862, at Corinth, Miss. M. Boatner, III, *The Civil War Dictionary* (NY: 1959), 176.

4. Gen'l Johnston. Probably Albert Sidney Johnston who graduated at West Point in 1826. He died on the battlefield after successfully attacking Grant at Shiloh, April 6, 1862. Ezra Warner, *Generals in Gray* (Baton Rouge: 1959), 161.

5. Identity unknown.

6. Elodie is probably referring to the Conscription act, which passed the Confederate Congress April 16, 1868. The Act required all white males between the ages of 18 and 35 to serve three years in the Confederate Army. Boatner, *The Civil War Dictionary* (NY: 1959), 172.

7. Identities unknown.

8. Yorktown, Va. The Battle of Yorktown was fought from sometime in the middle of April until May 4, 1862. This was also known as the Peninsula Campaign. Boatner, *The Civil War Dictionary* (NY: 1957), 752.

9. William Henry Chase Whiting graduated from West Point in 1845. Jefferson Davis appointed him Brigadier General on July 21, 1861. Davis appointed him Major General on April 23, 1863. Whiting died of wounds on March 10, 1865. Warner, *Generals in Gray* (Baton Rouge: 1959), 334.

10. See note 6.

11. Identity unknown.

12. Identity unknown.

13. Mr. Peques cannot be identified. Col. Morgan is probably John Tyler Morgan who was a lawyer and representative to the Alabama Secession Convention. He served as brigadier general later in the war. After the war, Alabama sent him to the United States Senate, where he fought for white supremacy. Warner, *Generals in Gray* (Baton Rouge: 1959), 221.

14. Dawson must be referring to fortifications left by Lord Cornwallis during the Revolutionary War.

15. Identity unknown.

16. Identity unknown.

CHAPTER 10

1. Mary Pringle Mitchell Papers, Department of Archives and Special Collections, Dacus Library, Winthrop University, Rock Hill, S.C. Biographical sketches of the Pringle family were obtained from Mary Pringle Fenhagen's two articles which appeared in *South Carolina Historical Magazine*, LXII (July 1961) 151–64, and (October 1961) 221–36.

2. Charles Alston Pringle (1841–1862) was appointed Brevet 2Lt in Company E, later H, 1st South Carolina Regiment (Butler's). On September 26, 1861, he was

appointed 2d Lt of Company E, and later died on June 29, 1862, of fever in Charleston. It is not known if he participated in the defense of Charleston during the siege of James Island.

    3. Donald Grant Mitchell (1822–1908) married Mary Frances Pringle on May 31, 1853, in Charleston, South Carolina. Mitchell, better known by his pseudonym, Ik Marvel (or Ike Marvel), wrote many books relating to travel and agriculture, and contributed to the *New York Enquirer* and the *Morning Courier*. Son of the Rev. Alfred N. Mitchell of Norwich, Connecticut, he attended Yale and studied law in New York and was appointed consul to Venice in 1853. At the time of the Civil War, Mitchell was teaching and writing in semiretirement at his famous farm "Edgewood," near New Haven.

    4. Edward Jenkins Pringle (1826–1899) graduated third in his class at Harvard and practiced law in Columbia and Charleston in the 1840s. In December 1853, he arrived in San Francisco and one year later formed a law partnership with two former Harvard classmates, A. C. Whitcomb and John B. Felton. By the 1870s, Pringle's law firm was one of the largest in California. In 1899 he was appointed commissioner of the Supreme Court in California. He married Cornelia Lititia Johnson and had seven children.

    5. Maria Duncan Pringle, nee Duncan (1826–1908), married John Julius Pringle (see note 6), second oldest brother of Mary Pringle Mitchell. Maria Duncan was daughter to Natchez planter Stephen Duncan, a pro–Unionist during the Civil War.

    6. John Julius Pringle (1824–1901), educated in England as was his older brother, William Alston Pringle (see note 15), graduated from the Naval Academy and later served at Vera Cruz during the Mexican War. He married Maria Duncan in 1849 and lived much of the rest of his life abroad in Europe, although references in Mrs. Mitchell's letters suggest otherwise.

    7. A small photograph roughly 2¼ × 3½ inches mounted on a slightly larger card which was very popular in the nineteenth century and used as a calling or visiting card.

    8. This is apparently an incomplete letter.

    9. A fort in Boston Harbor used during the Civil War as a Confederate prisoner of war camp.

    10. Donald Grant Mitchell, Jr. (1861–1950), also referred to as Stonewall, was the second son of Donald and Mary Pringle Mitchell.

    11. Also known as the battle of Secessionville, it was the scene of the defense of Charleston in June 1862 by General N. G. Evans and Col. T. G. Lamar, South Carolina Artillery, against Union forces commanded by Brig. Gen. H. W. Benham who was immediately discharged by President Lincoln after the Union defeat.

    12. Isaac Ingalls Stevens (1818–1862) graduated first in his class at West Point and later fought in Mexico and became governor of Washington Territory. Promoted to brigadier general of volunteers after the first battle of Manassas in September 1861, he participated under protest in the fiasco at James Island in June 1862. He was killed at the battle of Chantilly, Virginia, on September 1, 1862.

    13. On August 8, 1862, the *New York Times* reported that the *Golden Gate* sank in the Pacific Ocean, fifteen miles off Manzanilla, Mexico, with the loss of 180 passengers and a large amount of gold bullion.

    14. Mary Pringle Mitchell (1855–?) and Elizabeth Woodbridge Mitchell (1856–1943), eldest daughters of Mary Pringle Mitchell.

    15. William Alston Pringle (1822–1895), oldest brother of Mary Pringle Mitchell.

    16. Burton H. Harrison (1837–1904), private secretary to Jefferson Davis.

CHAPTER 11

1. From internal evidence Camp Lee is within the fortifications of the city of Richmond but exactly which part the editor cannot determine from the maps available. Richmond, on the James River, is the capital of the Commonwealth of Virginia and was the capital of the Confederate States of America.

2. "Janders" is jaundice, the results of a disorder of the bile causing the skin to be yellowish green. *Webster's Third New International Dictionary of the English Language Unabridged* (London, 1971), II, 1211.

3. The writer usually spells this without a capital P. Petersburg is on the Appomattox River about thirty miles south of Richmond. *Battlefields of the Civil War* Atlas Plate Fourteen (*The National Geographic Magazine*, hereafter, *National Geographic Map*).

4. Regiment is spelled this way throughout both letters with an occasional difference. James Morrison Stitt served in the Forty-ninth North Carolina, hereafter "the Forty-ninth," as an infantry private. The author enlisted into Company F, 19 April 1862. Colonel Stephen D. Ramseur of Lincolnton, North Carolina, commanded. John W. Moore, *Roster of North Carolina Troops in the War Between the States* (Raleigh, N.C.: 1882) III, 411 and 394. Hereafter Moore's *Roster*. Clark's *Histories*, III 125 and 151.

5. Hospital is consistently misspelled this way and is left in the text uncorrected.

6. "And" is written twice and is left to give the reader a feeling for the manuscript.

7. Benton Bridge is not on the *Official Records Atlas*. Drewry's Bluff is on the great bend of the James River about halfway between Richmond and Petersburg. Captain Calvin D. Cowles (ed.), *Atlas to Accompany the Official Records of the Union and Confederate Armies* (Washington, 1891–1895), Plate CXXXVII. Hereafter *OR Atlas*.

8. Thomas Jonathan "Stonewall" Jackson commanded the Second Corps, Army of Northern Virginia. *Dictionary of American Biography*, IX., 556 and 559. DAB, hereafter.

9. The author uses the word "and" and the ampersand interchangeably. Hereinafter, it is left as written.

10. The word "brigade" is consistently spelled this way and is left throughout the text.

11. Rapidan Station is on the Orange and Alexandria Railroad where it crosses the Rapidan River at its confluence with Robertson's River in Orange Court House, Virginia, between Fairfax to the north and Gordonsville to the south. Brigadier General Vincent J. Esposito, ed., *The West Point Atlas of American Wars* (N.Y., 1964) I, 1689–1900. Map 58.

12. Stitt fared well on the road. In all stories of soldiers, what one gets to eat is very important. To a young man in his early twenties who has obviously never known hunger, what he ate on this march is of no small significance. The word is corrected each time by the editor.

13. The lower case "I" is used often and is uncorrected when it occurs in the middle of sentences.

14. The phrase is "work at all." Suddenly one has a real feeling of the tiresomeness of marching on a road and the physically wearing aspect of it.

15. Frederick, Maryland. Hereinafter as Stitt spells it. The city is east of South Mountain over which the Army of Northern Virginia moved to Sharpsburg. Private Stitt is now sick again and ordered to the hospital in Frederick. He misses the battle at Sharpsburg. *National Geographic Map*.

16. Pinch Spratt and John Squires. Joseph L. Spratt of Lincoln County, North

Carolina, enlisted in Company K of the Forty-ninth, 15 March 1862. The editor chooses this person over one S. L. Spratt of Rutherford County, North Carolina, who was in the Fiftieth North Carolina. Moore's *Roster*, III, 423 and 441. John Squires, whose name the author crossed out, could be John B. Squires of Company B, Bethel Regiment or Marcus D. Squires of the Forty-ninth from Mecklenburg County, North Carolina. Squires had been wounded at Malvern Hill. The Bethel Regiment was the first of the North Carolina regiments. It was in the field only six months in 1861. Moore's *Roster*, I, 413. If John B. Squires, Moore's *Roster*, I, 411 is the most likely, how did he get there? Why is he not listed among any regiments after the Bethel Regiment? Was he there as a friend visiting? If Marcus Squires, Moore's *Roster*, III, 411, is the one, a regimental friend, did Stitt write the name of a friend from home and strike it out to correct the error? A mystery never to be solved. John B. Squires is listed among those who attended a reunion in 1903. Clara Laney, *Union County Cemeteries 1710–1914* and *Roster of Confederate and Revolutionary Soldiers* (North Carolina Historical Press, 1958), 145 and 176.

    17. Another doubling of words.

    18. The writer typically uses "ware" for "were."

    19. The Potomac River is the border between Virginia and Maryland.

    20. "Lieutenant." Hereinafter, the same.

    21. "Yankee" or "Yankees." Hereinafter, the same.

    22. "Prisoner." Hereinafter, the same with both singular and plural forms.

    23. "Hotel." For "was" the editors have written "were."

    24. "Secessionist Ladies." This is the editors' interpretation of the text. These would be Marylanders who supported the southern cause.

    25. Baltimore was a major port city for the state of Maryland lying on the western shore of the Chesapeake Bay at the northern end of the bay.

    26. Fort Delaware was in the narrows of the Delaware River, between Delaware City, Delaware, on the west and Salem, New Jersey, on the east. It was on an island and served as the outer defense of the city of Philadelphia. *Official Records Atlas*, plate CXXXVI.

    27. "And and" in original.

    28. This closing section tells much. First it indicates that the author and his family were financially well off. Mrs. Dunn seems to have practiced what she taught about keeping money, and Still has a practical eye for dealing in business. The reference to the Forty-eighth North Carolina cannot go unnoticed. The author's future brother-in-law, George Washington Howey, is a sergeant in the Forty-eighth. Family tradition tells that he was twice wounded and since he is not among the paroled at Appomattox it is to be assumed he was home recovering from the second wound. Howey's cousin, Colonel Samuel H. Walkup, commanded the Forty-eighth. Moore's *Roster*, II, 376 and 355. *Hudson Family Papers*. Of Capt. Cannon nothing has been discovered. The end of the letter indicates a desire for a letter from home quickly.

    29. Letter two begins with a list of towns. Weldon, North Carolina, near the Virginia border on the Roanoke River is railhead for the Wilmington and Weldon Railroad and the Weldon and Petersburg Railroad. *OR Atlas*, plate CXXXVIII.

    30. New Bern, Goldsboro, and Kinston, North Carolina. First one needs to note the absence of capitals for the names and second that New Bern is spelled several ways. The editor left them as Stitt spelled them. New Bern is at the mouth of the Neuse River on the Pamlico Sound. West of New Bern, about halfway to Goldsboro, is Kinston and then comes Goldsboro to the west and about halfway to Raleigh, the capital of North Carolina. *OR Atlas*, plate CXXXVIII.

    31. Rations.

32. The Trent River mouth is on the south side of New Bern. This river runs inland for a few miles. *OR Atlas*, plate CXXXVIII.

33. "Ours" is the brigade of the Ransom brothers, Robert, Jr. and Matt Whitaker. The Ransoms' home was Warren County, North Carolina. Robert Ransom's promotion to major general came in March 1862. Matt Ransom succeeded his brother when his promotion to brigadier general from colonel of the Thirty-fifth regiment came on 13 June 1863. The brigade consisted of the Twenty-fourth, Twenty-fifth, Thirty-fifth, Forty-ninth, and Fifty-sixth regiments from North Carolina. In 1863 M. W. Ransom took this brigade into eastern North Carolina to defend the Wilmington and Weldon Railroad. M. W. Ransom commanded the brigade to Appomattox. "He was not a trained soldier and never became a tactician, but he was a born leader of men." Allen Johnson and Dumas Malone, eds., *Dictionary of American Biography* (N.Y., 1958), VIII, 379, Part I of XV, Original Edition, Mecklenburg County Library, Charlotte, N.C. Moore's *Roster*, IV, 3 and 9. D. H. Hill, "*North Carolina*," in General Clement A. Evans, ed: *Confederate Military History: A Library of Confederate History in Twelve Volumes, Written by Distinguished Men of the South* (Atlanta, 1899), IV, 219. Hereafter, Clement, *Conf. Mil. Hist.*

34. M. D. Corse, Brigadier General, Provisional Army of the Confederate States, 1 November 1862. He commanded a brigade of Virginia troops. Clement's *Conf. Mil. Hist.* IV p. 219. Lee *Conf. Soldier*, p. 358. Thomas Lanier Clingman of Buncombe County, North Carolina, began his military career as colonel of the Twenty-fifth North Carolina. Clingman's Brigade consisted of the Eighth, Thirty-first, Fifty-first, and Sixty-first regiments. He commanded at Wilmington in 1862 and in 1863 joined Hoke's Division. *DAB*, II pp. 220–21. Moore's *Roster* IV p. 7. Robert Frederick Hoke of Lincoln County, North Carolina, began as colonel of the Twenty-first North Carolina. January 1863 saw him made brigadier general. The winter of 1864 found Hoke in tidewater North Carolina. His promotion to major general came on the battlefield in April 1864. *DAB*, IX p. 126.

35. Dover Road is the road through Dover Swamp west of New Bern, North Carolina. *OR Atlas*, plate CXXXVIII.

36. Commissaries. The food supplies.

37. The Twenty-fourth North Carolina. See note 33 above.

38. The War Between the States saw a great deal of the shooting of deserters. What is called a "Drumhead" Court Martial occurred frequently. Severe treatment of men thought to be cowards was not uncommon.

39. "Rejoiced."

40. Blackwater River and Ivor Station are in southeastern Virginia. The Blackwater River and the Nottaway River form the Chowan which flows southeast to Albemarle Sound. Ivor Station is on the Norfolk and Petersburg Railroad where the railroad crosses the Blackwater River near Suffolk, Virginia.

41. News.

42. Captain Andry, the editors conclude, is James P. Ardrey, commissioned first lieutenant, 10 November 1861 and later promoted captain. He enlisted from Mecklenburg County, North Carolina. On 12/13 May 1864 he met his death in the battle at Drewry's Bluff. Clark's *Histories*, III, 152.

43. Relations: Dovey is a half-sister to Morrison Stitt. Her full name is Dovey E. Dunn. Nancy is Nancy Lucinda Dunn, another half-sister, and Jeffrey is a half-brother, Jefferson Ezell Dunn. Hudson Family Papers.

44. J. M. Stitt. James Morrison Stitt died 5 June 1864. As the editors looked over the two essays on the Forty-ninth in Clark's *Histories*, some reconstruction of Stitt's last weeks could be made. During the first days of March 1864, soon after this letter,

the Forty-ninth helped retake Suffolk, Virginia. In this engagement the regiment met Negro troops for the first time. In April of that year the Forty-ninth fought at Albemarle Sound defending the North Carolina coast. In May the regiment fought at Drewry's Bluff where Captain Ardrey gave his life. On 16 May 1864 the Union Army was routed but escaped. Captain B. F. Dixon in his essay in Clark's *Histories* III said the town and city boys stood the army life better than the country boys. It was his opinion that the country boys lived a more regulated life from sunrise to sunset and had their three square meals a day. Army life simply ruined that. On 1 June 1864 the story begins to end. James Morrison Stitt is ill and headed home for North Carolina. On 4 June 1864 the Forty-ninth crosses the James River at Drewry's Bluff and begins its march to Appomattox; the next day James Morrison Stitt died. Clark *Histories*, III, 134, 135, 137, 139, and 151.

CHAPTER 12

1. Identity unknown.
2. The Potomac is a strategic river that separates Washington, D.C., from Virginia.
3. Perhaps Mrs. Collins is a neighbor of Mr. White's.
4. Red Rock is a small farming town in northern Oklahoma with a small (present-day) population of about 300 persons.
5. Identity unknown.
6. Identity unknown.
7. Identity unknown.

CHAPTER 13

1. Journal of Ella Gertrude (Clanton) Thomas, 1861, Mary Elizabeth Massey Papers, Archives and Special Collections Department, Dacus Library, Winthrop University, Rock Hill, S.C.
2. *Ibid.*
3. *Ibid.*
4. *Ibid.*
5. Letter from Kiah Sadler to Sadler Family, n.d., David Hope Sadler Family Papers, Archives and Special Collections Department, Dacus Library, Winthrop University, Rock Hill, S.C.
6. Letter from Mary Sadler to her son Kiah Sadler, 1862, David Hope Sadler Family Papers, Archives and Special Collections Department, Dacus Library, Winthrop University, Rock Hill, S.C.
7. Memorial for Lena T. Copeland, 1899, Lena T. Copeland Memorial Papers, Archives and Special Collections Department, Dacus Library, Winthrop University, Rock Hill, S.C.

CHAPTER 14

1. Wilks Papers. Winthrop University Department of Archives and Special Collections. Rock Hill, S.C.
2. Fought at Cedar Mountain on August 9, 1862, this was an engagement of the Second Bull Run Campaign. While the confederates could claim victory because they held the field, confederate commander Stonewall Jackson had miscalculated and nearly suffered a defeat from an opponent less than half his force.

3. This Virginia battle took place on December 13, 1862. Out of an estimated 106 federal troops who actually participated in the battle, 12,700 were killed or wounded. Confederate losses were put at 5,300.

4. Nicknamed the Swamp Fox for his elusive and guerrilla-like military tactics, General Francis Marion played a key role in the American Revolution, helping to drive the British out of South Carolina.

5. Actually poltroon, which means a spiritless coward.

6. In July 1862, General Wade Hampton (1818–1902) of South Carolina became second in command of J. E. B. Stuart's Cavalry group, and after Stuart's death in May 1864, he became corps commander.

CHAPTER 15

1. Thomas Belue, "The Diary of Thomas Belue," Winthrop University Archives; Shelby Foote, *Conversations with Shelby Foote* (Baton Rouge: 1987), 110.

2. There is no information as to the exact location of the hospital. An educated guess would lead one to believe that it is in Virginia, close to Richmond, Virginia.

3. Angelo Heilprin, Louise Heilprin, eds., *Lippincotts New Gazetteer* (Philadelphia and London: Lippincotts Company, 1905), 1758. "Stanton" is Staunton, Va., an independent city of Virginia, county seat of Augusta County. It is situated in the beautiful and fertile Shenandoah valley, 135 miles northwest of Richmond.

4. Camp Ewell: no reference or information as to the exact location of the camp. It is most likely in the western part of Virginia.

5. Angelo Heilprin and Louise Heilprin, eds., *Lippincotts, New Gazetteer* (Philadelphia and London, Lippincott Company, 1905), 2010. Winchester, Virginia, is an independent city, seat of justice of Frederick County, Virginia, 80 miles north by west of Washington, D.C., situated in the beautiful and fertile country that is part of the great valley of Virginia.

6. Major H. H. Smith, no reference as to who he was. We can only guess he was in Company F-15, South Carolina Volunteers, Kershaw Regiment.

7. Captain W. Willis, no reference as to who he was. We can only guess he was in Company F-15, South Carolina Volunteers, Kershaw Regiment.

8. Angelo Heilprin and Louise Heilprin, eds., *Lippincotts, New Gazetteer* (Philadelphia and London, 1905) 801. Harrisonburg, Virginia, is a banking post town, county seat of Rockingham County, Virginia, situated in the Shenandoah Valley, 68 miles southwest of Winchester, Virginia.

9. *Ibid.* 1234. Mount Jackson, Virginia, a banking post town of Shenandoah County, Virginia, on the north fork of the Shenandoah River, 51 miles NNE of Staunton.

10. *Ibid.* 578. Edinburg, Virginia, a post town of Shenandoah County, Virginia, near the north fork of the Shenandoah River, 36 miles SW of Winchester.

11. *Ibid.* 1289. New Market, Virginia, is a banking post town of Shenandoah County, in the fertile Shenandoah Valley 43 miles north by east of Staunton and near the base of the Massanutten Mountains.

12. The Shenandoah Mountains are located in the northwest part of Virginia.

13. Spereville is a location that was not identifiable. It is probably a town in the western part of Virginia but no evidence was given as to the exact location.

14. March was obviously a man who treated Thomas Belue very kindly, but there is no official record of his existence.

15. Angelo Heilprin and Louise Heilprin, eds., *Lippincotts, New Gazetteer* (Philadelphia and London; Lippincott Company, 1905), 1560. Rockingham County, in the

northwest part of Virginia, has an area of 870 sq. miles. It is intersected by the Shenandoah River and also drained by the North Fork of that river. The Blue Ridge extends along the southeast border of the county, which is a part of the Great Valley of Virginia.

16. *Ibid.* 735. Gordonsville is a banking town of Orange County, Virginia, seventy-five miles southwest of Washington, D.C.

17. *Ibid.* 1520. Rapidan is a post village of Culpeper County, Virginia, on the Rapidan River and on the Chesapeake and Ohio and the Southern railroads; *Ibid.* 1520, Rapidan River is a river of Virginia, rises on the southeastern slope of the Blue Ridge, has a general eastward direction and enters the Rappahannock about ten miles above Fredericksburg, Va.

18. Summerville Ford has no existence in any formal material. This is probably a small town in western Virginia.

19. Angelo Heilprin and Louise Heilprin, eds., *Lippincotts, New Gazetteer* (Philadelphia and London: 1905) 679. Fredericksburg, Virginia, a banking city of Spotsylvania County, Virginia, is on the right or south bank of the Rappahannock River and on the Richmond, Fredericksburg and Potomac and the Potomac, Fredericksburg, and Piedmont railroads, 61 miles north of Richmond, 54 miles south southwest of Washington, D.C.

20. *Ibid.* 381. Chancellorsville, Virginia, is a post station of Spotsylvania County, Virginia, near the south bank of the Rappahannock River, about seventy miles north by west of Richmond, Va.

21. Noah Church is not identifiable, but it is probably located on the outskirts of Fredericksburg in Spotsylvania County, Virginia.

22. Angelo Heilprin and Louise Heilprin, eds., *Lippincotts, New Gazetteer* (Philadelphia and London: 1905), 745. Hanover Junction in Hanover County, Virginia, is in the east central part of Virginia, has an area of 478 sq. miles. It is bordered on the northeast by the North Anna and Pamunkey rivers and on the southwest by the Chickahominy Creek.

23. Good Hope Church probably is in the area of Spotsylvania County, Virginia.

24. Fredericks Hall depot is probably in the area of Spotsylvania County, Virginia, but no concrete proof is given.

25. Central Railroad is located most likely in the central part of Virginia but there is no evidence given as to the exact location.

26. Lieutenant Stern obviously was a member of the same company as Belue but there is no official record of him, nor is he even mentioned in an official document or book.

27. Angelo Heilprin and Louise Heilprin, eds., *Lippincotts New Gazatteer* (Philadelphia and London: 1905), 183. Beaver Dam is a post village of Hanover County, Virginia, located forty miles north, northwest of Richmond, Virginia.

28. *Ibid.* 1,435. Petersburg, Virginia, is an independent city and port of entry of Virginia, situated on the right or south bank of the Appomattox River, ten miles from its mouth and twenty-two miles south of Richmond.

29. Weldon Depot is the depot at which Company F-15 boarded the train at Petersburg, Virginia, en route to Weldon, North Carolina.

30. Angelo Heilprin and Louise Heilprin, eds., *Lippincotts, New Gazetteer* (Philadelphia and London: 1905), 1,972. Weldon, North Carolina is a banking post town of Halifax County, North Carolina, on the southwest bank of the Roanoke River, ninety-six miles northeast of Raleigh.

31. *Ibid.* 2,008. Wilmington, North Carolina, a city, a port of entry and county seat of New Hanover County, North Carolina, is situated on the east bank or left

bank of the Cape Fear River, about twenty miles from its mouth and 134 miles south, southeast of Raleigh.

32. *Ibid.* 338. Cape Fear River is formed by the Deep and Haw rivers which unite at Haywood in Chatham County, North Carolina. It runs generally southeastward and enters the Atlantic Ocean at the south extremity of New Hanover County and Cape Fear.

33. At this point in the diary, Thomas Belue's handwriting is not readable. The city he seems to be trying to mention is Manchester, S.C., but there is no proof to back this observation.

34. Angelo Heilprin and Louise Heilprin, eds., *Lippincotts, New Gazetteer* (Philadelphia and London: 1905), 6.52. Florence, South Carolina, is a county in the northeastern part of South Carolina with an area of 630 sq. miles. It is bounded on the east by the navigable Peedee River and is intersected by the Lynch River and other streams.

35. *Ibid.* 113. Ashley River is a river of South Carolina that rises in Colleton County and runs southeastward and enters Charleston Harbor at the city of Charleston, which is on a point of land formed by the confluence of the Ashley and Cooper rivers.

36. *Ibid.* 1085. Macon, Georgia, the county seat of Bibb County, is situated on both sides of the Ocmulgee River and on the Central Georgia Railroad. It lies 103 miles south, southeast of Atlanta.

37. *Ibid.* 502. Dalton, Georgia, is a banking city, the capital of Whitfield County, Georgia. It is thirty-nine miles southeast of Chattanooga, Tenn.

38. *Ibid.* 1,545. Ringgold, Georgia, is a post town and county seat of Catoosa County, Georgia. It is situated fifteen miles northwest of Dalton, Georgia, on the Western and Atlantic Railroad.

39. *Ibid.* 2100. Chickamauga, Tennessee, is a hamlet of Hamilton County, Tennessee, situated twelve miles east of Chattanooga, Tennessee.

40. Sergt. G. S. Spears in all probability was in company F-15 along with Thomas Belue, although no official record has been found to prove this fact.

41. Sergt. B. F. Jones in all probability was in company F-15 along with Thomas Belue, but again there is no real evidence.

42. Lt. Goudeloch was most likely a member of company F-15, but there is no real proof or evidence that he served with Thomas Belue.

43. At this point in the diary, Belue has scribbled three words that are not readable.

44. Mr. Randatt was an Alabamian who was detailed to wait on the wounded of his own company and gave Belue as much attention as he could in the hospital.

45. Angelo Heilprin and Louise Heilprin, eds., *Lippincotts, New Gazetteer* (Philadelphia and London: 1905), 487. LaGrange, Georgia, is a banking city, the county seat of Troup County, Georgia, situated fifteen miles northeast of West Point, Georgia.

46. Oliver Hospital Ward E, housed in LaGrange, Georgia.

47. At this point in the diary, there is a thumbprint that obscures the words and makes it impossible to figure the word out.

48. Angelo Heilprin and Louise Heilprin, eds., *Lippincotts New Gazetteer* (Philadelphia and London: 1905), 100. Augusta, Georgia, is a city located in the east region of Georgia.

CHAPTER 16

1. When Faucette speaks of "favor," he is referring to a letter.
2. Location unknown.

3. Identities unknown.

4. Unknown.

5. Weldon is a town in Halifax County, N.C., named for a resident family. (See *The Origin of Certain Place Names* by Henry Gannett, 320.)

6. The Suffolk trip was an attack made on the town of Suffolk, Virginia, which was in Nansemond County, named from the county in England, 293.

7. Chowan; river and county in N.C., named from the Chowanoke Indian tribe. The word is a variant of the Algonquian sorwan, "south." One authority derives the word from sowan-ohke, "south country."

8. Franklin, Virginia; town at the foothills of the Alleghany Mountains. A battle was fought there on November 30, 1864 (*The Life of Johnny Reb*; Bell I. Wiley, page 289). The Confederates lost five generals in this campaign (*A Concise Encyclopedia of the Civil War*, Henry E. Simmons, 219).

9. In the minds of the Confederates, "citizens" were southern people.

10. They had set up quarters in Suffolk, Virginia.

11. Identity unknown.

12. Apparently there had been heavy rains which could have amounted to flooding.

13. Evidently they were pleased with their success at Suffolk.

14. Identity unknown.

15. Identity unknown.

16. Identities unknown.

17. Governor Zebulon Baird Vance, born in Buncombe County, N.C. At one time, he was a Unionist and in 1861 refused to join the Confederate Congress. When the Civil War began, he joined the state army as a colonel. He fought at New Bern, N.C., in March 1862 and in the Seven Days Battle before Richmond. (*Biographical Dictionary of the Confederacy*; Jon L. Wakelyn, page 419.)

18. Gov. Vance was elected governor of N.C. in September 1862 and was reelected in 1864, retaining the governorship until the end of the war. He worked hard to maintain the loyalty and fighting spirit of N.C.

19. Unknown information.

20. The sharp shooter corps was expert riflemen.

21. Unknown information.

22. Unknown.

23. Unknown.

24. If Kiah had a lady friend, he did not marry her, because he was killed. Richard H. P. Sadler (Kiah) was the son of Richard Sadler. He had three brothers: Oscar Williams, John Milton, and Rufus Earle. Kiah died in action on June 11, 1864.

25. Cousin.

26. Cousin.

27. The Richmond Campaign of 1864 probably refers to the Battle of Cold Harbor.

28. Cousin.

29. Of pay for troops.

CHAPTER 17

1. Author's sister was Mary Elizabeth White.

2. Probably his mother's sister.

3. His other sister, Adeline White.

4. John G. Barret, *Sherman's March through the Carolinas* (Chapel Hill: 1956), 643.

5. His brother, David Hutchinson White.

6. Retreating, hungry, and undisciplined Confederate soldiers.

7. Lee was a very religious man. Throughout the war he drew strength from his Christian beliefs and his views influenced his troops. See Thomas Nelson Page, *Robert E. Lee: Man and Soldier* (New York: 1929), 674–75.

8. Diary of Julius Mills, Winthrop University Archives, Rock Hill, S.C.

9. *Ibid.*

Conclusion

1. *Richmond Whig*, May 1, 1865.

2. See Sir Richard Livingstone's edition of Thucydides, *The History of the Peloponnesian War* (London: 1943), XVIII–XVIV.

3. On the eve of the 1860 presidential election, South Carolina's James Chesnut, a U. S. senator, warned about the threat posed by "Black Republican" Abraham Lincoln, *Charleston Mercury*, October 16, 1860; two significant slave uprisings had occurred in South Carolina: the 1739 Stone Rebellion and the 1822 Denmark Vesey insurrection; Calhoun, as vice-president and U. S. senator, was the architect of South Carolina's states' rights position, which argued that harmful federal laws (e.g., the 1832 Tariff) could be ignored or "nullified" by states.

Index

African Americans 29, 30, 32–35, 52, 58, 62, 64, 66, 68–69, 78, 82, 146
Agriculture 29–75
Alabama 93, 97, 108, 106
American Revolution 131
Appomattox River 89
Atlanta, GA 49, 53, 141, 143
Augusta, GA 144

Baltimore, MD 121, 152
Beaufort, SC 82
Beauregard, Gen. Pierre Gustave Toutant 102
Bell Creek Run, VA 86
Belue, Thomas 138–144
Bethel, SC 76
Booth, John Wilkes 152
Boston, MA 173
Burgess' Farm, VA 78
Burnside, Gen. Ambrose 126

Calhoun, John C. 156
Cameron, Gen. 95
Camp Lee, VA 123
Canada 110
Catawba River 91
Cedar Mountain, VA 85
Chancellorville, Battle of 80, 88
Charleston, SC 32, 35, 38, 55,65–66, 141, 145, 147
Charlotte, NC 91
Chattanooga, TN 141–142
Chester County, SC 133–134
Chicago, IL 105
Chowan County, NC 146
Christmas 32, 64, 134

Civil War records 22
Clanton, Ella Gertrude 129–137
Clark, Gen. Charles 102
Clarksville, OH 103
Columbia, SC 31, 72, 144
Columbus, GA 131
Columbus, OH 102
Concord, NC 91
Confederate flag 120
conscription 108
Copeland, Lena T. 132

Dalton, GA 141
Davis, Jefferson 96, 105, 154
Davis, Varina 154
Dawson, N.H.R. 106–109

Ebenezer, SC 86
Edenburg, VA 139
8th South Carolina Regiment 142, 253

Florence, SC 141
Fort Donelson, OH 102–103
Fort Sumter, SC 66, 78
Fort Warren, MA 112
France 110
Franklin, VA 107, 121, 128, 140
Franks, Augustus 99–105
Fraser's Farm, VA 84
Fredericksburg, Battle of 126, 135
Fredericksburg, VA 83, 85, 91, 140

Gaines' Mill, VA 83
Georgia 106
Gettysburg, PA 88
Goldsboro, NC 123
Grant, Gen. Ulysses 88–89